Democracy and Displacement in Colombia's Civil War

Democracy and Displacement in Colombia's Civil War

Abbey Steele

Cornell University Press
Ithaca and London

First published 2017 by Cornell University Press

Printed in the United States of America

Library of Congress Cataloging-in-Publication Data

Names: Steele, Abbey, 1979– author.
Title: Democracy and displacement in Colombia's civil war / Abbey
    Steele.
Description: Ithaca : Cornell University Press, 2017. | Includes
    bibliographical references and index.
Identifiers: LCCN 2017029978 (print) | LCCN 2017033860 (ebook) |
    ISBN 9781501712395 (epub/mobi) | ISBN 9781501709753 (pdf) |
    ISBN 9781501713736 (cloth : alk. paper)
Subjects: LCSH: Political violence—Colombia—History. |
    Political persecution—Colombia—History. | Forced migration—
    Colombia—History. | Unión Patriótica (Colombia)—History. |
    Colombia—Politics and government—1974–
Classification: LCC HN310.Z9 (ebook) | LCC HN310.Z9 S74 2017
    (print) | DDC 303.609861—dc23
LC record available at https://lccn.loc.gov/2017029978

In memory of my father,
J. Fred Steele

To those familiar with the awful abuses suffered by victims of these and other wars, academic theorizing may seem callous, opportunistic, even obscene. The neutral language of social science can never do justice to articulating the enormity of wartime suffering; but that effort is perhaps best left to journalists, novelists, and poets. As social scientists, our job is more modest. We provide explanatory tools to illustrate the social forces causing and shaping patterns in human misery. Whether or not this provides any tangible benefit to the world is difficult to say.

JAMES RON, *FRONTIERS AND GHETTOS*

Whoever said that everything is lost, I come to offer my heart!!
I offer it to forgive both the guerrillas who displaced us and kidnapped my father, and the paramilitaries who snuffed out his life and stole our lands from us. It does no good to keep cultivating the rage and hatred that these wounds left us. It is time to heal, it is time to look at ourselves and recognize each other and to know that this is our land and only together and in peace can we make it flourish!

¡¡Quién dijo que todo está perdido, yo vengo a ofrecer mi corazón!!
Lo ofrezco al perdón tanto de la guerrilla que nos desplazó y secuestró a mi padre, como de los paramilitares quienes cegaron su vida y nos quitaron nuestras tierras. Ya no vale la pena seguir cultivando la rabia y el odio que nos dejaron estas heridas. ¡Es tiempo de sanar, es tiempo de mirarnos y reconocernos y saber que ésta es nuestra tierra y solo juntos y en paz la haremos florecer!

ENILDA JIMÉNEZ PINEDA

CONTENTS

ILLUSTRATIONS

PREFACE

I arrived in Colombia for the first time in January 2002. That year, friends and I started an informal workshop with teenagers in Altos de Cazucá, to the south of Bogotá. The thousands of residents come from all over the country and construct the least flimsy houses they can manage, clinging to the foothills of the central chain of the Andes. Many of them are displaced, victims of the civil war. I wondered what brought the families to the neighborhood, aspirationally named "El Progreso," or Progress. Where were they all from? Why did they come to El Progreso? Who did they leave behind? Would they ever return? But I was too shy to ask, worried that I would make everyone uncomfortable.

Only one month after I arrived, the peace talks that had started three years earlier between the government and the FARC, Colombia's largest insurgency, fell apart. Bogotá buzzed with nervousness about the possibility of a terrorist attack by the FARC. One finally came months later, at the inauguration of newly elected president Álvaro Uribe in August. The mortars killed fifteen and injured forty more.

Once a week, I took an evening class at the venerated Universidad Nacional, where the main campus plaza features an image of Che Guevara. My class, taught by Donny Meertens, was held in a magnificent building designed by Rogelio Salmona, one of the few on campus left free of the "*fuera gringos*" and "*Camilo Torres, presente*" graffiti. More than once I arrived on campus to find the gates locked; student protests occasionally led to shutdowns. Once, an abandoned police tank remained, facing the campus gates.

Even with the uncertainty following the end of the peace talks and the twitchy energy of the city, Bogotá still felt distant from the war. We were ensconced on a high-altitude plateau (nearly three thousand meters high) and told by US embassy officials not to risk traveling by road outside of the city. That year, I took flights to visit other cities: Calí, Cartagena, Barranquilla. But rather than travel to areas more directly affected by the war, the closest I got was by talking to the people arriving in the cities, displaced from their homes, their land, and their communities and in many cases barely eking out new lives in unstable houses and strange cities.

When I returned to Colombia to start my fieldwork in 2006, my focus was on understanding the causes of displacement. This time, though, I finally visited places that experienced the war directly. The Urabá region experienced an early, intense onslaught of violence, but was relatively calm in 2007. Still, I should have taken more precautions than I did. I traveled alone on public transportation, only sometimes remembering to let friends in Bogotá know where I was. I let strangers guess where I was from rather than present a consistent story, because I found it difficult to come up with something that sounded credible. It was a reckless choice. Once, improbably, the driver of the jeep transport (the area's answer to a bus, for all the unpaved roads) guessed I was from Bogotá ("do your parents know you are here?"). I visited a rural area where an acquaintance's father met me and took me to a bar at ten in the morning, where I was thankful I could substitute beer for the anise-flavored national liquor *aguardiente* he urged me to drink. When I met one of the people I wanted to interview, my contact introduced me as his European daughter-in-law (which I later tried to correct in private).

In spite of my missteps, I found that the region was vibrant with engaged residents who were willing to speak with me at great length about their experiences. Many spoke with pride about their past roles in developing the city of Apartadó, establishing labor regulations, and building the banana economy. I also visited Medellín to try to track down people who left Urabá and take account of their stories too. I met many with the help of NGOs like Cedecis, which works in the *comunas* that crawl up the mountains surrounding the city. The hardest part of this work was to ask for people's time away from work and family and to ask them to share their painful stories, knowing that I would not be able to offer much at all in return.

I hope their sacrifices were not in vain; I hope this book reflects their experiences faithfully. I also hope it can illuminate displacement patterns in civil wars, especially Colombia's. Though the findings are harrowing, maybe they can contribute to ongoing efforts for justice and peace in the country.

This book has the imprint of many people, to whom I am incredibly grateful. First, I acknowledge the countless people in Colombia who made this work possible. Most of all, I am indebted to the hundreds of people who graciously shared their stories. Enilda Jiménez, Mario Agudelo, and William Forero were exceedingly generous; I hope I captured the essence of their insights and memories. Donny Meertens, Jorge Restrepo, Mauricio Romero, Consuelo Valdivieso, and Pedro Valenzuela provided supportive guidance in Bogotá. I am grateful especially to Ana María Ibáñez and Fabio Sánchez, who welcomed me to the Centro de Estudios de Desarrollo Económico (CEDE) at the Universidad de los Andes and its lively environment during my stays in Bogotá and who always helped me track down the data I needed or shared their own. Andrés Gómez, Lizeth Herrera, Gloria Lema Vélez, and Nidia Montoya were extremely helpful in Medellín. Ana Aldana, Mariana Blanco, Valentina Calderón, Juan Espinosa, Carolina Gómez, Luisa Lema Vélez, Claudia López, Andrés Mesa, Alf Onshuus, Eli Prado, Saúl Sánchez, Rebecca Tally, Harold Tenorio, and Juan Vargas offered levity, wisdom, and friendship and made Bogotá a second home for me.

Many more people equipped me with the tools to try to understand the stories I was collecting, and displacement and politics. My greatest intellectual debt is to Stathis Kalyvas, who profoundly influenced how I think. I am the social scientist I am because of him. Libby Wood was an incredible mentor in the classroom and in the field, consistently inspiring me to try to be a better scholar and a better person. I would have been extremely fortunate to have either Stathis or Libby as an adviser; it is hard to fathom how lucky I was to have both. The broader community at Yale was invaluable, too. Adria Lawrence and Matt Kocher were confidants who not only influenced how I think but also boosted me at critical times. Sue Stokes pushed me to think beyond Colombia and civil wars. Pierre Landry and Ian Shapiro encouraged and supported me as well. The Comparative Politics Workshop, and the Order, Conflict and Violence community shaped the kind of political scientist I am. I am also very grateful to Jake Shapiro, who offered me the chance to continue my research in Colombia as a postdoctoral fellow. His seemingly ceaseless energy and sharp insights pushed me to work harder and, hopefully, to greater effect.

Years before graduate school, Sheryl Kohl, David Patten, Jan Denman, Jeanne Hey, Sheila Croucher, and Emile Haag all captivated me and influenced how I see the world, the questions I ask, and how I try to write it all down. Adam Isacson became a role model because of his tireless, humane advocacy based on rigorous description and in-depth knowledge of Colombia.

Financial support from the National Science Foundation, the Fulbright-Hays Doctoral Dissertation Research Abroad program, the Program on Order, Conflict and Violence, the MacMillan Center for International and Area Studies at Yale, Syracuse University's Institute for National Security and Counter-Terrorism's Andrew Berlin Award, and the Political Economy and Transnational Governance Research Group at the University of Amsterdam made this work possible. Princeton University and the Empirical Studies of Conflict Project also provided support through the Air Force Office of Scientific Research (AFOSR) under Award No. FA9550-09-1-0314. I am also grateful to Atsushi Tago and the CROP-IT program for generously supporting my sabbatical at Kobe University in 2015, which gave me much-needed time to write.

Diego Avanellada efficiently and expertly transformed hundreds of photos into manageable data. Nicole Martinez Moore, Leigh Newman, Nury Bejarano, Jessica Di Salvatore, Karen Lugo-Londoño, and David Ifkovits all also contributed outstanding, essential research assistance. Institutional support from the Universidad de los Andes and the CEDE in Bogotá was tremendous, as was my time at Econometría toward the end of the project, and CERAC at the beginning.

My book workshop was sponsored by the Institute for National Security and Counter-Terrorism at Syracuse University, which allowed me to invite Tom Pepinsky and the late Will Moore to campus. I am grateful for that day, not only for the substantive and invaluable feedback from Tom and Will, but also for the chance it gave me to spend time with Will. Colleagues at Syracuse also commented on various sections of the book and helped me improve it, including Matt Cleary, Seth Jolly, Dan McDowell, Quinn Mulroy, Shana Gadarian, and Renee de Nevers. Dominika Koter and Juan Masullo read chapters of the manuscript and gave generous, incisive comments. Rob Karl offered unwavering support for this project from the beginning, piqued my interest in the lore of the FARC, and was my expert consultant on the historical chapters. Editor Roger Haydon helped me find my voice with patience and encouragement. I am also grateful for the helpful comments of two anonymous reviewers.

Portions of chapter 1 were previously published in "Seeking Safety: Avoiding Displacement and Choosing Destinations in Civil War," *Journal of Peace Research* 46, no. 3 (2009): 419–29. Portions of chapters 1 and 5 were previously published in "Electing Displacement: Political Cleansing in Apartadó, Colombia," *Journal of Conflict Resolution* 55, no. 3 (2011): 423–55. Portions of chapters 1 and 6 were previously published in "Warfare, Political Identities, and Displacement in Spain and Colombia," *Political Geography* 51 (2016): 15–29 (with Laia Balcells).

During and since my time in graduate school, I was also fortunate to meet people I admire not only as scholars but also as friends. Ana Arjona, Juanita Aristazabál, Laia Balcells, Rob Becker, John Boy, Sarah Zukerman Daly, Steve Engel, Francesca Grandi, Sandy Henderson, Turku Isiksel, Corinna Jentszch, Oliver Kaplan, Steve Kaplan, Dominika Koter, Harris Mylonas, Rob Person, Livia Schubiger, Ryan Sheely, Paul Staniland, and Michael Weintraub all helped shape this project (and helped make the journey enjoyable), and I am grateful to each of them.

The humor, love, and perspective of Kim Abbott, Julie Beck, Cat Byun, Amanda Chawansky, Christine Kim, Doug Kysar, Sarah Govil, Chris Donahue, and Manuel Somoza both inspired and grounded me over the years. Fuphan Chou, Beth Feingold, and Hannah Stutzman—my heifers—have managed to hold me up and push me forward, even from great distances. Fu never shies from deep analyses of all kinds, and brings me along to reveal important gems. Bethy inspires me with her big-hearted, contagious enthusiasm for adventures and research dedicated to the greater good. Hannah, my midwestern-cachaca touchstone and fellow calamity speaker, offers so much wisdom, wit, and love in the most understated way. I would be lost without them. I also owe special gratitude to Alex Fattal, my dear friend who introduced me to Cazucá, the virtues of Dylan, and much more since our early days in Bogotá together.

My mom, Pamela Krohn, has always supported and encouraged me, and trusted me to follow my own path, even when it led to a country with an ongoing war. I'm so grateful. My stepfather David has been a constant source of support too, as have my stepsiblings Brian Krohn, Michael Krohn, and Cheryl Klauminzer. The Peters clan's constant love over the years has almost been overwhelming. My beloved brother, James Steele, has traveled with me our whole lives and taught me how to observe along the way. And I will forever be grateful for my joyful dad and grandparents, who always conveyed their love for and faith in me. I still work hard to make them proud. If not for Seiki Tanaka and his incredibly generous and intelligent support, I could not have finished the book. I also could not have become a mother along the way. I am forever grateful, especially for Rowen and Kai, my dear sons and bright lights.

Abbreviations

ACCU	Autodefensas Campesinas de Córdoba y Urabá (Peasant Self-Defense Forces of Córdoba and Urabá)
AUC	Autodefensas Unidas de Colombia (United Self-Defense Forces of Colombia)
CNP	Colombian National Police
ELN	Ejército de Liberación Nacional (National Liberation Army)
EPL	Ejército Popular de Liberación (Popular Liberation Army)
FARC	Fuerzas Armadas Revolucionarias de Colombia (Revolutionary Armed Forces of Colombia)
GMH	Grupo de Memoria Histórica (Historical Memory Group)
GoC	Government of Colombia
IDP	Internally displaced person
PCC	Partido Comunista de Colombia (Communist Party of Colombia)
PC-ML	Partido Comunista de Colombia–Marxista-Leninista (Communist Party of Colombia [Marxist-Leninist])
UP	Unión Patriótica (Patriotic Union)

A Note on Pseudonyms
and Translations

In some cases, I have assigned pseudonyms to interviewees to protect their identity. Pseudonyms are indicated by attribution to stand-alone first names. Those identified by both first and last names are public figures, and their names have not been changed.

I conducted all interviews with Colombian subjects in Spanish and translated the excerpts that appear in the book based on my notes.

Finally, several quotes appear from Spanish-language archival and secondary sources. I am responsible for all translations and any errors.

Democracy and Displacement in Colombia's Civil War

UNSETTLING

Displacement during Civil Wars

The neighborhoods that climb the mountains surrounding Medellín are among the city's poorest, in spite of the rich views they afford. I met Arturo in one such steep *comuna* in 2007. He had come to Medellín more than a decade earlier from a region called Urabá in northwest Colombia, where he worked on one of its famous banana plantations. One day in 1994, he told me, armed men arrived in the neighborhood where he lived. They shot into the air, scaring Arturo and his neighbors. A couple of days later, the army arrived in tanks, spreading more fear. Then, ominously, armed men started prowling the neighborhood on motorbikes, perfect for assassinations and quick getaways in the 1980s. The final straw for Arturo came when his neighbor turned up dead; after that, he left for Medellín, three hundred kilometers away. He tried to return to his home and work after only four months, in spite of the risks. But it was still too dangerous, so he returned again to Medellín, where he has lived ever since.

If Arturo were Darfuri or Bosniak or Shi'ite, we could imagine a narrative to make sense of his story: sometimes people are displaced because of their ethnicity. But Arturo is Colombian. The city where Arturo lived was racially and socioeconomically diverse, and the armed groups did not target people because of their race, ethnicity, or class. Still, while Arturo and his neighbors anxiously began to stay indoors, a nearby neighborhood was left alone by the same armed men, even though its residents seemed remarkably similar. How can we understand what happened to Arturo, his neighbors, and the millions of others currently displaced? Were they just unlucky victims of random violence?

Arturo and his neighbors were unlucky, but the violence they faced was not random. In Colombia, I uncovered unique evidence from remote archives and nearly two hundred interviews that shows that armed groups target some types of civilians for expulsion from their homes and communities because they perceive them to be disloyal, even if these groups are tied not by ethnic or sectarian bonds but by political ones. Arturo and his neighbors shared a history of organizing in a union, fighting for housing and land rights, and, eventually, voting for the same political party in elections. Tragically, elections—often considered by policymakers as tools to alleviate conflict and transition to peace—triggered violence instead of reducing it. Elections revealed civilians' political loyalties, stigmatized some as insurgent sympathizers, and spurred others to ally against them. As a result, counterinsurgents collectively targeted supporters of the political party, like Arturo and his neighbors, with violence until they left, and then took control of the city. What happened in Arturo's town shows that cleansing is not limited to ethnic groups. *Political* cleansing captures the broader phenomenon of the expulsion of a particular group from a territory. In this book, I distinguish political cleansing from other forms of displacement and set out to explain when and where armed groups attempt political cleansing.

Political cleansing is one form of civilian displacement and accounts for a portion of the nearly sixty million people worldwide who have left their homes and communities during war over the past seventy years. Civilian displacement—defined as migration provoked by one or more armed groups during war—has been a regular, unfortunate feature of politics for centuries. But never before have there been so many displaced. As of 2014, the Internal Displacement Monitoring Center (IDMC), the UN's official point organization on the issue, estimated that 19.5 million displaced people live in new countries as refugees, while roughly double that number—38 million—remain within the borders of their home countries as internally displaced persons (IDPs) (IDMC 2014b). In 2014 alone, 13.9 million people were newly displaced, 11 million of whom were IDPs, another grim new record during a calendar year (UNHCR 2015). Colombia ranks among the countries with the highest IDP populations in the world, with more than six million scattered since the mid-1980s.

For individuals and families, displacement means separation from communities, loved ones, and property and an uncertain future in strange new places, often after experiencing gruesome violence and treacherous journeys. These families' wrenching experiences have broader political effects as well. For example, roughly half of all Syrians in 2016 were either internally displaced or living across borders. The dramatic shift in that country's demographic composition will undoubtedly affect everything from economic development to postwar politics. Countries that host refugees struggle too. In addition to the logistical and humanitarian challenges, receiving states can face their own domestic unrest as a result of the new immigrants, which have been linked to a higher probability of violence and civil war.

Despite the importance and scale of civilian displacement, it remains a murky phenomenon. Scholars have associated displacement with broad contexts, such as nation-state formation, human rights violations, violence, wars, and, more specifically, civil wars. While these factors are common backdrops for displacement, they do not explain it. Displacement is typically depicted either as an unintended byproduct of other forms of violence, or the result of a centralized ethnic cleansing campaign. However, neither view can account for important variation in forms and levels of displacement, sometimes during the course of the same civil war. In Iraq, for example, even though the country was invaded in 2003, it was only following the bombing of the major Shi'ite shrine Al-Askari in early 2006 that displacement skyrocketed. What accounts for this shift? Within wars, too, displacement does not affect all families or communities. To account for this variation, some recent scholarship has moved from contextual factors to look for common characteristics, such as wealth or assets, of individuals and households who decide to leave their communities. This line of inquiry, however, is too far abstracted from the wartime context and glosses over armed groups' influence on households' decisions. It is difficult to account for why Arturo and his neighbors left, while residents down the street did not, without the vital information about how armed groups behaved and in particular how they targeted the violence they perpetrated. To characterize and explain displacement, then, this book moves to the middle ground between large-scale contextual factors and individuals' characteristics, to study the interaction between armed groups and civilians within wars. In particular, I focus on civilians' shared characteristics and connections, and how armed groups treat them.

Across wars, armed groups target for cleansing civilians who are members of rival ethnicities, sects, or political groups. Often the targeted group is some combination of identities, or a network within a broader group, which can make political cleansing difficult to detect, especially from afar. The United Nations High Commission for Refugees (UNHCR) notes, "Violence that appears indiscriminate may also be deliberately targeted at certain groups of civilians" (UNHCR 2012, 6). In Nigeria, for example, the counterinsurgency effort against Boko Haram seems to target Muslims: "For the soldiers, the young men's long, flowing robes—the traditional garb of Muslim West Africa—were enough to establish guilt, the refugees said" (Nossiter 2013). But ethnicity is also relevant: "citizens with the vertical ethnic scarring of the Kanuri, a group dominant in the Islamist militant group Boko Haram, were being taken away [by the military]" (Nossiter 2013). The US State Department's human rights report on the Congo from 1993 noted that "at least 200 and perhaps many more persons died" in violence where "victims appeared to have been targeted on the basis of ethnic *and* political affiliation" (Fariss et al. 2015, emphasis added). In Colombia, because ethnic and religious identities did not coincide with the sides of the war, displacement seemed haphazard. In key instances, however, counterinsurgents were very particular about their political targets. Arturo's city was full of leftists, including many who had supported a rebel group, but only the supporters of one political party were targeted. Regardless of how narrow or broad the targeted group is, the threat is clear: leave or risk death.

To be sure, displacement is not always the result of a purposeful campaign against a group. Individuals also escape threats directed against them, sometimes just barely. In other cases, civilians relocate to avoid violence around them but not directed at them. Civilians' best options for safety depend on the type of threat they face from armed groups, not just the intensity of violence. Based on this insight, the book characterizes forms of displacement during war. *Individual escape* and *mass evasion* are forms of displacement that are unintended by armed groups or are incidental to the violence they perpetrate. In the case of individual escape, civilians manage to thwart selective targeting by an armed group. With mass evasion, civilians get out of the way of indiscriminate violence. In contrast, *political cleansing* follows strategic and purposeful collective targeting of civilian groups. Furthermore, political cleansing can be widespread, even in nonethnic civil wars like Colombia's. The primary focus of the book is to explain when and where armed groups engage in this form of displacement.

Collective Targeting, Political Cleansing, and Democratic Reforms during Civil War

I argue that collective targeting and political cleansing are most likely under two conditions: (1) when an armed group attempts to conquer a territory, and (2) when and where armed groups have information about civilians' loyalties, specifically if there is reason to believe that some types of civilians are likely to be supporting a rival armed group. If an armed group can link a group of civilians to one side of the conflict, it can infer the loyalties of the individual group members. Civilians who are perceived to be disloyal will make conquest difficult; they could help the rival armed group resist the incursion and they will be difficult to coerce or persuade into switching sides. Removing the disloyal will help the conquering armed group make inroads to gain control. In addition, expelling local rivals will make other residents of a community more likely to collaborate without fear of retaliation.

But even if it would make strategic sense for armed groups to expel their rival's civilian base, how can they identify the disloyal without any ascriptive clues? Elections are one mechanism, expressly meant to reveal preferences of the population. When electoral results map onto neighborhoods and villages, as they tend to in local elections, the residents of these areas are revealed as supporters of a particular party or candidate.

In addition to directly revealing information about residents, elections can also trigger new alliances. If an insurgent-aligned political party is successful, for example, the losing politicians have incentives to ally with counterinsurgents to change the constituency and have a better chance of winning in the next round.

The framework yields implications for when displacement is likely, and where. In terms of timing, collective targeting and political cleansing should only occur once a cleavage that links groups of civilians to either side of the war has emerged. These sorts of cleavages are not always constant throughout a civil war. Following an election is one possible example. Cleavages can also shift for other reasons. Returning to the Iraq case, for the first three years after the 2003 invasion, the insurgency was not strictly related to sectarian identity. It was only following the bombing of the Samarra shrine in 2006 that Shi'ites and Sunnis cemented on opposite sides of the war. Notably, some observers claim that the shift began in 2005, when political parties started to coalesce around sectarian identities. One consequence was a massive increase in displacement, once the allegiances of members of the predominant sects became suspect by the other sects' armed groups.

Arturo and his neighbors did not become targets for political cleansing until they had the opportunity to vote for a political party associated with insurgents. The Patriotic Union (Unión Patriótica, or UP) was founded by the Revolutionary Armed Forces of Colombia (Fuerzas Armadas Revolucionarias de Colombia, or FARC) in the context of peace talks with the Colombian government. Though lethal violence was endemic in the region where Arturo lived throughout the 1980s, displacement was uncommon until paramilitary groups opted to conquer the community by targeting the FARC political party supporters to expel them from the community. Residents of a nearby neighborhood were not targeted by paramilitaries, even though they shared the same socioeconomic, racial, and even employment background as Arturo and his neighbors. They were also leftists and associated with their own insurgent group, the Popular Liberation Army (Ejército Popular de Liberación, or EPL). At the time the paramilitaries arrived in the area, the EPL was officially demobilized and so was not the primary focus of the counterinsurgency. In fact, some former EPL members formed new militias, which they claimed were necessary to protect themselves from the FARC, who accused them of providing intelligence to the state. The new militia formed an alliance with the paramilitaries, which provided additional protection for the civilians historically associated with the EPL.

Once groups of civilians and likely support for insurgents or the state are linked, then collective targeting is possible. It becomes probable, however, when an armed group attempts to conquer a community. In irregular civil wars (i.e., insurgencies), counterinsurgents are the most likely to use this approach because it requires substantial resources and attracts attention. Insurgents cannot typically afford either. Those communities or segments of communities where the supposedly disloyal civilians live are the ones likely to be targeted for political cleansing. This is even more likely in communities where locals will benefit in some way from the expulsion of their neighbors. In Arturo's case, the political party he supported was especially problematic because it challenged local elites' power and prompted them to ally with the counterinsurgents. Without Arturo and his neighbors, those elites could win elections and restore their political power in the future.

Evidence from Colombia

The book documents collective targeting and political cleansing, and it uses evidence from Colombia to test the argument for when and where it is likely. Colombia's is not an ethnic civil war, so evidence of collective targeting there indicates that it may exist in other nonethnic civil wars as well. Further, Colombia is a country of diverse regions, terrain, and state presence, which makes it possible to evaluate the argument under different conditions within the context of the same war. Finally, given the importance of elections in the Colombian civil war, the experience holds some lessons for other civil wars, which often incorporate elections as a mechanism for peace building or conflict resolution.

The forms of displacement that the book describes and explains are difficult to observe directly. In addition, collecting data in civil wars is difficult. Records are lost or destroyed, and people's memories shift as the war develops. To collect reliable information myself, I went to the Urabá region in northwestern Colombia, one of the first regions to experience the surge of violence in the 1990s. Urabá is a diverse area, with rural communities and town centers, subsistence and commercial agriculture. Pockets of different political party supporters live throughout the region, which allowed me to test if they were more likely to be targeted and to leave than their neighbors. When I set out to collect evidence on variation in political loyalties, I found what I was searching for in a busy administrative office whose harried manager gave me access to the "archives," a rooftop that looked like the handiwork of a hoarder. Mounds of papers occupied most of the space; garbage bags bursting with papers spilled out of a room so full it was impossible to enter. Eventually, I spotted some binders that contained what I needed: the list of registered voters (by ID number), organized according to their polling station. These lists existed before and after the arrival of paramilitary groups to the region, so I could compare who stayed and who left following the conquest. Another binder listed the local electoral results, also by polling station. These records allowed me to demonstrate that residents who lived in areas that favored the UP were more likely to leave. Still, the striking finding could have been coincidence, or the consequence of some other factor. To investigate whether the paramilitaries purposefully targeted and expelled UP supporters, I sought archival information to shed light on what was happening in the municipality at that time. I found the local archivist, Albeiro, at the municipal city hall complex in a small stall in the open air with a copy machine and a few bound copies of municipal proceedings. After several visits, Albeiro took me to the archives of the municipality, in the belly of the town gymnasium. We walked under the stands (which were packed that day with Jehovah's Witnesses holding a meeting), and Albeiro unfastened the padlock and led me to a stuffy room that reeked of mildew. Most of the records were stored in old boxes stamped with banana brands; some were bound in fake green leather. Albeiro let me write up an impromptu "contract" and turn over my Colombian ID card for collateral so that I could take the documents to my tiny hotel room, where I took hundreds of digital photos of them over several days. The documents were the minutes of meetings held by a local committee to discuss the evolution of violence in Apartadó. They provided a detailed picture of how local officials, including the mayor, the local police chief, and the coroner, perceived the violence at the time, and they provide an opportunity to evaluate the extent to which paramilitaries expelled UP supporters. The records show that the paramilitaries used tactics consistent with collective targeting and an intent to expel the residents of UP neighborhoods: fliers and graffiti warning people to leave, and firing weapons in the air within UP neighborhoods, just as Arturo described.

Together, the evidence I collected in Colombia shows that collective targeting and political cleansing took place and that it happened according to my expectations: where the disloyal were revealed and when armed groups were attempting conquest. An interesting exception was a group of rural hamlets tucked into the mountains to the west of Apartadó. Even though they overwhelmingly supported the UP in elections and faced intense collective targeting by counterinsurgents, the residents were able to resist political cleansing. Based on interviews in the community and with advocacy organizations, I speculate that withstanding collective targeting requires coordination among targeted group members, which in turn demands organization. The organization needs to adopt strict measures within the community to create disincentives for leaving and incentives to stay, even under the threat of violence. Connections with external support networks also help bolster community members' resolve. Indigenous communities with pre-existing institutions and external supporters, and a handful of peace communities have managed to create the rare conditions needed to avoid political cleansing.

Based on what I found in Urabá, I collected quantitative data on displacement and electoral results across Colombia, which indicate that UP supporters were collectively targeted in other communities as well and that the process of political cleansing was repeated. Because comparable fine-grained evidence is difficult to collect or unavailable, I cannot rigorously test the argument in other civil war settings within this book. What happened in Colombia, however, is possible and even likely across civil wars.

The displacement of civilians during civil wars deserves rigorous analytical attention. Recent advances in the study of civil war violence have improved our understanding of when and where lethal violence is most likely; this study broadens the focus to a central outcome of violence in civil wars. The current understanding tends to equate wars or violence with an increase in displacement, but we can and need to be more precise. Violence is not a random occurrence during civil wars; understanding the conditions under which it is used to purposefully provoke displacement is an important step. Ethnic cleansing is a clear example of when violence is implemented to remove a population from a territory, but this book shows that ethnicity is the basis of only one type of political cleansing. Difficult-to-observe political loyalties are also crucial bases for collective targeting and political cleansing.

Outline of the Book

The rest of the book delves into displacement conceptually, theoretically, and empirically. Chapter 1 provides an in-depth logic and theory of displacement. Here I define the key terms and concepts of the book, as well as the conditions under which the theory applies. The basic argument is that during contestation between armed groups, they displace civilians they believe are loyal to their rivals.

To ground the book in the context of Colombia, chapter 2 presents a historical overview of the Colombian civil war. The current civil war's roots extend back to *La Violencia*, the previous civil conflict in the mid-twentieth century, in which millions of Colombians were internally displaced. The chapter traces the legacy of civilian displacement for both the development of political loyalties and the emergence of the contemporary insurgencies. Chapter 3 traces the evolution of the key actors into the contemporary civil war, presents the overall patterns of violence since the 1980s, and raises key questions about civilian displacement that the rest of the book sets out to answer.

Chapter 4 grapples with the puzzling onset of displacement in Colombia. Even though some date the war to the founding of the FARC (officially in 1966), and 1978 is the year the war crossed the violence threshold to enter cross-national datasets, displacement was not registered by advocates and the Catholic Church until 1986. The Colombian government did not take action until 1997 after prodding from the UN and advocacy organizations. What accounts for the lag between civil war onset and displacement? If my theory is correct, then the onset of displacement should be associated with the revelation of civilians' loyalties. I collected information about the formation of the UP and the implementation of local-level elections and show that these were crucial steps in the adoption of displacement as a tactic by paramilitaries. Displacement on a wide scale can be traced to 1988, the year elections were extended to the local level. There is evidence, in addition, that supporters of the insurgent group's political party were the earliest targets for displacement. The increase in displacement is linked to the growth and spread of counterinsurgent forces, which until 1997 were regionally based.

Chapter 5 moves to Arturo's hometown to test the theory based on detailed information about which civilians and neighborhoods armed groups targeted and on who left the municipality as a result. I show, using local electoral returns and voter censuses, that residents of UP neighborhoods were much likelier to leave Apartadó between 1991 and 1998. To investigate if the variation in displacement across political groups was caused by the conquering paramilitary groups, I draw on archival and interview evidence and show that the displacement of UP supporters was the result of a concerted paramilitary campaign. This chapter also explores how two rural communities were able to withstand collective targeting and thwart political cleansing, against the odds.

The Urabá work also revealed how I could take advantage of the rich quantitative data that exist in Colombia. If what I found in Apartadó reflected a more general pattern, then municipalities with UP voters should have suffered more displacement, all other things being equal. This is what I find in chapter 6, even accounting for levels of violence perpetrated by the armed groups. The order of chapters 5 and 6 is unconventional for political science, but it reflects how my research unfolded. It was only after traveling to Urabá, interviewing residents there, and combing local archives that the overlooked form of displacement in nonethnic settings—political cleansing—became apparent. Once I developed the theory, I was able to collect new data on political representation across Colombia to test the implications of the theory on a larger scale. My hope is that this order of chapters will prove helpful to students of political violence by revealing some of the process behind the research and emphasizing the crucial role fieldwork played in the development of both my ideas and the empirical evidence presented here.

The conclusion situates Colombia, displacement, and elections during civil wars in comparative perspective and discusses the long-term implications of displacement for peace building and state building. The politics of displacement are enduring. In Book 17 of *The Prince*, Machiavelli ([1532] 1910) urged the prince to avoid taking people's property "because men more quickly forget the death of their father than the loss of their patrimony." Thomas Paine ([1776] 1998) mentioned the sacking of property before any other grievance in *Common Sense*. At the aggregate, "States make wars and wars—massively—make migrants," James Scott observes

(2009, 146), extending Charles Tilly's adage. Indeed, contemporary wars have led sixty million people to leave their homes and communities. In this book, I show *how* contemporary wars "make" migrants. The process of understanding displacement during wars, in turn, sheds light on how these migrants shape contemporary states as well.

1

Characterizing and Explaining Wartime Displacement

Residents of La Chinita, a neighborhood in the municipality of Apartadó, in humid northwest Colombia, were celebrating at a block party on January 23, 1994, when several men arrived and began to shoot. The final death toll was thirty-two. "Of course we thought about leaving," the mother of one of the victims told me thirteen years after the event in the community center of the same neighborhood. "But we just couldn't." In spite of the gruesome violence, many of her neighbors also stayed. The massacre in La Chinita was one of many perpetrated in the region beginning in the late 1980s.

Less than a mile down the road, another neighborhood "was abandoned," a former armed group leader told me.[1] The neighborhood, Policarpa, was where the alleged perpetrators of the La Chinita massacre lived. Its residents, including Arturo, whom we met in the introduction, were mostly poor laborers on the surrounding banana plantations. They

---

1. Interview with Mario Agudelo, Medellín, July 4, 2007.

left the homes they struggled to build over the years and set off for other regions of Colombia in spite of the uncertainty.

We tend to think of civilian displacement during wars as a humanitarian crisis, which it certainly is. But this view ignores the political aspects of displacement and gives the impression that it is haphazard and cannot be systematically studied. Yet how can we account for why people in La Chinita stayed in town despite the gruesome violence, while so many from Policarpa opted to leave? The people who lived in these neighborhoods shared the same ethnic profiles, the same socioeconomic class, and the majorities of each even worked in the same sector, the banana industry.[2]

If the residents of the two neighborhoods had been members of different ethnic groups, we might attribute the variation to antipathy or a racist campaign. Ethnic cleansing tends to be perceived as a thoroughly orchestrated process, perpetrated by groups with strategic interests or hatred or both. Even though the basic observed outcome of what happened in Policarpa and ethnic cleansing are equivalent—a group of civilians leaves their communities after facing a targeted threat—their predominant characterizations are quite distinct. This book shows that even in the absence of a centralized campaign against ethnic groups, cleansing still occurs based on group identities. After spending years in Colombia, interviewing dozens of people and collecting original, fine-grained data from remote archives, I found that group identities and perceived loyalties do play a role in displacement, even in nonethnic civil wars.

In this chapter, I provide the conceptual and theoretical groundwork of the book. First, I argue that civilians' decisions to stay in or leave a community depend not on the level of violence, but rather on the way armed groups target them. Armed groups target selectively, indiscriminately, and collectively. Each type prompts different reactions from civilians and different forms of displacement. I focus on collective targeting, which is when armed groups target civilians because of a shared trait. When faced with collective targeting, a household's risk assessment depends on the decisions of other civilians who are also targeted: if everyone stays, it reduces any one household's risk of suffering direct violence.

---

2. Neighborhoods were integrated by Afro-Colombians and mestizos.

Given sustained violence directed at their group, however, it is likely that households will decide to leave, triggering others to follow suit. The resulting form of displacement is what I term "political cleansing" and can be based on any group-level trait, such as ethnicity, perceived ideology, or neighborhood. Ethnic cleansing, then, is a form of political cleansing.

Second, I develop a theory for when and where armed groups are likely to employ collective targeting to cleanse a territory and thereby gain an advantage over a rival. When armed groups compete for control over a community, they seek to displace disloyal civilians because such displacement undermines the rival armed group's presence and is more effective than killing or attempting to convert those who are disloyal. To eliminate nonsupporters, armed groups need to be able to tell who is loyal and who is not. Although information about civilian preferences is difficult to obtain in the context of civil wars (especially those without an ascriptive cleavage), elections conducted before or during a violent conflict are one way armed groups can identify those who are disloyal. Contemporary democratization politics promote elections at the earliest opportunity, which could expose civilians to violence. Colombia's experience suggests that careful attention to electoral rules and institutions are necessary to prevent such a backlash.

A Definition of Wartime Displacement

The number of people displaced during war has climbed steadily since millions left their homes during and following World War II.[3] In the 1951 Convention Relating to the Status of Refugees, the UN defined a refugee as anyone who, "owing to a well-founded fear of being persecuted for reasons of race, religion, nationality, membership of a particular social group, or political opinion, is outside the country of his nationality, and is unable to or, owing to such fear, is unwilling to avail himself of the protection of that country" (UNHCR 2010, art. 1). The convention did not originally include internally displaced people (IDPs), those who do not cross an international border. The UN eventually adopted "guiding principles"

---

3. Initially meant to serve the European refugee crisis, the UN adopted a 1967 protocol to extend the 1951 convention beyond Europe and World War II–related displacement.

on the internally displaced in 1998, which defines IDPs as refugees aside
from their location within their origin states.[4] The number of IDPs and
refugees around the world nearly tripled between 1980 and 1990 "to
22 million from 23 countries and about 17 million from 50 countries, respectively" (Vincent 2001).[5] This book characterizes and explains wartime displacement, defined as civilian migration that is provoked, directly
or indirectly, by one or several armed groups.[6] This definition is distinct
from the legal one adopted by the UN, which is concerned with identifying displaced individuals. Instead, the definition that anchors this book
is *displacement*, which is fundamentally an interaction between armed
groups and civilians. The focus of the book is on this interaction, rather
than the ultimate destination of the displaced, whether within their home
country or in a new one. The starting assumption is that the initial displacement shares common foundations regardless of the final destination
of the displaced.[7]

---

4. The delay between the recognition of refugees and IDPs reflects the delicate relationship between the UN and its member states, which seek to protect their own sovereignty.
Refugees are beyond the origin state's sovereign territory and are therefore recognized by
international law as eligible for humanitarian assistance. IDPs are not. It is interesting to note,
however, the importance that the UN definition places on membership in a group as a basis
for persecution or fear of it.

5. In spite of the UN's refugee definition, estimates of the displaced do not depend on
investigating the causes. Rather, they are estimates of the number of people living within host
countries, organized and compiled by the United Nations High Commission for Refugees
(UNHCR), the UN agency that delivers assistance to refugees in multiple camps throughout
the globe. For details, see Crisp (2000).

6. This definition excludes displacement that stems from natural disasters or planned
development projects. These types, which can affect huge numbers of civilians, are beyond the
scope of this project because they are linked to fundamentally different causal processes. I use
"wartime displacement" and "displacement" interchangeably. Another distinction between
my definition and existing academic, press, and advocacy work is that the latter tend to refer
to displacement as "forced migration" or "forced displacement." I prefer the term "displacement" to these options because I think it better avoids implying underlying causes for the observed movement of civilians and sidesteps the debate about how "forced" any given wartime
migration truly is (e.g., Petersen 1958; Kunz 1973).

7. Armed groups should condition their targeting behavior on their expectations about
where civilians are likely to go, which I discuss further later in the chapter. For some wars,
the proximity to international borders and the presence of transnational groups and identities
play a key role in the patterns of displacement that develop. The theoretical and empirical
focus of this book is primarily on dynamics within the borders of one country.

The Context: Irregular Civil Wars

The contexts in which armed groups and civilians interact are crucial for understanding the nature of those interactions and the outcomes they produce. Civil wars are the contexts this book studies. Indeed, the growth of refugees and IDPs has coincided with the increase in the number of civil wars in the second half of the twentieth century. The dynamics of the Cold War led to an increase in a form of warfare known as "guerrilla wars" or "insurgencies," as the Soviet Union and the United States supported politically friendly rebels that would otherwise have faced defeat by stronger states (Kalyvas and Balcells 2010; Hobsbawm 1996). These "irregular" civil wars (Kalyvas 2005) account for roughly half of all wars.[8]

This book aims to conceptualize and explain variation in *forms* of displacement within these irregular civil wars rather than the overall *scale* of displacement produced by them. The focus of this book is distinct from that of studies that explain large-scale campaigns like mass killing (Valentino 2004), deportation (Greenhill 2010), ethnic cleansing (Bulutgil 2016), or genocides and politicides (Harff 2003; Straus 2006).[9] Though these types of victimization often overlap with forms of displacement, these phenomena require different explanations because they are typically centralized decisions. In contrast, the forms of displacement I document and explain here are related to armed groups' strategies *within* ongoing wars, which I expect to vary across communities and over time.

---

8. Kalyvas and Balcells (2010) and Kalyvas (2005) identify three types of civil wars: irregular, conventional, and symmetric nonconventional. Irregular wars are discussed below. Conventional refers to matched military forces, which leads to the formation of front lines and regular battles. Civilians are theoretically less implicated in the production of violence in these types of wars, though Balcells (2017) finds that armed groups nonetheless do target civilians behind the front lines. Symmetric nonconventional wars are those in which both sides are weak and struggle to establish territorial control. Here again, though civilians are victimized, the logic of the patterns are distinct from wars in which the armed groups are competing over territorial control. The balance of civil war types, according to Kalyvas and Balcells (2010), has shifted over time and may continue to change toward what Kalyvas (2005) calls "symmetric non-conventional," given fewer international sponsors of otherwise weak groups. This view, however, may undervalue the sponsorship of nonstate organizations and networks such as Al-Qaeda.

9. Valentino (2004) includes mass killing campaigns whose aims are "dispossessive," meaning that the aim of lethal violence is to expel people from the land. I agree that lethal violence is often part of cleansing efforts, as does Downes (2008, 20), though I study these tactics on a smaller scale rather than as a widespread campaign.

In the context of civil wars, it is difficult to collect reliable information about war-affected communities, and this is often a secondary priority to providing assistance to the victims of violence. But as a result, we do not have a clear understanding of how displacement comes about, especially in nonethnic civil wars. To lay the groundwork for understanding it, we first need to understand the characteristics of these types of wars and how these characteristics influence the ways armed groups and civilians interact.

Irregular civil wars feature an imbalance between strong state militaries and any allied militias, and weak insurgents. In some contexts antirebel militias are also important (Jentzsch, Kalyvas, and Schubiger 2015). Armed groups, including state armed forces, are "formal organizations using armed force to influence the outcome of a stated political incompatibility."[10] Insurgents avoid military confrontations with the state, and front lines do not form as a result (Kalyvas 2006). This dynamic has dire implications for civilians: the competing armed groups rely on them and demand their participation in the war. The insurgents ply them for resources and use them for cover. (Mao famously quipped that guerrillas swim in a sea of civilians.) The central challenge for counterinsurgents is the "identification problem," separating civilians from insurgents. To resolve the problem, they require information from civilians (Kalyvas 2006). Both sides attempt to establish territorial control where they are the only actor in charge. To this end, armed groups use several tactics to gain or retain control or to disrupt a rival's presence or control, including various forms of violence against civilians (Kalyvas 2006, 124–32).[11] Though both insurgents and counterinsurgents face similar incentives to use violence, they differ in when, where, and how they do so because of the different resources available to them. (I return to this below.)

Civilians are individuals who do not participate in the military activities of any armed group but who may be "part-time" affiliates or collaborators. To avoid violence, individuals continually assess their risk and

---

10. See definitions at Uppsala Universitet, Department of Peace and Conflict Research, http://www.pcr.uu.se/research/ucdp/definitions/, last accessed August 1, 2015.

11. Not all armed groups or parties to civil wars qualify. I assume that armed groups' main goal is not the elimination of some subgroup of the general population for its own sake, as in genocides and some ethnic cleansing campaigns.

weigh the actions they can take to reduce that risk. Civilians also have political preferences and resource constraints that shape the decisions they make. All things being equal, they prefer to stay in their communities and on their land. Unfortunately, armed groups often make this option impossible.

During irregular civil wars, "What armed groups fear the most is disloyalty, not exit" (Gutiérrez Sanín 2003, 22). Because the armed groups do not face each other for set battles, their ability to defeat one another hinges on civilians. The main basis of competition is for territorial control, and disloyalty by civilians can mean the difference between victory and defeat (Downes 2008, 36). Disloyalty could be informing a rival armed group where another is camped, or who is working for them among her neighbors. It could also be providing food, like the extra tortillas that some Salvadorans voluntarily gave to the FMLN (Wood 2003). Armed groups do their best to seek out and punish the disloyal.

Loyalty and Collaboration

Given the risks involved, why would civilians betray a powerful armed group? In other words, what explains disloyalty? Kalyvas (2006) shows numerous examples of civilians providing information to whichever armed group has relatively more territorial control, because the likelihood they will be punished for failing to comply with the stronger group is higher than the likelihood that they will be punished for defecting from the weaker group. This dynamic suggests that one important factor shaping civilians' choices is the degree of control an armed group exercises, and it explains the amount of collaboration they receive from civilians. In other words, civilians respond to incentives like security, because collaborating with the stronger group is less risky than helping a weaker one.[12]

I argue that in addition to incentives, civilians also develop loyalties, to their kin, to their neighbors, to members of social networks, and to fellow ethnic group members. Loyalties can also be transmitted through generations, within households and clans. Darden (forthcoming) shows

---

12. Not all collaboration, Kalyvas (2006) demonstrates, is useful for the armed groups. Civilians often use civil war dynamics to settle personal scores or accumulate property.

that nationalist education at the time of literacy led to lasting identities and loyalties in Ukraine. Identities can also develop based on loose ties: Skarbek (2014) argues that ascriptive differences between group members are useful in the context of large populations, in this case prisons, because it allows group members to generate trust. Two mechanisms for sustaining group identification are internal group norms and in-group policing; members know they are subject to the group's rules and will be punished if they violate them (Fearon and Laitin 1996). Over time, the act of trusting other group members and relying on internal regulation seems to generate identification with the group and loyalty to its members.

These dynamics of identity formation and reinforcement structure wartime cleavages, or the "the salient system of group classification in a society and its conflicts" (Kalyvas and Kocher 2007n10). Gould (1995, 15) relates the dynamic process of collective identity formation to the concept of cleavage when writing about the mobilization of the Paris Commune:

> The collective identity of workers as workers only emerges if the social networks in which they are embedded are patterned in such a way that the people in them can plausibly be partitioned into "workers" and "nonworkers"; but once this is possible, social conflict between collective actors who are defined in terms of this partition will heighten the salience and plausibility of the partition itself. The intensification of the boundary's cognitive significance for individuals will, in other words, align social relations so that the boundary becomes even more real.

Similarly, Tilly and Tarrow (2007, 80) build on their idea of boundary formation: "Everywhere in identity politics we will meet the mechanism of boundary activation, in which an existing boundary becomes more salient as a reference point for collective claim making."

"Boundary activation" can emerge from prewar cleavages and wartime dynamics (Balcells 2017; Bulutgil 2016). Lubkemann's (2005, 2008) studies of wartime migration in Mozambique emphasize the importance of prewar society on wartime cleavages. Whereas in Machaze (and the larger central provinces), the extended family was the primary site of prewar conflicts, in the Gaza and Nampula provinces, ethnic cleavages structured social relations. Lubkemann finds evidence that FRELIMO and RENAMO, the primary armed groups fighting in Mozambique, each shaped their behavior depending on these community social structures. The result was variation in the forms of violence and displacement in each region. For example, extended families dissolved in Machaze through atomistic displacement, while the ethnic cleavage in Nampula led to entire villages leaving together.

Loyalties can also emerge in the context of ongoing wars. Wood (2003) finds that some peasants engaged in risky activities to support rebel groups in El Salvador because it gave individuals *pleasure in agency*, which Wood describes as an emotional benefit to individuals who feel they are contributing to a broader, just cause when they engage in risky action. In turn, this could produce identification with or loyalty to a group that promotes the cause. Similarly, Goodwin and Skocpol (1989, 494) argue that "it is the ongoing provision of collective and selective goods, not ideological conversion in the abstract, that has played the principal role in solidifying social support for guerrilla armies." The provision of these goods can create loyalties over time. In some cases, communities earn a reputation as loyal to one side, which can reinforce residents' identities (Kalyvas 2006, 128–29).

In other cases, prewar cleavages may not become salient until the war itself begins (Kalyvas and Kocher 2007). Balcells (2017) documents dynamics of "revenge" that began during the Spanish Civil War, and Bulutgil (2016) explains how emotions triggered by alliances and violence during war can lead to a greater likelihood of ethnic cleansing campaigns. On an individual level, Petersen (2002) explores how fear, hatred, resentment, and rage—typically generated during war—account for ethnic violence, perpetrated by individuals who identify with an ethnic group and perceive members of other ethnic groups to be justifiable targets of violence. Bringa and Christie's (1993) fascinating documentary *We Are All Neighbors*, about a Bosnian village during the civil war, shows that as violence approached, the distance between Muslim and Catholic neighbors grew. Within groups, neighbors became closer, gathering for religious services and singing nationalistic songs. In other words, the violence caused the polarization and shaped group members' loyalties, rather than the polarization causing the violence.

Kalyvas (2003) cautions that it would be a mistake to assume that the cleavage that characterizes the "sides" of a war at the national level translates directly onto the local level. Yet Gould (1995, 21–34) points out, and the documentary demonstrates, that collective identities leading to political action are likely to be formed, and remain relevant, at the local level.

As violence becomes imminent and is directed at specific groups like ethnicities or sects, individuals become more likely to choose a side. Kalyvas and Kocher (2007) argue that when individuals are potential targets of violence, it becomes safer to align with an armed group, which could provide relatively better possibilities for safety. Lichbach (1994, 413) argues that selective and collective benefits are insufficient, though, because the groups providing the benefits (in this case, safety) face competition. Hirschman ([1970] 1980, 81) adds, "Expressed as a paradox, loyalty is at its most functional when it looks most irrational, when loyalty means strong attachment to an organization that does not seem to warrant such attachment because it is so much like another one that is also available." For Lichbach, the distinguishing factor is ideology. Gutiérrez Sanín and Wood (2014) explain how ideology can attract civilian support as well as create normative commitments to the group or cause. They also point out that ideology is not restricted to nonethnic conflicts, but that ethnic violence, and indeed all political violence, also implies an ideological basis.

Individuals, then, can embrace a collective identity as the result of affective loyalties, ideology, civil war violence, emotions, or even pragmatic decisions. Regardless of the source of individuals' attachment to a collective identity, and by extension to an armed group in the case of civil wars, individuals' security interests and their group membership reinforce one another and produce or strengthen cleavages during wars. These cleavages, and the individual attachments that underlie them, have important implications for how members of each side are likely to act and for the subsequent threats they are likely to face over the course of a war.

Selective, Indiscriminate, and *Collective* Targeting

Armed groups—both insurgents and counterinsurgents—aim to prevent defection and to generate compliance among civilians. Prewar and wartime processes create incentives and group identities that lead civilians to be disloyal in spite of the risk. The central challenge for armed groups, then, is to identify and punish the disloyal civilians.

To do so, armed groups use violence and the threat of violence to generate compliance and punish disloyalty in the service of winning or retaining territorial control. Again, disloyalty matters because it can hinder an armed group's ability to avoid rival armed groups' challenges to their quest for territorial control. Depending on the form of disloyalty the armed group anticipates or detects, it will target individuals or groups. In other words, a key distinction among forms of violence is who the possible victims of violence are: individuals, groups, or no one in particular and everyone in general. I call this distinction "targeting," which refers to the selection of civilians that an armed group defines as the potential objects of violence. Three types of targeting underlie most violence in civil wars: selective, indiscriminate, and collective (Steele 2009; Kalyvas 2006; Wood 2010; Gutiérrez Sanín and Wood, forthcoming).[13] When faced with any threat of violence, civilians try to secure their safety and the safety of loved ones. But the best way to do so depends on the type of targeting they face from armed groups. In turn, how civilians respond to the targeting leads to different forms of displacement.

Selective targeting is the most dangerous for civilians. They are targeted by an armed group because of something they have done or, probably just as often, are accused of doing. Those who have collaborated with a rival armed group, or have engaged in some activity that an armed group does not approve of such as leading a social organization or engaging in politics, are frequent targets of selective violence. In other words, selective targeting is characterized by high specificity. Individuals might be targeted for political reasons or for private ones. Political selective targeting occurs when individuals are targeted for failing to collaborate with an armed group or for defecting to a rival. As Kalyvas (2006, 142) writes, "Violence is selective when there is an intention to ascertain individual guilt." Private selective targeting is based on a denunciation by another civilian, for motives unrelated to supporting one armed group or another, such as revenge or greed (Kalyvas 2006).[14]

---

13. These types are informed by the concepts of selective and indiscriminate violence outlined by Kalyvas (2006), but I use "collective" to make a sharper distinction between random and nonrandom violence. Importantly, the form of targeting does not imply the scale of the violence; each type can relate to many or few victims. In the case of collective targeting, the proportion of the population targeted depends on the group-level trait on which the targeting is based. It may encompass an entire community or be limited to a narrow profile, such as profession. Conceptually disaggregating the scale of the violence from its targeting basis is necessary to avoid inferring targeting type from the number of victims observed.

14. Kalyvas (2006) explains how selective violence is "jointly produced" by armed groups and civilians, who take advantage of armed groups to settle private grievances. Civilians' *perception* of the violence as selective is important for understanding the effect the violence is likely to have (Kalyvas 2006, 145). The important factor for this work is how well the targeted civilian can assess the likelihood of suffering violence.

Indiscriminate targeting is not related to any trait or behavior, so anyone is potentially a victim.[15] Targeting that is indiscriminate (from civilians' perspective) can either be randomly directed at communities or can occur when armed groups confront one another near residential areas.[16] Any "collateral damage" from these confrontations constitutes indiscriminate violence because civilians are not the intended targets. Civil war violence is frequently described this way by observers. In 2008, the *New York Times* reported that the LRA massacred hundreds in the Congo, for no discernible reason (Gettleman 2008). The IDMC noted in its 2009 *Global Overview* that in Yemen, "At the height of the . . . fighting in 2008, 130,000 people had reportedly been internally displaced in a conflict involving indiscriminate bombardment of civilian areas, arbitrary arrests, enforced disappearances, and alleged child recruitment by all parties" (IDMC 2010). Jason Lyall (2009) described rocket attacks launched by Russian soldiers in Chechnya as random, fueled by binge drinking.

Collective targeting is violence or threatened violence against members of a group because of membership in that group.[17] In other words, group membership is "integral rather than incidental" to the targeting (Brubaker and Laitin 1998, 428). Collective targeting is distinct from being caught in the crossfire of battling armed groups, targeted indiscriminately with all other civilians, or selectively targeted for not collaborating or for defecting. Armed groups (as well as civilians) use civilians' group affiliations to infer support for a rival. Affiliation can be related to neighborhood, ethnicity, or a trait that indicates an

---

15. Here indiscriminate is not used in the international legal sense of discriminating between armed combatants—legitimate targets of violence—and civilians, who are illegitimate targets under any circumstances in international law. Instead it refers to discriminating among civilians on some basis, such as behavior (selective) or membership in a group (collective, explained below), or not at all.

16. Given the structural characteristics of irregular civil wars, indiscriminate targeting is relatively less frequent than in conventional or symmetric nonconventional wars.

17. At times, Kalyvas defines "indiscriminate" the same as I am defining "collective": "In indiscriminate violence . . . the concept of individual guilt is replaced by the concept of guilt by association. . . . The specific rule of association varies and ranges from family to village, region, and nation" (Kalyvas 2006, 142). But he frequently describes indiscriminate violence as if it were random (Kalyvas 2006, 143–72). In some cases, it overlaps with selective targeting: "too much reliance on [secondary] profiling defeats the basic premise of selective violence" (Kalyvas 2006, 187). In addition, the concept of indiscriminate violence is used interchangeably with "random" and with what I am defining as "collective" in the literature (e.g., Lyall 2009; Downes 2007). The debate about the efficacy of "indiscriminate violence," I think, is partly due to this conflation. See Wood (2010) for a similar definition of collective violence.

armed group's "social constituency" (Schubiger 2015). When a civilian is targeted because of a shared, suspect characteristic or membership in a group, she has a higher probability of experiencing violence than a civilian who does not share her type. Ethnicity is an all-too-common basis for targeting. Bosnia, Croatia, Sri Lanka, Cyprus, and Sudan have experienced ethnic fighting and cleansing. In Uganda, the Acholi were expelled from their villages into resettlement camps (Branch 2006). In Cote d'Ivoire, supporters of the government were accused of "ethnically-motivated killings and rapes in Abidjan" (IDMC 2012a). In other conflicts, the types of organizations or professions that people belong to are the basis of targeting. The IDMC characterized violence perpetrated by insurgents in Thailand as indiscriminate, though only some types of people were targeted: "representatives and symbols of the Thai state, including teachers and schools" (IDMC 2014a). Stepputat (1999a, 62–63) argues that in spite of the association of counterinsurgent action in Guatemala with "scorched earth" tactics, in fact both the insurgents and the military seem to have pressured community leaders to choose sides prior to targeting villages. In effect, the villages were then linked to one side or the other.

Selective, indiscriminate, and collective targeting together account for variation in forms of violence that civilians experience during civil wars. This book argues that civilians' reactions to violence—including displacement—depend on which of these forms they experience.

Civilians' Responses and Forms of Displacement: Escape, Relocation, Cleansing

When faced with violence, what should civilians do? How can they reduce the risk that they or someone they love will die? The best course of action for civilians depends on the form of targeting they face.[18] How they respond, in turn, creates different types of displacement: individual escape,

---

18. Civilians' perceptions of targeting should also be important. To the extent civilians do not perceive the actual form of targeting they face, their reactions will not be consistent with the expectations outlined here. I thank Juan Masullo for bringing this to my attention. I assume for now that perceptions are accurate. This is probably too strong an assumption, but explaining variation in the accuracy of perceptions is something I do not undertake here. In chapters 4 and 5, I describe some tactics used to communicate the intent behind collective targeting, including graffiti and leaflets, so there is empirical support for my assumption in my cases.

TABLE 1.1. Targeting by armed groups and forms of civilian displacement

Targeting type	Selective	Collective	Indiscriminate
Displacement form	Individual escape	Political cleansing	Mass evasion

mass relocation, and political cleansing. Table 1.1 summarizes the forms of displacement that emerge based on armed groups' targeting and civilians' responses.

Civilians face the greatest risk when confronted with selective targeting, because an armed group is out to get them specifically. Those selectively targeted are the least likely to stay in a community relative to other targeted types, because if they do, their risk of suffering direct, lethal violence is very high. As a result, selective targeting is likely to lead to individual escape, if the targeted person discovers the threat in time. Examples abound within civil wars: People denounced for being an accomplice might receive a tip and escape just ahead of their would-be assassins. A schoolteacher in the Casamance region of Senegal was advised by a schools inspector to leave because of threats by rebels (Evans 2007, 69). In Colombia, a woman I interviewed described how twelve FARC combatants surrounded her home; her husband saw them from afar and hid in the surrounding mountains until he could secure safe passage out of the region. She and her children followed, carefully navigating hundreds of miles through rivers to safety on the Caribbean coast.[19] In other cases, affiliation with an organization can be the difference between life and death or escape. Kaplan (2013) documents how members of a highly organized peace community learned of threats against them and escaped ahead of imminent violence when the organization could not intervene successfully on their behalf. It may be safer to affiliate with an armed group for this reason: armed groups tend to have more access to information and may be able to facilitate escape (Kalyvas and Kocher 2007).[20]

---

19. Interview with the author, Cartagena, July 2002.

20. The FARC also seem to use this as a recruitment mechanism. Several ex-combatants I spoke with described how they had been an informant for a nearby front, or active in a student political organization associated with the insurgents, when the FARC informed them that they were on a state list of rebels, so it would be safer to go to the "monte" and join the ranks (interview with the author, June 8, 2007, Bogotá).

In cases in which the targeting is indiscriminate, the best way to avoid the violence depends on its intensity and frequency. If it is infrequent, civilians may decide the risk of future suffering is relatively low compared to the costs of relocating. If the fighting or violence is regular and intense, a better option may be to relocate until the danger subsides. Because the violence is associated with their location, not who they are, civilians can move out of the way, which might not be possible with collective and selective targeting. In the Spanish Civil War, some residents of cities that faced aerial bombardment sought safety in the countryside. The NRC/IDMC noted in its 2012 *Global Overview* (IDMC 2013) that hundreds of Israelis were temporarily displaced to avoid Palestinian armed groups' indiscriminate rocket fire into Israel. At the outset of the Syrian civil war, the NRC/IDMC reported that IDPs and refugees were "returning home after the security forces loyal to the government have left" (IDMC 2011), as if they had temporarily moved out of their way to avoid general violence. Some indigenous communities in Colombia establish "humanitarian zones" where members relocate when armed groups' violence approaches. Melander and Oberg (2007) find that the intensity of fighting, measured by battle deaths, is not a good predictor of displacement. The finding makes sense within this framework: when armed groups do confront one another, civilians themselves are not targets. If the threat of suffering violence is high, however, households may move to a nearby town, perhaps temporarily. Other coping mechanisms include sleeping in towns at night and returning to fields during the day.

Civilians who face collective targeting have possibilities and constraints different from those who face other forms of targeting. One key difference is that the risk members of collectively targeted groups face is interdependent. If a person is selectively targeted or faces indiscriminate violence, the decision to stay in or leave a community does not depend on others who are selectively or indiscriminately targeted; the likelihood that the person will suffer direct violence will not change whether or not others stay. In contrast, when armed groups collectively target, the decision to stay or leave of any given individual who shares the targeted trait depends on the response of everyone else similarly targeted. In this way, the situation that civilians are confronted with matches the conditions for Granovetter's

(1978) threshold model of collective behavior.[21] As more people who are collectively targeted leave, it will trigger others to do so, because they will feel less safe without the "cover" of others like them and more vulnerable to violence as a result.[22]

Given sustained, collective violence directed at their group, households have strong incentives to leave, which only increase if others begin to do so.[23] Darby provides an example from Northern Ireland: "more families left their homes, not because they had actually experienced violence, but from anticipation of trouble in the future; that is, not because individuals had been attacked or threatened, but because the community to which they belonged had itself become isolated and vulnerable" (Darby 1990, 98). In Missouri during the US Civil War, Fellman notes, "The grind of guerrilla war, coupled to the flight of politically like-minded neighbors, frightened and depressed those who remained" (Fellman 1989, 74). Decades later, lynchings of black residents in the US South were associated with out-migration of blacks, but lynchings of whites were not associated with any such movement (Tolnay and Beck 1992), reflecting the fact that the violence directed against blacks was based as much on their identity as on any "crime" they supposedly committed. In contrast, white

---

21. Granovetter's (1978) model also suggests why different communities will experience different scales of cleansing even if they are exposed to the same type and level of collective targeting. Individuals' thresholds for staying in spite of the violence and others' leaving are likely to be distributed differently across communities, and these distributions are likely to have a significant impact on the overall levels of cleansing observed. Further, these distributions can also be influenced by an individual's social ties, which essentially weights the impact of leaving on a person depending on how close others are to that person, which in turn can influence the scale of cleansing a community experiences. Explaining individuals' thresholds and community-level distributions is beyond the scope of this project (and, as Granovetter [1978] notes, often intractable), but it is important to underscore that the distribution of thresholds for leaving or staying in a population is one reason that the scale of displacement does not reveal the type of targeting or form of displacement in a straightforward way, even if it is the best indicator available in some cases.

22. There is probably a point at which the armed group will stop collectively targeting the group, because the proportion of those who remain is so small that they do not constitute a sufficient threat. In these cases, the armed group could pursue a lower-cost strategy of conversion by demanding that those who stay declare their allegiance to the new group in charge. As with the distribution of thresholds across communities, this more general threshold is difficult to calculate ex ante, but it may depend on other factors of the community such as proximity to the stronghold of the rival armed group, for example.

23. If the armed group with which they are linked offers protection, staying could be an option. An alternative would be to defect to the targeting group.

lynchings were selective, reserved for individuals who transgressed a norm or violated the law. As a result, other whites did not migrate out of the region.

Collective targeting involves multiple tactics. One is the use of lethal violence against members of the targeted group, even if the primary goal of the armed group is to expel group members rather than kill them all. People are extremely reluctant to leave their homes, land, and communities, but they will leave when faced with the possibility of death. In an interview with Human Rights Watch, María Girlesa Villegas, a public advocate (*defensora del pueblo*) for the department of Antioquia, stated, "The movement of masses of people is only the last step in a long process. It starts with one or two families, then a group of people. Again and again, these communities see atrocities. And when they can stand it no longer, that is when they leave" (Human Rights Watch 1998). Stepputat (1999b, 52) observed that in Guatemala, "massacres seem to be the most important single events that lead to the massive displacement of the rural population." The former minister of agriculture in Colombia, Alejandro Reyes, agrees that massacres produce the most displacement there.[24] Moreover, this violence cannot be perceived to be indiscriminate if it is to effectively provoke displacement. Weidmann and Salehyan (2013, 59) model violence in Iraq and find that random violence does not account for the segregation that emerged in Baghdad; the violence has to be targeted based on ethnicity.

Threats are also an important component of collective targeting; they communicate that the killing will not end until the group leaves the community. They also tend to signal that the intent is not to kill all members of the group, unless the violence is genocidal. A report on displacement in Colombia notes, "Frequently . . . mass displacements are announced in advance, [and] those who fail to follow the order to move find themselves at risk of massacre or other serious attack upon their physical security" (UNHCR 2003). In Myanmar, Cusano (2001, 148) reports that "The Burmese army's counter-insurgency tactics usually follow a pattern: after targeting an area for depopulation, the army orders villagers to move by issuing a written notice, convening a meeting of village headmen or

---

24. Interview with the author, Bogotá, May 27, 2013.

visiting the village themselves." In Colombia, paramilitary groups favored graffiti to announce their arrival and to warn residents that they should leave ahead of time (Amnesty International 1997).

Another tactic is to burn homes to evict residents, as paramilitaries eventually did in the municipality of Ituango in Colombia (e.g., *El Tiempo* 2000). In Turkey, state forces burned thousands of "recalcitrant" villages (IDMC 2009):

> Helicopters, armored vehicles, troops, and village guards surrounded village after village. They burned stored produce, agricultural equipment, crops, orchards, forests, and livestock. They set fire to houses, often giving the inhabitants no opportunity to retrieve their possessions. . . . By 1994, more than 3,000 villages had been virtually wiped from the map and more than a quarter of a million peasants had been made homeless.

Ultimately, individuals who are members of targeted groups may choose to leave the community because they have been directly threatened; or they may leave because they are afraid; or they may leave because they would prefer to live in a more secure community where the likelihood that they will suffer violence is lower. The precise motivation can vary, but I argue that armed groups create situations to prompt civilians to leave and that targeting members of a group in this way—what I call collective targeting—will increase the probability that members of the targeted group will leave, for whatever reason.[25]

When civilians leave in response to collective targeting, the armed group has effectively "cleansed" the territory. By now the term is a familiar one, even if it usually applies only to ethnic violence. The tactics armed groups use to cleanse nonethnic groups, however, closely resemble what happens with ethnic cleansing. "Political cleansing" is the expulsion of a particular group from a territory.[26] It is a general phenomenon that occurs

---

25. A substantial segment of the literature on displacement dwells on the conceptual distinction between "forced" or "impelled" and relatively "voluntary" migration during war. Empirically, it is ambitious to establish what portion of an individual's ultimate decision was "voluntary" or "forced" (Petersen 1958). The problem is probably not just tricky but intractable (perhaps even epistemologically so). Displacement defined as wartime migration sidesteps this problem.

26. Bulutgil (2009) defines ethnic cleansing as the forced population movements and killings of a particular ethnic group. However, I prefer to avoid the term "forced." Further,

to different degrees across wars and based on different targeted groups within and across wars. The concept of political cleansing, in other words, encompasses the category of ethnic cleansing. Depending on the cleavage of the war, I expect the relevant indicator of loyalty to be the basis of collective targeting and of the cleansing that results. When ethnicity is politicized as the primary cleavage in the war, armed groups are more likely to target members of an ethnic group. Supporters of political parties can be similarly profiled, as the book documents. Regardless of the basis of collective targeting, political cleansing can result.

One important distinction between forms of cleansing is that in some cases, cleansing is a policy choice at the center, and the form it takes is a generalized campaign. Most commonly, these campaigns are directed against ethnic groups (Bulutgil 2016). The type of cleansing I conceptualize and explain here is a strategy during war to win territorial control, rather than a large-scale campaign directed from the center.

Resisting Political Cleansing

In some cases, communities can manage to stay in spite of collective targeting. This is relatively rare, because it requires coordination to keep a minimum core of the targeted group from leaving, so that the interdependent risk among households is relatively lower than moving elsewhere. In these cases, staying with the community reduces a household's risk of suffering direct violence because, perversely, there are more possible alternative victims. Such a community would be more likely to have residents with a high threshold for violence, in Granovetter's (1978) terms. It may also be possible for communities to take specific actions to increase residents' thresholds for violence. Based on my fieldwork, I think two elements are essential: First, the community must have or adopt a strong set of internal norms or rules that prevent "defection" of residents.[27] If some begin to leave (defection in this case), it will likely trigger others to follow, as

---

killings are an aspect of the collective targeting that armed groups engage in, which I argue can lead to political cleansing. Romero (2000, 98) also uses the term political cleansing in reference to paramilitary activity in Colombia.

27. See Kaplan (2013) for a description of one community organization that helped to coordinate its members against armed groups' threats and probably greatly reduced displacement.

I wrote above. Rules prohibiting or incentivizing people to stay can stave off this chain reaction. (I describe this further in chapter 5.) The development of these rules or norms could have occurred prior to any violence, or it could be a reaction to the targeting. It could also be fostered by outside organizations. For instance, organizers with the Indigenous Organization of Antioquia (OIA) worked with an indigenous community in Apartadó, where I conducted fieldwork, to activate institutions for internal policing and external neutrality that the community itself did not already rely on.[28]

This leads to the second condition: An external group must offer some sort of protection or support to maintain the communities' resolve in the face of ongoing violence. The outside group may be a nongovernmental organization, as in the case of the OIA, Justicia y Paz, and CINEP (Masullo 2015) and international groups like the Fellowship of Reconciliation (FOR) or Peace Brigades International (PBI), which "accompany" communities that try to stay. Or the outside group could also be an armed organization.[29] These speculations are supported by Juan Masullo's (2017) systematic study of communities engaged in organized forms of noncooperation with armed groups. We coincide in our accounts of the importance of internal mechanisms and external support to organize and withstand ongoing violence, though he emphasizes that external support is more essential for the formation of the organized noncooperation, while internal regulations sustain it. Interestingly, Masullo (2017) finds that organized noncooperation is more likely as a reaction to collective targeting than to either selective or indiscriminate forms.

While it is possible for communities to resist collective targeting, it is also unlikely. The possibility, though, reinforces the conceptual distinction between collective targeting and political cleansing. The former is a strategy, and the latter is an outcome that is not always achieved.[30] The next section further delimits these central concepts.

---

28. Interview with Carlos Salazar, Apartadó, July 24, 2007.

29. According to Masullo's (2017) typology, the peace community in the Urabá region I visited is engaged in the most confrontational type of noncooperation, openly opposing the armed groups. The indigenous community that also managed to resist the political cleansing effort engaged in what Masullo (2017) calls "brokered non-cooperation," which relies on intermediaries to negotiate with armed groups and avoid or end violent threats. A third type is "oblique non-cooperation," characterized by more indirect acts of resistance.

30. A related point is that we should not infer that communities without high levels of displacement were not targeted collectively.

Conceptual Boundaries

Even though collective targeting and the political cleansing that can result typically involve lethal violence, political cleansing is not the same as genocide (or politicide). Genocide is defined as the attempt to physically destroy members of an organic group (Straus 2001). Rather than destruction of a group, political cleansing aims to remove the group in question from a territory.

Collective targeting is also not equivalent to communal violence. The distinction is the participation of at least one armed group; communal violence is typically perpetrated by community members who may temporarily organize to fight a rival community or subset of their own, but they do not remain organized. Further, at least one party that is allied with the state or is representing the state must be a participant. Gould (1991) also refers to this as "collective violence." Communal violence has been documented in Nigeria (e.g., IDMC 2012b), Indonesia (e.g., Tajima 2014), and India (e.g., Wilkinson 2006; Varshney 2003).

The focus of the book is on *strategic* targeting of civilians rather than opportunism. Opportunistic armed groups and criminal organizations often take advantage of civil wars to acquire new land illegally through forced property sales and falsified documentation. Such greedy behavior can be the cause of displacement, or a secondary effect of it, in the sense that armed groups or allies can claim ownership of the assets abandoned by those expelled for strategic reasons (e.g., Molano 1992). Though opportunism is likely a source of some displacement within and across wars, I focus on the strategic aspects of displacement as important to understand as a first step, rather than the decision to engage in other actions that could produce displacement.

The conceptualization of targeting and the displacement it provokes both complements and departs from assumptions underlying existing work. Ana María Ibáñez characterizes displacement as either "reactive," in response to a direct attack by armed groups, or "preventive," to avoid a future attack (Ibáñez 2008, 13).[31] I think this distinction captures an important aspect of civilians' experiences across different forms of targeting. The advantage of theorizing both reactive and preventive displacement

---

31. She finds that most IDPs in Colombia were reactive.

from a perspective of targeting is that it provides an analytical tool to incorporate armed groups' strategies in a systematic way. This approach also sheds light on which civilians are most likely to be at risk of different forms of violence and displacement. Whereas Moore and Shellman (2004) and Davenport, Moore, and Poe (2003) also theorize that individuals' choices depend on their assessment of the risk they face, they assume that individuals face a lottery of risk. In contrast, I theorize that risk systematically varies among individuals of a given community and over time, depending on their networks, identities, and even choices.[32] Choices that appear minor at one point in time can end up having enormous—and dangerous—repercussions over the course of a civil war. Sometimes in retrospect, the "choice" was in fact nothing but the luck of the draw: the banana plantation that happened to be hiring that day led a laborer to join the union that represented the workers there, which led to moving into a neighborhood founded by union members (and backed by an armed group), which led the worker to identify with his fellow union members and neighbors. Such choices, coincidences, and risks shape individuals' and groups' identities in important ways in the context of a civil war.

In this framework, displacement resulting from selective and indiscriminate targeting is most similar to common perceptions: it is unintended or incidental to the goals of an armed group. Individuals escape selective targeting, and groups move out of the way of indiscriminate violence. In contrast, given expectations about civilians' behavior, armed groups can implement collective targeting to generate the displacement of a subset of the community for a strategic advantage. This is the form of displacement that the book sets out to explain.

A Theory of Collective Targeting and Political Cleansing

When and where do armed groups use collective targeting? Armed groups are likely to use different forms of targeting in particular settings and at particular times, because the costs and benefits of each form are context-dependent. While I expect selective and indiscriminate targeting

---

32. The authors acknowledge that the distribution of risk may not be random, but they do not theorize it.

to produce displacement, as I wrote in the previous section, in those instances the displacement is incidental to the goals of armed groups. Kalyvas (2006) provides a theory of selective violence that accounts for variation in selective targeting, and a logic of indiscriminate violence in irregular civil wars. I argue, however, that armed groups are aware that collective targeting is *likely* to produce displacement of the targeted group of civilians. In pursuit of political cleansing—the expulsion of a particular group from a territory—armed groups employ collective targeting. In this section, I develop my central argument that two variables drive the process: contestation between armed groups for control over a territory, and the identification of civilians' loyalties.

Competition and Conquest

Armed groups need the collaboration of civilians in order to consolidate territorial control, the key aim of both insurgents and counterinsurgents. How to gain such collaboration is a key challenge for armed groups. I argue that cleansing will help them secure the collaboration they need. As I described above, collaboration is not just a function of incentives such as security, but also of civilians' political preferences and loyalties, which may have been shaped by insurgents. The population's loyalties also create limitations for the counterinsurgents' relative advantage in resources. David Galula, a captain in the French army during the Algerian War of Independence, observed, "The theory that the population would join our side once it felt protected from the threat of rebel bands had proved wrong. The idea that we could forcibly implicate the population on our side had not worked" (Galula 1963, 97). In other words, even with superior coercive resources, counterinsurgents cannot switch civilians' allegiances—and deter defection—by force alone. Force, however, is effective for expelling the disloyal. Expulsion is most likely during competition between armed groups to gain control of a territory, and especially during an effort by counterinsurgents to conquer a new territory and wrest control from insurgents.[33]

---

33. The logic of political cleansing applies to all armed groups, but as I explain further below, the relative balance of power between insurgents and counterinsurgents leads the latter to be more likely to attempt it to conquer a territory. Insurgents would prefer to slowly

Armed groups stand to gain from political cleansing in two important ways. First, to the extent that civilians contribute to insurgents, removing them from a community directly reduces the resources available to insurgents, and, consequently, their presence.[34] The counterinsurgency literature features the central assumption that insurgents rely on civilians as a resource; the implication that follows is that states should target those civilians to curtail the resources of insurgents and defeat them. Sometimes this implies "draining the sea," referring to Mao's dictum that insurgent fish swim in a sea of civilians (Sepp 1992).

The second key benefit of political cleansing is that the remaining population may be more likely to comply with the incoming armed group, and would therefore lower the costs of establishing control, via three mechanisms. First, upsetting the balance of power should reduce civilians' fear of retaliation by insurgents. I expect civilians who may have developed grievances against insurgents or their followers to denounce individuals to counterinsurgents more regularly, enabling the counterinsurgency to transition to selective violence. In turn, the application of selective violence can reinforce counterinsurgent control of an area (Kalyvas 2006).[35] Second, with the most likely supporters of insurgents gone, counterinsurgents can spend fewer resources on monitoring potential traitors. Third, cleansing should also have a demonstration effect: the violence observed by the nontargeted civilians establishes a credible threat against defecting in the future.[36]

Insurgents are also most likely to attempt political cleansing during contestation, but as a defensive rather than offensive tactic. In order to defend a territory, insurgents have an incentive to target groups that could

---

infiltrate a community rather than invite repression by counterinsurgents with such a large-scale assault.

34. Armed groups must have sufficient resources to make a sustained assault. I assume this to be exogenous. If the group displaces and reconfigures communities, it may acquire more resources and consolidate control, but a minimum amount is necessary to initiate it. Otherwise, civilians will be likely to weather the occasional violence.

35. This dynamic can facilitate conquest, both locally and potentially, across a civil war.

36. Additional motivations are emotional. While the specific motivations are difficult if not impossible to pin down, the recurrent killings of "disloyal" civilians following numerous civil wars suggests that revenge and hatred also play a role in targeting, in addition to instrumental reasons. These mechanisms may have played a role in the massive killings of "landlords" in 1948 China and the loyalists in Algeria after the French pulled out (Keegan 1994).

potentially ally with the challenging armed group to attempt to stave off the advance of the challenger.[37] Although in general insurgents are less likely to politically cleanse, they are most likely to do it during competition for control with a rival armed group.

When an armed group is attempting to gain a foothold in a community where a rival does not exist or is very weak, collective targeting is unlikely.[38] First, when a group has yet to establish a presence in a community, the local-level cleavage is yet to become salient and polarized. Even if there is a cleavage to exploit in terms of tapping allies, it may not be clear which community group to tap. Kalyvas (2003) refers to this mechanism as alliance. Second, nonstate groups, like insurgents, generally have few resources, and collective targeting can be costly because it would reveal insurgent presence and may draw retaliation by the state (or counterinsurgent militias), as I discuss further below.

Cleansing is also unlikely to pay off when a group exerts control in a territory or is generally unchallenged. When an armed group controls a territory, selective violence is the most effective way to deter defection and generate compliance (Kalyvas 2006). When the threat of competition is low, the controlling armed group does not have an incentive to collectively target civilians under its control. Instead, it should use a combination of tactics ranging from coercion to persuasion to elicit resources from the community (Arjona 2016). Metelits (2009) argues that predation is more likely during periods of competition, while governance is more likely when there is control. Often, rivalry matters more than resources in determining victimization (Balcells 2010, 2017).

Repopulation   Armed groups' interest in shaping their local "constituencies" is reflected in a common step following political cleansing: repopulation of the territory, often in abandoned homes. Kalyvas and Kocher

---

37. Kalyvas (1999) writes about this dynamic in terms of massacres committed by insurgents losing ground in Algeria. In addition to meting out punishment for defection, however, those massacres may have been instrumental to try to achieve the abandonment of property; he describes the collective targeting of neighborhoods. In this situation, cleansing is a tactic that relies on demographic change to achieve goals of control (but in this sense to retain rather than gain it).

38. State forces may prefer to resettle entire communities because of their "human ecology" (Kocher 2004). In such cases, though, the goal of the armed group is not to control a community, but rather to prevent it from being controlled by an insurgent group. I consider these types of goals below.

(2007, n105) cite a paper on the occupation of the Philippines by Japan during World War II that "reports that the anti-Japanese guerrillas in the Philippines 'encouraged the migration of loyal Filipinos from the enemy-controlled areas to the unoccupied districts.'" ISIS makes regular appeals "to recruit not only fighters, but also citizens, to come and live in a functioning and thriving community" (Caris and Reynolds 2014, 9). Cusano (2001, 147) also reports that among insurgent groups representing the Karen ethnic group in Myanmar, "[The DKBA] tries to woo KNU members and sympathizers from refugee camps, promising a better deal under the DKBA if they return—and threatening retribution if they don't. By attacking KNU-controlled refugee camps in Thailand, DKBA has influenced displaced Karens' choices about where and how to flee."

Repopulation is also frequent within Colombia. The UNHCR reports,

> Entire areas are "cleansed" of the support they are suspected of providing to the "enemy" via mass displacement of whole communities. When the land concerned is of strategic value in military or economic terms, it is repopulated by supporters of the forces conducting the displacement. (UNHCR 2003)

Following displacement, the paramilitaries in particular "repopulate the territory with 'trustworthy' dwellers" (Gutiérrez Sanín 2003, 22).[39] Amnesty International (1997) reports that "zones chosen as objectives are 'cleansed' of the real or potential support of the guerrillas, and are repopulated with peasants favorable to paramilitaries or with family members in the paramilitaries." Romero (2003, 110) also reports that repopulation took place in neighborhoods of Barrancabermeja, a large city on the Magdalena River in Colombia.

In general, competition between armed groups is most likely to provoke collective targeting, either to facilitate conquest in the case of counterinsurgents or, less commonly, to resist conquest in the case of insurgents. Before reshaping the population of a territory or community, though, the armed groups need to know who is loyal and who is not.

---

39. This was supported by Mario Agudelo, who said that trying to legalize the property in the Policarpa neighborhood in Apartadó while he was mayor was complicated by the fact that people the paramilitaries brought in were occupying homes (interview with the author, Medellín, May 14, 2008).

Identifying the Disloyal

Galula wrote, "To sum up the situation, the big problem was how to assess the loyalties of [the locals]" (Galula 1963, 97). Armed groups, then, face two problems: (1) how to gain control of a territory if conversion of civilians is extremely difficult, and (2) how to identify the loyalties of civilians. I argue that resolving the first problem depends on resolving the second: armed groups can attempt to displace civilians when and where they can infer loyalties.

In some wars, ascriptive clues are used to infer loyalties by one or both armed groups and by civilians themselves.[40] In the absence of such clues, identifying potential allies and adversaries is a crucial challenge. French counterinsurgent theorist Trinquier writes, "In modern warfare, the enemy is . . . difficult to identify. . . . It is a non-physical, often ideological boundary, which must however be expressly delineated if we want to reach the adversary and to defeat him" (Trinquier 1964, 26). Even where it is relatively well known that a rival has a presence, it is difficult for an outside armed group to separate possible allies from likely adversaries. For displacement to pay off, this information is crucial. Otherwise, the outside armed group would have to resort to indiscriminate targeting, which is an instrument too blunt to create the changes in the community that would allow the armed group to conquer the community. Rather than expelling a portion of the population suspected of supporting the rival, indiscriminate targeting might cause too many civilians to leave, complicating the armed group's ability to establish control and lowering the benefits of doing so. An example comes from Missouri during the US Civil War. Fellman (1989, 95–96) writes that General Order No. 11 targeted residents of several counties for displacement, but authorities "did not distinguish between the loyal and the disloyal—all became war refugees." After the expulsion, "those who could obtain certificates of loyalty were permitted to return home," but most did not until the war was over. As a result, the Union could not establish control over those counties. In the twentieth century, such resettlement programs varied in success, depending on how

---

40. Frequently such patterns lead scholars to classify these wars as "ethnic," when in fact they may share much in common with nonethnic irregular civil wars (Kalyvas 2008; Kalyvas and Kocher 2007). In some cases, insurgents calculate that they will benefit from converting a conflict into a primarily ethnic one (Kalyvas and Kocher 2007).

well the programs distinguished between the loyal and disloyal (as well as how many resources were mobilized) (Sepp 1992). The Strategic Hamlet Program in Vietnam, which resettled thousands and thousands of peasants, was regarded as a failure despite the massive resources involved, because it did not distinguish between loyal and disloyal civilians. As a result, the Viet Cong were able to continue their activities in the new locations (Stubbs 2004).

Even in wars without an ethnic cleavage, information linking groups of civilians to armed groups can emerge, especially at the local level. Local-level cleavages tend to influence alliances with armed groups, but are largely unobservable to outsiders.[41] When armed groups acquire information about local groups and form beliefs about the probability of individuals' allegiances based on membership in such groups, then using collective targeting can be an effective tactic to compete with the rival armed group.

The UNHCR reported that in Sri Lanka, another process revealed civilians' loyalties:

> The LTTE also has a practice of mandatory civil defence training, even in areas under government control. This includes the issuance of a training card as proof of participation. Non-possession of the training card in LTTE-controlled areas can lead to, among others, restrictions on freedom of movement. These may seriously impact the ability of individuals to secure a livelihood. In government-controlled areas, individuals suspected of having participated in LTTE training may be perceived as LTTE sympathizers, even though the participation was coerced. (UNHCR 2006, 4)

In some cases, the act of leaving or staying serves as a signal to warring armed groups. In Guatemala, the UNHCR (2000, 59–60) reports,

> The view of the military and, through its propaganda, of much of the population under its control was that most of those who had fled had been

---

41. An additional possibility is when a group-level identifier becomes politically relevant as a result of the macro-level cleavage of the war. In general, identification processes can either be related to a national-level event that makes local-level identities salient (i.e., external processes), or they can emerge from within the community, related to the presence of an armed group (i.e., internal processes). I expect that depending on the process of local-level cleavage activation and formation, the timing of cleansing should vary over the course of the wars.

supporters of the rebels. As a result any false move by returnees, such as failure to show up for civil patrol duty or even a dispute over land with a neighbor, could result in being branded a guerrilla sympathizer. The consequences were serious and ranged from repatriates being singled out for intimidation or harassment to physical attacks and even killings.

Carlos Castaño, a Colombian paramilitary leader, agreed, saying that an additional benefit of massacres is that it separates the loyal from the disloyal. "If the people leave, it confirms their suspicions."[42]

Regardless of the source, when a local-level cleavage is revealed, information emerges in three areas. First, potential targets and potential allies become apparent to outsiders. Second, the cleavage also provides some information about the relative strength of a rival in a given community or neighborhood. Finally, the public revelation of a cleavage also provides information to civilians residing in a community, which in turn enables them to take stock of their relative distribution, form beliefs about future safety, and potentially seek allies outside the community. In other words, when a group-level identifier links some civilians to an armed group, it can either entice outside challengers to strike or prompt locals to try to form alliances with outsiders.

The local peculiarities of cleavages might suggest that every town must be different in terms of the likelihood and extent of political cleansing. On some level, of course this is true. Yet the view that armed groups can operate on the basis of difficult-to-observe local cleavages across a region or country gives an unrealistic picture of their abilities and resources. In the next section, I explain how elections facilitate the identification of loyalties, and targets.

Democratic Reforms and Information   While the interaction between local-level cleavages and the "macro" cleavage of the war —what Kalyvas (2003, 2006) calls alliance—is often critical to wartime dynamics within communities, supralocal organizations and networks can also be important points of interaction with the macro cleavage. A key for fostering and shaping collective identities beyond the locality are formal organizations (Gould 1995, 15). Gould (22) writes that formal organizations lead

---

42. Interview with Alejandro Reyes, Bogotá, May 27, 2013.

to "the creation of social ties that encourage the recognition of commonalities on a scale considerably broader than would be expected on the basis of informal social networks alone."[43] Indeed, the success of the rebellion may depend on bridging the local to the larger: "Dissident peasant organizations that attach local issues to national ones will be more successful than organizations that rely solely on national issues" (Lichbach 1994, 407).

One such type of formal organization is the political party. When a political party is aligned with a party to the armed conflict, the "master cleavage" can translate to the local level; in other words, it provides a "meso-level" link between the "micro" and "macro."[44] Trinquier (1964, 27) cites political parties as key harbors in which "our opponents can thus get themselves within our frontiers and under the protection of our laws."

In addition to forming a basis of identification that links localities to one another, political parties also engage in conflict. Lipset and Rokkan (1967) argue that political parties have two sociological functions: expressive, because they translate conflicts into action; and instrumental or representative, because opposing sides must strike bargains and aggregate and prioritize demands. One of the reasons political parties can be particularly effective is because they generate an identification with the organization. Party identification (or loyalty) can stem from pre-existing cleavages or from voting and mobilization itself (Lupu and Stokes 2010). Regardless of the source of loyalty for any particular individual supporter or partisan, parties represent policy positions and ideologies that can overlap with those of parties to the war. Elections contested by Trinquier's "parties of the enemy" (Trinquier 1964, 27) facilitate collective targeting by counterinsurgents for two reasons: they provide information about civilians' loyalties, and they create opportunities for new alliances with locals.

Local elections with territorial representation are especially useful for inferring loyalties, because in addition to allowing armed groups to form beliefs about civilians' loyalties, they also link those loyalties to particular

---

43. Staniland (2014) also highlights the importance of social networks for undergirding organizations.

44. Edwards (2007) points out that such a level is crucial, and overlooked, in work on displacement. He theorizes about social networks, but I think the critical point is that such networks are somehow identifiable to rival armed groups; in the absence of sectarian or ethnic social networks, political parties can fill this role.

locations within a community.[45] For displacement to be effective, an armed group must be able to direct sustained violence against a precise civilian group within a region or city.[46] In communities without an ascriptive cleavage, counterinsurgents attempting to displace a targeted segment of the population need to direct violence against particular locations, and because candidates represent specific neighborhoods and communities, local electoral results reflect where parties have a territorial base.[47] Importantly, armed groups do not need to identify specific voters to achieve their goals; targeting areas where voters have revealed that a proportion of them, rather than individuals, are sympathetic to a rival armed group generates a payoff for the armed group, because it is likely to change the relative balance of power in the community and the calculations of those who stay.

If voting could reveal group-level loyalties and endanger civilians, it raises the question of why voters would nevertheless participate in elections and cast their vote for an insurgent-affiliated political party. In order for voters to cast their vote for such a party, the threat of violence has to be perceived as remote. The formation of beliefs about the likelihood of violence, in turn, depends on previous violence. In Colombia, voters did not anticipate the violent backlash because in most of the country

---

45. Elections are especially useful for states and counterinsurgents to get a sense of communities in the periphery, because they translate local cleavages into something the center can "see." This overlaps with the paradox articulated by Kocher (2004) and illuminated by Ron (2003): on the periphery, states are both less likely to monitor their citizens and more likely to use repression.

46. Ascriptive traits are the cheapest to target, because once one is linked to an armed group they are easy to identify and difficult for civilians to hide or shed. Traits such as gender and age group can sometimes become targets, but targeting a demographic so broad can be costly to the community (for example by eliminating a male workforce) and therefore can lower the benefits of controlling it. Such traits might be targeted for specific roles, such as for forcibly recruiting children or young men or women, but not to gain control of a community per se.

47. Paradoxically, precisely where insurgents organize voters and mobilizations, they expose supporters, potentially inviting counterinsurgent intervention and thus undermining the likelihood of maintaining their influence. Whether or not these events are voluntary is a separate question. Many reported cases in Colombia suggest that mobilizing civilians is a tactic of the insurgents in some regions to put pressure on the government or military. What is important is how such mobilizations are perceived, not in terms of how voluntary they are, but what they reveal about the guerrilla's strength in any given community. Because armed groups care about their rival's base, and hence the behavioral support (as opposed to attitudinal support) of civilians, whether or not they really support the guerrilla is less relevant.

there had been no prior example of political cleansing. The exception was in pockets near the Magdalena River, where the first self-defense forces formed. Instead, there was a sense of hope that supporting the UP could lead to an end in the war by expanding political participation and convincing the FARC that it could have an impact through nonviolent politics. As I describe in chapter 4, in spite of UP leaders facing violent threats and assassinations from early on, rank-and-file supporters did not anticipate violence against themselves. The violence was regionally based at the outset, because the counterinsurgency was not yet operational in many areas of the country. Even as UP supporters in the north were receiving threats and facing displacement and execution, voters in the south of the country did not feel threatened. But once northern paramilitaries joined forces with local politicians in the south and relocated and expanded there, UP supporters were similarly targeted. At this point, the national-level reach of the paramilitaries became apparent. As assumptions about rational voters would suggest, once violence began in a particular region, UP support dropped substantially. Ultimately, the FARC prohibited electoral participation beginning in 1997 in areas where it was still influential (FARC-EP 1997n9). Not all elections trigger the revelation of information or fine-grained information required for collective targeting. In some cases, the level of aggregation is too high, for example at the district level for national legislative assemblies. Even with the outcome of election results in these cases, armed groups will not be able to discern blocs of political party supporters. In other cases, political parties are not linked to armed groups or voters do not respond to the influence of armed groups. Lomo and Hovil (2004, 16–22) describe such an episode in Uganda: The LRA tried to mobilize civilians to vote for the opposition in 1996, but they failed to garner political support. In some cases, political party membership is not voluntary, as was reported to the IDMC for some areas of Nepal: "The mission was told that commonly villagers who were forced to attend CPN/M [The Communist Party of Nepal/Maoist] political programs found themselves enlisted in the Maoist political party and sometimes given important local party roles, often without their knowledge" (IDMC 2006). If counterinsurgents were aware that party membership was involuntary, then it should be a less useful basis for targeting. Nevertheless, the same IDMC report found that many villagers on CPN/M lists fled military patrols to avoid their wrath.

Alliances Elections do not only reveal information to armed groups; they also reveal information and distribute political power among locals. As a result, the second key process triggered by elections is set in motion: the formation of new alliances. In particular, those on the losing side of elections may be "sore losers" (Przeworski 1991) who seek to overturn the electoral outcome or ensure that it will not happen again. This is a particularly likely possibility when an insurgent-backed political party has been successful. Writing of Francis Deng, the UN's special rapporteur for internal displacement, Korn (2001, 9) reports that "Deng has pointed out that 'it is never the mere differences of identity based on ethnic grounds that generate conflict, but the consequences of those differences in sharing power and the related distribution of resources and opportunities'" that lead to problems. Though this refers to ethnic differences, political rivals are as likely to target each other. When local elites have recourse to armed action, they may well seek it out (Romero 2003; Robinson 2013; Balcells 2017; Collier 2009; Snyder 2000). In the context of an ongoing civil war, local political elites can invite armed groups into their communities to re-shape their constituencies and increase their chances of winning elections in the future.[48]

Violent elections are common (Hyde and Marinov 2012). "Militarized elections" undermine democratization (Staniland 2015), and the process of democratization itself can lead to mobilization around ethnic identities and exclusionary policies (Mann 2005) or to sore losers who reject electoral outcomes (Przeworski 1991; Collier 2009; Snyder 2000), which make first or second elections particularly dangerous (Cederman, Gleditsch, and Hug 2013; Flores and Nooruddin 2012). Autesserre (2010) also argues that setting up elections constitutes potentially huge opportunity costs in postconflict environments, because it focuses on this new institution without resolving enduring local conflicts. Here I consider a different influence of elections on violence than either the onset of civil war or postconflict environments. Rather, I focus on the effect elections and political parties have on violence during an ongoing civil war. I show in the subsequent

---

48. Balcells (2017) theorizes that political elites use the warring sides of a civil war to promote changes in their districts as well, focusing on lethal violence, and shows that in the Spanish Civil War, prewar political competition in the form of close elections explains where bombings were more likely.

chapters that *improvements* in achieving democratic aspirations, such as participation and representation, can be perversely dangerous within an ongoing civil war.

Alternatives and Constraints on Collective Targeting and Political Cleansing

Why Not Mass Killing?   Political cleansing and repopulation are not the only approaches that would change the composition of a community. Given the armed groups' goal of eliminating the disloyal in the territory, an alternative tactic would be mass killing. Political cleansing, however, is less costly than mass killing for three reasons.[49] First, in contemporary civil wars, mass killing invites condemnation that could lead to intervention, which would jeopardize an armed group's goal of territorial control. It is more plausible to deny responsibility for political cleansing; armed groups can and do claim that civilians are leaving of their own accord rather than in response to targeted violence. Second, because displacement is frequently perceived to be a by-product of violence rather than a strategy, armed groups, especially state armed forces, can deny responsibility more easily than when they use widespread lethal violence. Eliminating disloyal civilians from a territory trumps the potential costs of those civilians becoming the armed group's enemy elsewhere, for several reasons. After experiencing displacement, civilians who have been targeted for political activities or identity are likely to change their behavior to avoid suffering again, even if they only falsify their true political preferences (Kuran 1991). Alternatively, civilians could change their preferences after an experience of displacement; they may resent their experience of supporting an insurgent group only to suffer for it. Kocher (2002) finds surprising evidence that this was the case among "evacuated" Kurds in Turkey. Kalyvas (2006, 123) observes that civilians appear to acquiesce to incumbents (state forces) after forced resettlement to incumbent-controlled areas.

---

49. This does not imply that lethal violence will not be employed as an element of collective targeting. Indeed, it is typically necessary to provoke cleansing. See Valentino (2004) for examples of mass killing related to a goal of widespread dispossession. Downes (2008, 20) also points out that lethal violence typically accompanies displacement.

Not killing disloyal civilians, though, demonstrates one of the drawbacks of political cleansing for armed groups: the problem of where the disloyal will resettle. If civilians can resettle anywhere, why would armed groups expel the disloyal only to potentially undermine control in other regions? The second cost is the attention from rivals that the large-scale violence that accompanies collective targeting would garner. I discuss each in turn.

Resettlement In many conflicts, counterinsurgents controlled resettlement. The resettlement of civilians in the mid-twentieth century by colonial powers, notably the United States in Vietnam, is an example. These resettlements had one thing in common: they were directed toward populations whose potential proximity to insurgents made them "susceptible" to insurgent influence. The large-scale programs were based on rurality (Vietnam), ethnicity (Malaysia and Kenya), and political affiliation (Ukraine) (Zhukov 2014). They had the effect of making these populations more "legible" to the central state by making the "human ecology" of these populations more governable (Scott 1998, 2009; Kocher 2004).[50] But resettlement schemes required vast amount of resources in order to be effective. These efforts at internal governance and counterinsurgency were largely within the domain of nation-state sovereignty until the international human rights model intervened: resettlement became an international war crime in the Second Protocol to the Geneva War Convention, signed by member states in 1977. There are some exceptions, but they require that the armed group responsible for resettlement provide for the well-being of civilians.[51]

Even without such large-scale resettlement programs, counterinsurgents continue to engage in the expulsion of suspect residents, as in Myanmar: "Those living in the affected areas become collectively regarded as potential insurgents or sympathizers: the boundary between frontline and

---

50. Heilbrunn (1962, 153) argues that the real benefit of resettlement is to protect the civilian population against guerrillas, or to "reform" (convert) the population. The Ugandan government used this justification to relocate four hundred thousand Acholi civilians in Gulu District into "protected villages" from 1996 to 2000, and another four hundred thousand after 2002 (Human Rights Watch 2003).

51. International humanitarian organizations, which offer such assistance to refugees and increasingly to the internally displaced, often end up taking on this responsibility instead.

rear areas is blurred. The tatmadaw's counterinsurgency strategy, the Pya Ley Pya or 'Four Cuts' strategy (officially endorsed in 1968 and still in operation today) is designed to suppress internal insurgency by cutting the insurgents off from their support system (food supplies, funding, intelligence and recruits) linked to the civilian population" (UNHCR 2001).

Insurgents have also engaged in resettlement. In some cases in Colombia, the FARC has used massive displacement to avoid the conquest of a territory by a rival group. For instance, Human Rights Watch reported that in 1996, many of the displaced attending a meeting in Tierralta, Colombia, said that they were "ordered to abandon their homes by the FARC. At the time, the FARC was pressured by the ACCU [paramilitaries] and apparently believed that a mass displacement of civilians would delay the paramilitary advance and win them increased access to provisions." These instances resemble resettlement more than cleansing because they aim to deny a rival armed group control over a territory by depopulating it. This is a different tactic than cleansing a portion of a population to gain or retain control over the territory they inhabited. As in many cases with cleansing, however, the insurgents did not maintain control over where people resettled (though there are accusations that FARC members accompanied the march of the many thousands of people, perhaps influencing where they went and their resolve to stay). When will armed groups discount the problem of resettlement and engage in collective targeting? First, armed groups—even state armed forces—are often sufficiently decentralized not to take into consideration the potential negative consequences of political cleansing for another part of a country or to value the future possible success less than the success of their own group's present campaign. For more centralized groups, we can imagine situations in which control of some territories is more strategically important than others.[52] Second, to appreciate the calculations of the armed groups, we need some expectations of where civilians will resettle following political cleansing.

Civilian-Led Resettlement   In contrast to organized resettlement programs, most civilian resettlement is unaccompanied and unorganized during civil wars. Still, I argue that there is an underlying logic to it. When

---

52. Stipulating which types of territories are more valuable is beyond the scope of this project.

civilians are targeted collectively, they are likely to resettle together with others similarly targeted or to move closer to the armed group they are associated with (Steele 2009). The reason is that any given household risks detection wherever they resettle, but "hiding" among others who are similarly targeted, or seeking the protection of an armed group, will help reduce the chances that that household will suffer direct violence. This should lead to patterns of clustering, which helps the displaced tap into social networks for support and assistance navigating new environments. So even though it is rational for households to resettle with others like them, it endangers the group as a whole because the group becomes more visible to rival armed groups. Thus, the armed groups that engage in displacement can make a decision to target the disloyal to win control of a community and resolve to pursue the displaced in their new communities without much trouble finding them down the line. Indeed, there is evidence that in Colombia, IDPs remained vulnerable to collective targeting in areas where they resettled (Steele, 2017).

Another possible destination for collectively targeted civilians is near the armed group with which they are accused of associating (Mason and Krane 1989). This decision would also be consistent with the points raised by Kalyvas and Kocher (2007) about the high costs of remaining neutral, which include not having access to information about possible future violence. Even if an insurgent group may not be able to offer protection against a counterinsurgent group, for example, it is more likely to be able to collect intelligence about the activities of rival armed groups and warn civilians. Certainly this is not always the case, however, and if the civilians who were collectively targeted resent the armed group they are accused of supporting for failing to protect them in the first place, then moving toward the armed group is less likely.

Finally, a third pattern that occurs is that many displaced will relocate to cities for safety and for access to resources. Because cities tend to be controlled by the state more easily than can the countryside, this trade-off is acceptable to counterinsurgents (Kocher 2004). Further, the displaced also tend to cluster when resettling in cities, so even if insurgent "infiltration" of urban spaces is a concern, identifying "problematic" pockets of the city is not. This dynamic played out in Medellín; after years of IDP resettlement to the outskirts of the city and a widespread impression that Comuna 13 housed IDPs who sympathized with the FARC and filled the ranks of its urban militia, the military launched Operation Orion to again target the residents of the area. Massive displacement took place and disrupted the neighborhood's networks.

Whether the targeted group lives in a rural community, a town, or a large city helps account for which of these three resettlement options they are likely to choose. Rural residents are most likely to move closer to insurgents, because insurgents are likely to have a stronghold in a rural area. People who have been expelled from towns are less likely to move closer to insurgents, because they are less likely to have lived near them in the past or less likely to prefer to live in a rural area compared to a more densely populated one. Instead, they are more likely to relocate to a new town or city. Urban residents who have been targeted are more likely to resettle within the same city, but in a different neighborhood, as described above in Medellín, or in Baghdad as well (Weidmann and Salehyan 2013; Lischer 2008).

In general, armed groups are willing to use collective targeting to gain control of one community, at the possible—but not definite—expense of a problem down the line. In the worst case, insurgents gain additional supporters in a stronghold area. In the most likely case, those who have been targeted will not be difficult to find if they prove problematic in their new destination. Whether or not they turn out to be problematic will depend on how deep their ties are to the group they are accused of supporting. In some cases, any sympathy or even support for an armed group is destroyed when the armed group is unable to protect them, which might also discount the importance of where people resettle. Another factor in the trade-off for cleansing, I argue, is that it is often also meant to benefit a local elite, for instance to improve the chances of winning elections. In this case, the local elite will not be affected by where the displaced resettle, and the extent to which these locals who prefer cleansing have influence over the incoming armed group, it also makes where the displaced resettle less of a deterrent.

Possible Rebuke   The second constraint in using collective targeting is the attention it would potentially garner from rivals. This constraint is key to explaining why counterinsurgents are more likely than insurgents to use collective targeting: the latter have fewer resources and prefer to avoid direct military confrontation. Collective targeting would increase the likelihood of such a confrontation for insurgents, but if employed by counterinsurgents, insurgents will not be in a position to retaliate.

When insurgents seek to build a presence in a territory, they must do so slowly to avoid detection by authorities or rejection by the community. Insurgents do not have enough resources to face down the state's military if they are discovered. For this reason, Kalyvas (2005, 92) writes, "[Irregular wars] entail a slow and patient process of state building by rebels who lack the state's resources." Over time, rebels persuade some community members to join the cause, recruiting and building up their ranks. As a result, insurgents are less likely to engage in political cleansing as a tactic to conquer territory.

Castaño, the paramilitary leader in Colombia, noted the difference in counterinsurgent and insurgent approaches to Alejandro Reyes in 1994:

> The only way to defeat [the guerrillas] is going after the social base of the guerrillas in each region, and with the ones who stay, create self-defense groups. The difference with the guerrillas is that they enter zones for the first time, where there is no violence, and they can fraternize with the people and win them over without having to sacrifice anyone. Only afterwards do they begin to demand more and more contributions over time and then come the threats and the kidnappings. When a war is organized with self-defense forces it is different. The self-defense groups [paramilitaries] enter zones that are beaten down by the violence and then they cannot distinguish between guerrillas and peasants. They do a general cleansing and only after can they enter and talk with the people. (Reyes Posada 2009, 93)

A former EPL member, Mario Agudelo, explained, "With the paramilitaries, they arrived with lots of force, all at once. The FARC and the EPL were much slower, over a longer period of time, so we could tell who you could believe."[53]

Insurgents' calculations change if they face a challenge in a territory they already control. Downes (2008, 30–31) notes that guerrillas "lash out" when they are losing. Lashing out may be strategic: when counterinsurgents attempt to conquer a territory, insurgents might conclude that cleansing will help them *retain* a territorial presence. They could expel

---

53. Interview with the author, Medellín, May 14, 2008.

those civilians whose loyalties they question (or in some cases, even know) in order to retain a core group of more reliable supporters. This strategy is risky, however, because counterinsurgents still have an advantage in coercive power and could then more easily target the rebels' supporters. Further, insurgents may find selective violence, rather than collective violence, more effective under these conditions. In short, insurgents are less likely to engage in collective targeting to cleanse a territory because it is less likely to pay off for them in their quest to gain territorial control. This logic is consistent with Ibáñez's findings: insurgents tended to displace people during armed confrontations, while paramilitaries used direct threats in Colombia (Ibáñez 2008, 79).

Types of Territories   The overall imperative to shape the population of a particular territory makes some communities more prone to collective targeting and political cleansing than others. In general, communities that are relatively "new," associated with new economic opportunities such as natural resource extraction or illicit crop growth, are easier to reshape through political cleansing and repopulation. In Colombia, these communities are referred to as "settler" communities, or newly colonized territories. Two factors explain why these types are prone to cleansing: First, state institutions are less likely to operate well in these areas because they tend to lag behind the population growth and development of the communities. The state may also face competitors in these areas, such as insurgent groups or other illegal armed groups, which take advantage of disorderly communities to impose their own rules and regulations (Arjona 2016). Indeed, insurgent groups did accompany the growth of many such communities in Colombia in the 1960s, as I describe in the next chapter. As a result of the uneven presence of the state, residents' ownership of property is much less likely to be formalized than in regions with stronger state institutions. In turn, people without titles to their land or property are less likely to be able to stake a claim to the property in the future, which may make them more vulnerable to targeting as well (Ibáñez 2008).

The second, related factor that makes these areas targets for cleansing is that they are relatively easy to repopulate. "Boom towns" of new economic or illicit activities produce a demand for laborers. Coupled with an offer to take over existing property, job opportunities in these communities are likely to be attractive to other potential migrants, who would feel grateful for the opportunity and, as above, more likely to be compliant as a result.

Implications

The new conceptual framework to characterize forms of displacement, and the theory to account for political cleansing, helps to illuminate why residents of La Chinita stayed in Apartadó, while their neighbors in Policarpa eventually left. While both neighborhoods were mobilized leftists and union members, those living in Policarpa supported a political party associated with one insurgency rather than another. Most often as a result of happenstance, over time the residents of the neighborhood became associated with and voted for a radical political party that challenged the status quo electorally.

The theory also leads to more general expectations for patterns within irregular civil wars. First, in the context of nonethnic civil wars, which are more likely to have local cleavages that are difficult to observe, elections can lead to reinforcement of group identities and loyalties. They can also reveal important local cleavages, which may make civilian voters vulnerable to repercussion from armed groups opposed to their political project and the insurgency that backs it. These processes lead to the implication that following competitive, local elections contested by an insurgent-backed political party, an increase in collective targeting and political cleansing is likely. Further, the timing of such armed group behavior will coincide with their entry and conquest of a community, rather than when a community is under control.

Second, the processes of group identity formation even in nonethnic civil wars indicates that particular civilian groups are more likely to be targeted by armed groups than others. This variation is likely to exist at the local level, but it has implications for aggregate patterns as well.

Finally, to evaluate whether or not collective targeting is employed in the service of promoting political cleansing, we should observe behavior by armed groups that indicates their preference that particular groups leave a territory. For example, we should observe evidence of threats in addition to lethal violence.

Existing explanations for displacement focus on the association between violence and displacement: as violence increases, so does displacement. This framework refines these insights to help illuminate when and where the violence—specifically in the form of collective targeting—is likely. The second contribution is to point to how loyalties matter and can be revealed even in nonethnic wars. In this case, I focus on the role of political parties and elections and argue that democratic politics can trigger political cleansing in the context of an ongoing civil war.

Research Design

Testing the theory poses considerable challenges. In addition to being difficult to observe, these dynamics are difficult to identify and study because of several reinforcing incentives. First, the 1977 Amendments to the Geneva Conventions prohibited the resettlement of civilians during wars. Rather than changing states' and armed groups' behavior, however, it changed how these groups depict the problem.[54] Now states and armed groups alike have incentives to represent displacement as out of their control and certainly not directly caused by them. Rather than resettlement, it was "evacuation" in Turkey; elsewhere it is "displacement." In addition, humanitarian and advocacy organizations also have incentives not to distinguish among civilians. Legally, it would complicate the category of noncombatant. Practically, it would risk continued targeting or rejection in their receptor communities. If they were targeted, civilians themselves would have strong incentives for concealing the underlying reason they left, especially if it was not based on identifiable traits. These incentives present challenges to conducting research on the relationship between political identities and the likelihood of collective targeting and political cleansing because it is difficult to observe collective targeting and political cleansing directly, especially when the relevant cleavage is not ascriptive.

To address these challenges, the research design incorporates both quantitative and qualitative methods to test the implications of the argument,

---

54. According to Branch (2008), it also provided an opportunity for the Ugandan government, which he argues relied on humanitarian intervention in order to carry out wide-scale displacement of Acholi civilians.

at various levels of analysis, within the context of Colombia. First, historical analysis shows that political cleansing (and displacement more generally) was not a large-scale phenomenon until after local-level elections
were held and when an insurgent political party, the Union Patriótica
(UP), contested them. Consistent with the argument, there was no obvious
basis for targeting groups before the UP revealed these loyalties. Further,
I show that political cleansing allowed paramilitary groups to gain territorial control and expand throughout the country. The next step I take is to
focus on one region in particular, Urabá, an example of a recently settled
region that shares many features of other newly "colonized" regions in
Colombia. There I assess the timing and the targets of displacement within
one municipality, Apartadó. Drawing on archival documents and interviews, I detail the methods employed by the armed group to evaluate if
they were consistent with collective targeting. I conclude that the municipality did experience collective targeting by paramilitaries in the town,
which led to political cleansing during an effort to wrest control of the
city from the FARC. Two rural communities were able to resist political
cleansing in spite of collective targeting. A third step zooms out to conduct
quantitative analysis of displacement across all Colombian municipalities
to test if electoral support for the UP relates to higher levels of civilian displacement. The order of chapters parallels how my research unfolded and
reflects the importance of information at the local level for this kind of research. It would have been impossible to establish that cleansing occurred,
let alone whether or not it followed my expectations, without the information I collected in Apartadó. Even though the in-depth nature of the
research required limits the possibilities for rigorously testing the theory
across civil war settings, the argument and the underlying mechanisms are
general to irregular civil wars. I return to this discussion in the conclusion,
with a focus on when and where democratic politics during civil wars are
likely to be particularly dangerous.

Colombia is an appropriate setting to test the theory, for both analytical and practical reasons. As an irregular civil war, it fits the scope conditions of the argument. Further, the war is not based around an ethnic
cleavage, so it is possible to better isolate political loyalties from competing or overlapping identities that may also be relevant in the course of a
civil war. Fine-grained information on group identities that are largely
unobservable, particularly in nonethnic civil wars, is difficult to gather in

the context of civil wars, let alone across wars. In Colombia, though, relatively rich data are available, and the possibility of conducting fieldwork
in some regions of the country makes an in-depth study possible. With a
population of internally displaced persons (IDPs) estimated to be about
six million—between 10 and 12 percent of the population—Colombia
ranks with Sudan, Iraq, Afghanistan, Syria, and the Democratic Republic
of the Congo as one of the countries most affected by internal displacement (UNHCR 2015). As Gutiérrez Sanín, Acevedo, and Viatela (2007)
point out, despite some obvious state capacity issues, the bureaucratic
nature of the state is intact and highly professional.[55] This includes the
National Administrative Department of Statistics (Departamento Administrativo Nacional de Estadísticas, or DANE) and the National Voter Registry (Registraduría Nacional), which allows for testing implications in a
wider, systematic way throughout the country.

Returning to Urabá, we can make sense of why those in Policarpa left:
they were targeted by counterinsurgents based on their political identities.
Their neighbors in La Chinita, conversely, were deemed reliable enough to
avoid targeted violence by paramilitaries. They did suffer violence at the
hands of the insurgents, though. But the massacres perpetrated—though
gruesome and terrifying—were not enough to push them out. This chapter provides the conceptual groundwork for the project by disaggregating
forms of displacement based on how armed groups target civilians during civil wars and how civilians respond differently to each type. This disaggregation permits analytical leverage to study patterns of displacement.
Focusing on strategic displacement, I also develop a theory of political
cleansing during civil wars.

The work advances the literature on violence during civil wars by offering a theory to account for a massive, yet overlooked, feature of civil
war violence: nonlethal violence. I argue that displacement is not just
an ancillary outcome of other processes, but one that requires explanation in its own right. In particular, we need to understand the conditions

---

55. That Colombia has these data available belies a peculiarity about the war itself and
suggests some possible scope conditions for generalizability. In general, the Colombian experience of relatively strong state capacity in some areas suggests how that broad perspective
stems from poor conceptualization about the overaggregated "capacity" notion (Gutiérrez
Sanín, Acevedo, and Viatela 2007).

under which armed groups use collective targeting to politically cleanse territories. I argue that it is most likely to occur during competition for territorial control, and where and when civilians' collective loyalties are revealed. The next two chapters describe the origins and evolution of the Colombian civil war, before turning to tests and refinements of the theory in Colombia.

THE LEGACY OF DISPLACEMENT DURING LA VIOLENCIA AND THE ORIGINS OF THE CONTEMPORARY WAR IN COLOMBIA

Colombia's vast and diverse landscape has been the stage for several rounds of violent political upheaval; the country has experienced nine civil wars since its founding in the early nineteenth century. The families displaced during the wars, and migrants searching for greater economic opportunities, chipped away at the frontier, clearing the forests for agriculture and cattle ranching. The population spread from the cool highlands of the Andes through the forests of the hot lowlands (LeGrand 1984, 31, 42). A war in the mid-twentieth century, known simply as La Violencia, accelerated the trend, as more than two million people—roughly 10 percent of the population—fled from violence (Oquist 1978, 82–84). The war also changed the nature of the process, though, because the displaced settlers were accompanied by new actors: armed insurgent groups.

This chapter lays the groundwork for understanding contemporary displacement in Colombia through three key features of the country and its history. First, it briefly introduces the physical, human, and political terrain. Second, it situates the widespread civilian displacement during

La Violencia as essential for the formation of the insurgent groups that became the protagonists of the contemporary war. It also contrasts the general patterns of displacement during La Violencia with the predominant forms during the contemporary war. Third, and finally, it describes the relationship between insurgent groups and civilians in areas settled by the displaced, which fostered lasting loyalties and resistance. The next chapter traces the confrontation among the insurgents, paramilitaries, and state forces and introduces the patterns of violence and displacement that characterized the conflict between the mid-1980s and 2012.

Colombia's Political Geography

In the San Juan Mountains in the northwest region of Urabá, Leonidas, the leader of an indigenous community, told me, "We came here during La Violencia. We opened this land."[1] He and his family were among the millions of "refugees" during La Violencia, the war fought between 1948 and 1964.[2] The simplicity of the name—the Violence—belies the complexity of the war. Even though the war was fought roughly along partisan lines between the dominant Liberal and Conservative political parties, the number of actors and the patterns of violence differed across regions and morphed over time (Roldán 2002; Henderson 1985; Ortiz Sarmiento 1985; Sánchez and Meertens 1983). Leonidas's family—led by his Liberal father—traveled by night to avoid detection by Conservative bands. In Urabá, they found a frontier territory and Liberal refugees from different parts of the country, some of them organized with arms to fend off the Conservative militias or even the police. It was a long trek for Leonidas's family: they moved from Cauca in the southwest to the northwest, across one of the three chains of the Andes running from the north to the south of the country (Eastern, Central, and Western).

The imposing Andes that Leonidas's family climbed trisect Colombia's 440,000 square miles (the size of France, Germany, and England

---

1. Interview with the author, Apartadó, June 26, 2007. Opening the land refers to clearing the dense forests for settlement and agriculture.

2. Internally displaced persons (IDPs) are often referred to as refugees in Colombia, even though they do not cross an international border.

combined) and delimit its diverse terrain and regions, from the Atlantic coast in the north to the Amazon in the south and the Pacific coast on the west to expansive plains in the east that cover about a third of the country. Figure 2.1 shows the topography of the country. The population of Colombia in the 2005 census was estimated at forty-eight million, roughly triple the population at mid-twentieth century. There are thirty-two departments—similar to US states but with less autonomy—and more than 1,100 municipalities, which have a *cabecera*, a town that serves as the municipal capital, surrounded by rural hamlets and villages.

Culturally, the country encompasses strong regional identities and traditions. The music, dance, and food of each region are distinct; the diversity across the country is protected by the towering mountains between them. Afro-Colombians are a substantial share of the population (some estimate as high as 20 percent) and also have distinct cultures by region.[3] The Pacific coast, with a population over 90 percent Afro and indigenous, has historically been neglected by the state, and it is now the region most affected by violence as armed groups fight for coveted routes for their illicit activities. Indigenous communities are a relatively smaller share of the population in Colombia than in its Andean neighbors like Ecuador and Peru. Now roughly one million indigenous individuals across the country live in communities that have special autonomy and collective land rights granted in the 1991 constitution. Nevertheless, the racial and ethnic hierarchies in the country favor lighter-skinned mestizos.

Roughly 20 percent of the population now lives in or around the capital, Bogotá, both the literal and mythical center of the country. Literal because the city sits on a plateau of the central chain of the Andes, three thousand meters above sea level (or "3,000 meters closer to the stars," as one of the city's slogans proclaimed) in nearly the exact center of the country. Mythical because the capital's authority and influence over the diverse regions of the country have often been a fairy tale to residents of those regions.[4]

---

3. Communities on the Atlantic coast tend to be more mixed, while communities on the Pacific coast are more isolated and more likely to have special status that allows communities to have shared land rights (under Law 70 of 1993). Within the Pacific coast, though, *chocoanos* and *tumacenses* will point out their differences as well.

4. It is also mythical in another sense: European explorers arrived in what would become Bogotá in the seventeenth century seeking the indigenous Muiscas' lake of gold and the legendary El Dorado nearby.

Figure 2.1. Map of Colombia

Bogotá's tenuous ties to the regions date to the founding of the country. On July 20, 1810, a junta declared Bogotá's independence after Napoleon conquered Spain. Though the declaration was followed by nearly a decade of war with other provinces, Colombia still celebrates July 20 as its independence day. Royalists eventually unified the rebellious regions of New Granada (as Colombia was known), only to fall to the "Great Liberator" Simón Bolívar's forces in 1819.

The debate surrounding the formation of Colombia and its degree of centralization led to the founding of two enduring rival political parties. Bolivarians aligned in a fight to keep New Granada ruled from the capital, while Liberals (led by Santander) favored more autonomy for the regions. Later, the Bolivarians became the Conservatives and supported the church and its active role in governance. Liberals, since about 1850, have preferred a more secular state. The two parties fought six civil wars, all relatively short-lived, in the nineteenth century. Colombia welcomed the twentieth century with the Thousand Days' War (1899–1902), an especially bloody confrontation.

One factor contributing to the parties' recourse to violence was the structure of competitive politics. Elections in the Colombian system were winner-take-all; whichever party won a majority in the presidential election was able to appoint governors, who then appointed mayors. Patronage and clientelism propped up the system and reinforced identities. Liberals and Conservatives appointed party faithful to state positions after electoral victories, so switching sides was extremely difficult (Henderson 1985).

The nature of elections and the recurring civil wars reinforced the population's loyalty to one party or another, and eventually the population was split between Conservatives and Liberals across the country's diverse regions. Liberal and Conservative identities became deeply ingrained, passed on from one generation to the next (Schoultz 1972, 32).

The electoral stakes were not limited to control of political appointments, but also over land policy and distribution, a crucial source of wealth. Between the Thousand Days' War and La Violencia half a century later, sporadic violence erupted in the regions, primarily over access to land. The 1936 "Law of Lands" (Ley 200) entitled rural residents to gain ownership of land if they converted it to productive "social use." Some land targeted by peasants for such small-scale production was owned or claimed by powerful landowners, who feared potential legal action against them. In reality, the barriers to peasants actually securing title to land were nearly insurmountable (LeGrand 1984), but landowners nevertheless saw the legal regime as a threat to their power. An additional grievance among landowners was emerging resistance to the traditional "obligation" system, which required peasants to work for one day each week on the landowner's estate in exchange for access to a parcel of land. "Agrarian leagues" were formed to rebel against the obligation, and the recently founded Communist Party was also involved in organizing peasants in the 1930s and 1940s (Molano 1987).[5] In a pattern that would replay itself again and again, the central state failed to protect the property rights of peasants, which would have challenged the interests of the powerful landlords. In 1944, Congress officially reversed course with the adoption of Law 100, which halted or rolled back some of the advances in land redistribution.

Liberal rural peasants found a champion in presidential candidate Jorge Eliécer Gaitán, a renegade Liberal who promoted economic redistribution and increased political participation and who mobilized a sizable following throughout the country in the 1940s. This mobilization threatened Liberal elites' interests as much as it did the Conservatives, and led to a split in the Liberal party, allowing Conservative candidate Mariano Ospina to win the 1946 election with only 41 percent of the vote (Sánchez 1992).

The outcome unleashed a backlash against peasant organization and resistance, led by Conservatives who had been shut out of political power for years (Schoultz 1972, 33). Much of the violence related to landowners' newfound support for reversing the land redistribution that had gained traction in the 1930s. Though violent confrontations flared in many pockets of the country, it was not until 1948 that it became the widespread La Violencia, which uprooted millions and laid the foundation for the current civil war.

La Violencia

On April 9, 1948, Gaitán was assassinated in Bogotá.[6] Supporters spontaneously began to riot and loot, and the capital convulsed for days. The

---

5. See LeGrand 1984 for details.
6. The date is still marked today. The killing was never definitively solved.

violence in Bogotá ignited regions already in arms.[7] By 1949, the central Andes regions devolved into violence spurred by local Conservative agents of the Bogotá regime and Liberal party members organized into armed bands (Henderson 1985). It would be several years before the violence was contained, only to mutate and erupt again (Sánchez and Meertens 1983; Henderson 1985).

Violence spread throughout the country, where it served the interests of both landed elites in the regions and party leaders governing from Bogotá. Regional elites (and some "entrepreneurial" peasants) aimed to expand their landholdings or reverse the gains made by peasants in the 1930s (Roldán 2002, 41). In the case of Antioquia, Roldán (2002) shows that regional elites were motivated by race and cultural dominance as well. Whether or not a region of the department erupted in violence was conditioned by how "core" or peripheral it was. If a region was perceived as different and unruly, then Conservatives in Medellín were more likely to send police forces, which often led to violence. Violence also depended on the communities themselves. Segovia was viewed as different and radical by Medellín elites, but also organized and able to resist. In Urrao in the south, moderate Conservatives and Liberals worked together to resist violence from the state, and this resistance eventually became armed. In Urabá, locals invited intervention by the army from neighboring Bolívar (now Córdoba) because the soldiers were more likely to be Liberal and black, like the local population, than the police or army battalions from other areas of Antioquia.

Conservative elites in Bogotá also had an interest in the partisan violence, but their interest was electoral.[8] Conservatives had a clear majority in only about one-third of the country's municipalities in 1948, and they feared eternal eclipse by Liberals. As a result, "the Conservatives had to fight back, and . . . they did so by means of a systematic attack on the Liberal regions of the country" (Hobsbawm 1963a, 250). The attacks were possible because as the governing party,

---

7. Sánchez (1992, 82) notes the inflammatory impact of radio broadcasts from Bogotá, led by the rector of Universidad Nacional, promoting the revolution and (falsely) announcing its triumph in the capital.

8. Violence also followed local feuds (Hobsbawm 1963a). Several historians have written excellent regional accounts of la Violencia: Henderson (1985) for Tolima, Ortiz Sarmiento (1985) for Quindío, and Roldán (2002) for Antioquia.

Conservatives controlled both the army and the police, and they called on extra-institutional groups like the *chulavitas*, fearsome militias modeled after one created in the Boyacá village of the same name. Soon these Conservative armed groups were referred to as *pájaros* (birds) and death squads.[9] The violence perpetrated by these groups was especially gruesome. The "necktie" was an infamous mode of assassination that involved slitting victims' throats and pulling the tongue through the opening. In spite of the brutality, the Conservatives enjoyed the open support of the Catholic Church, reflecting its long-standing ties to the party (Peñaranda 2007; Sánchez 1992).

Liberals responded by forming their own armed groups. As with the Conservative groups, many were sponsored by local Liberal elites. The small communist and agrarian league enclaves also formed armed groups, which were primarily self-defense forces. Isauro Yosa, known as "Mayor Lister," a founding member of the FARC, recounted to sociologist Alfredo Molano, "forty days [after April 9, 1948], the thing had already started. The dead were abundant and we knew them. Not the assassins, though. The police didn't realize or take responsibility for anything, as if what was happening were in a neighboring country. That's why we had to take up weapons: because no one responded" (Molano 1994, 22).

One story, also recounted to Molano (1994, 44), depicts the spontaneous eruption of violence in a town in Tolima:

> One Sunday around 11 in the morning, when the plaza was bustling, someone yelled *vivas* to the Liberal party (viva!) and right away, as if they had made an agreement, *vivas* to the Conservative party. *Vivas* to Gaitán and *vivas* to Laureano [Gómez, the Conservative leader], *vivas* to López [a Liberal leader] and *vivas* to Mariano [Ospina, the Conservative president], a dangerous volley, even more dangerous given how hot it was that day. Somehow, *panela* [cane sugar, usually in bricks] began to fly from those who had *panela*, bottles from those who sold beer, yuca and plantain from those who had food stalls. A country battle. At the end of the party, there were four dead and twelve wounded, all by knife. The next day the rumors started that Lamparilla and Pájaro Azul [Conservative bandits] were going to take over the town.

---

9. Peñaranda (2007, 37), citing Betancourt and García (1991) on the *pájaros*, links them to later paramilitaries and to the assassins that drug cartels would employ in the 1980s.

One apparent witness to this outbreak was Pedro Marín, a displaced Liberal seeking refuge from the Conservative bandits who had taken over his town in nearby Génova, in the coffee-growing Quindío department. Marín would become Manuel Marulanda, one of the founding members of the FARC and its leader for more than four decades.[10] After this episode, Marín left again, "this time with a 'very long procession.' The roads . . . filled with the persecuted." The displaced went to a municipality called Roldanillo, where

> a big surprise awaited. Thousands of families were sleeping in the plaza, in the corridors, in the atrium of the church. Cooking in whatever fire . . . all asking the government for a solution, an intervention against the bandits. The people needed to return to their farms because many had left their children and wives, their husbands, the harvest and the animals, and finally the land. All abandoned to the grace of God, or the Conservatives, that sometimes seemed like one and the same with all the power they had. (Molano 1994, 46–47)

By 1952 many had already fled their homes as a result of this sort of violence and rumors. Liberals and Conservatives began to segregate.

The Coup of 1953, *Repúblicas Independientes*, and the National Front

In the midst of the violence, another presidential election was held in 1949, one year earlier than planned. The Liberal candidate, Darío Echandía, withdrew from the contest after the assassination of his brother. The party conceded its inability to protect its partisans and advised them to abstain. For many, though, abstention was not an option, because without the official stamp issued after voting, they could be easily identified and targeted by Conservatives (Molano 1994, 48–49). The Conservative and only presidential candidate, Laureano Gómez, won the election.

For the next three years (1950–1953), Gómez continued the policy of physical and political extermination of the Liberals (Helguera 1961, 355). The police were "militarized" and brought under the Ministry of Defense

---

10. He died of natural causes in 2008 at age seventy-seven.

(Llorente 2005). In practice, governors still appointed troops and paid for them (Cardona 2008, 114–15), and violence continued to spread.

In 1953, the army intervened. General Gustavo Rojas Pinilla, a respected officer, mounted a coup against the Gómez administration, and the president was forced into exile on June 13. The army portrayed itself as nonpartisan, though Conservatives accused it of being Liberal (Gilhodés 2007, 302).[11] The Rojas regime, however, revealed that it would support those who had advanced their interests through violence, as it "sought not to aid those who had been ruined by the Violence but rather to reward and stimulate those who, either directly or indirectly, had come out on top in the process" (Sánchez 1992, 105).

The Rojas regime made initial strides against the violence by issuing a general amnesty for armed group members, which many accepted. In total, roughly 3,500 combatants turned in arms, including most of the Liberal guerrillas in the Eastern Plains (Llanos) (Sánchez 1992, 103). Communists demobilized as well but did not surrender their weapons. A subset of Liberals who did not accept the amnesty were derided as *Liberales sucios* ("dirty Liberals") by fellow "clean" Liberals who did demobilize. The group of displaced men that Manuel Marulanda led was *sucio*, all the more because it eventually allied with communists. Soon, the *sucios* and communists were targeted both by the army and the "clean" Liberals, who were soon remobilized by large landowners (Sánchez 1992).

In 1955, the largest military offensive targeted the peasant settlements of the region known as Sumapaz, where many displaced Liberals had resettled since the onset of the violence. Villages where the agrarian leagues were strong were hit, as well as the Communist Party stronghold of Villarrica. The ten thousand soldiers provoked those who had already been displaced once to leave again, in the "Columna de Marcha." The march lasted three or four months, involved about three thousand people, and was guided and organized by guerrillas (Molano 1987, 43). More people from other regions joined later. Molano (1987, 34) writes, "Eastern Tolima was lost, but the people, which was what was important, survived by displacing towards El Duda, el Guayabero and El Pato." There, several "independent republics" cropped up, such as Marquetalia,

---

11. Again, this perception varied depending on region and battalion, as Roldán (2002) documents for Antioquia and Ortiz Sarmiento (1985) describes for Quindío.

Riochiquito, Guyabero, and El Pato, where the displaced lived with the Liberal-communist armed groups, which provided order and protection. These communities welcomed peasants who were fleeing from other regions of the country and would become the "first redoubts of the FARC" (Flores 2014, 20–21).

The following year, in 1956, the *país político*—as the Liberal and Conservative elites were known—ousted Rojas and replaced him with a military junta until elections could be organized (Helguera 1961).[12] The 1958 elections marked the beginning of the National Front, the consociational regime that would rule until 1974. Many observers point to this exclusionary system as an important cause of the contemporary civil war (e.g., Pécaut 1992; Sánchez 1992; Restrepo 1992).[13] Alberto Lleras was the National Front's first president in 1958.

Lleras quickly enacted a new amnesty and a "rehabilitation" program aimed at encouraging demobilization and supporting ex-combatants and violence-affected communities with employment campaigns and development programs. (Marulanda himself was even employed through the program.) But the rehabilitation program did not survive accusations from within the government (mostly from Conservatives) that it was a payout to the bandits who had colluded with Liberals (Karl 2017).

In 1960, Lleras established Tribunals of Conciliation and Equity to adjudicate land and property disputes stemming from La Violencia.[14] Eight courts were created, with jurisdiction over regions of the country perceived as the hardest hit by violence: Pereira and Armenia in Caldas, Huila (in Neiva), Tolima (Ibagué, Armero, and Guamo), Cauca (Santander de Quilichao), and Valle del Cauca (Buga).[15] The tribunals lasted only two years before they were shut down. For six of the eight tribunals, scholars Donny Meertens and Gonzalo Sánchez were able to find reference to a

---

12. Rojas was tried by the Senate in 1959, which found him guilty of actions unbecoming the president, and stripped him of his citizenship, titles, and rank. He eventually returned to form an opposition political party, ANAPO, and contested the presidential election in 1970. The results were widely perceived to be fraudulent in favor of the Liberal candidate, Pastrana.

13. Since 1974, democratic elections have been held. Scholars such as Daniel Pécaut and Luis Alberto Restrepo continued to refer to the regime as the National Front throughout the 1980s until a new constitution was adopted in 1991 (Restrepo 1992; Pécaut 1992).

14. Decreto Numero 0002 of February 1960.

15. Decreto Numero 0672, Ministerio de Gobierno, March 18, 1960.

total of 1,303 cases.[16] Of those, 213 were "archived," or denied, because of lack of documentation or sufficient evidence. Only a tiny portion of the displaced population ever engaged with the government's primary mechanism for adjudicating their property. As the next section describes, the failure of the tribunal reflects the state's inability and unwillingness to intervene in the massive demographic and political changes caused by displacement.

Displacement and Its Legacy

Already in 1958, it was clear that displacement and resettlement had transformed Colombia's countryside and cities. The estimated two million people who had left their homes between 1951 and 1964 were straining cities, depleting established communities, and settling in new regions (Oquist 1978, 82–84).[17]

Displacement accelerated the urbanization of the country. In 1938, roughly 70 percent of the population lived in rural areas; in 1972, 45 percent did (Schoultz 1972, 28). In terms of the rural resettlement of the displaced, there were two major impacts on the future political development of the country. First, Liberals and Conservatives segregated from one another. Municipalities that had mixed partisan populations before 1948 became homogeneous. Second, some of the displaced—mostly Liberals—created new communities in previously sparsely populated or

---

16. I am extremely grateful to Meertens and Sánchez for sharing their hand-copied notes with me, which they collected in 1978 by tracking down the remaining archives of the tribunals in each of the regions. The missing tribunals were Ibagué and Guamo.

17. This estimate is not well explained or well documented. By 1961, the National Investigative Commission on the Causes of the Violence (Comisión Investigadora Nacional de las Causas de la Violencia) refers to a source that estimated 800,000 internally displaced people and 150,000 refugees (Guzmán Campos, Fals Borda, and Umaña Luna 1962, 2:319). In one Tolima municipality alone, the commission cites an investigation that found that "in El Ataco, 1,993 people were thrown off their property. Assuming an average of 5 people per family, that is an estimated 9,965 people exiled out of the [population of] 17,600 people (1951 census)." In other words, more than half of the population is estimated to have been displaced. Ataco was a bastion of Liberal guerrillas, and, following the amnesty, a site of contestation between the "limpios" and the "sucios." Ataco remains an area where the central state has a tenuous presence; along with Chaparral, Planadas, Florida, and Pradera, it was among the fifty-one municipalities selected by the government to receive an intensive state-building effort beginning in 2010.

unpopulated territories. This process is referred to as colonization, and in some cases it was accompanied by armed groups, primarily Liberal groups and communists who did not accept the pardon offered in 1958. Indeed, some of the founders of these incipient armed groups were themselves displaced, including the founders of the FARC. In other instances, new communities formed by the displaced welcomed the FARC, the ELN, or the EPL as they attempted to expand their influence.

Partisan Segregation   By 1958, 125 municipalities where Liberals had had a majority before 1950 had become solidly Conservative; only seven were the reverse (Karl 2017). In all, Conservatives increased their share of majority municipalities from one-third to one-half (Karl 2017). A February 1961 note cited in Karl (2011) describes the change in Caldas: "there are municipalities, villages, hamlets where there is peace but peace without the enemy. All of the inhabitants belong to one sole political flag, and violence is not possible amongst themselves."[18] Molano (1987, 41) characterizes how the segregation emerged:

> Those persecuted by the government, by the *chulavitas*, by the Conservatives, weren't only the organized campesinos but also the entirety of the Liberal population without distinction by nuance or by class. The Conservative party had decided to push back the Liberal party definitively, and not only in the polls: thousands and thousands of campesinos were displaced [*desalojados*] and assassinated by the *chulavita* terror.

The segregation was facilitated by local elites who failed to intervene to protect the targeted. In many places where the displaced did attempt to return, local elites blocked it unless the returnees pledged allegiance to Conservatives.

> Everyone wanted to return. The mayor of Roldanillo organized a meeting and said that those that wanted to return could return if and only if they signed a certificate in which they renounced . . . their Liberal creed and committed to vote for the Conservative party. It was a real *cedula* [ID card], a

---

18. Weidmann and Salehyan (2013) find a similar effect of segregation in a very different place: Iraq in 2006–2010.

safe passage: anyone who didn't have it was a liberal, and the liberals were [killed] without asking who they were. The little paper was a requirement for those who wanted to return and without it in your pocket you couldn't work the land. It was everything: property title, recommendation, life insurance. Many, but many, had to sign, or more likely, put their fingerprint. Marulanda commented later that that was the day that he stopped believing in the police and the authorities. (Molano 1994, 46–47)

Elsewhere, locals who had been mobilized from previous rounds of fighting threatened to block Liberals' return. Karl (2011, 11) quotes from a report to the Armed Forces Joint Command:

"The *alcalde* [the mayor of the Boyacá municipality Coper] publicly announced that . . . his term in office has as its principal aim the facilitation of the return of all the Liberals who for one reason or another had to leave the town during the past violence." The *alcalde*'s policy, the commander continued, "while very good in intention, is at the moment impractical if one remembers that the spirits and arms of the town have not been disarmed. . . . [The policy] is so intolerable that spirits are stirred up more every day."

The mayor—who had himself "converted" to the Conservative party—was only protected from assassination by the town priest, who intervened with the local Conservatives several times (Karl 2011). The impracticality of the mayor's proposal was evident in many municipalities after 1958. Massacres began to increase, especially in Tolima, and particularly in municipalities, according to Karl (2011, 12), that had undergone "Conservatization" during the early period of the war. The massacres may have been part of an effort to prevent Liberals from resettling on their own property.

The government's failed attempts to adjudicate the property of the displaced effectively made the segregation permanent. When the Conciliation and Equity Tribunals were shut down in January 1962, the unsettled cases were supposed to be transferred to civil courts, but it does not appear that the cases were continued. If contemporaneous estimates of displacement are correct, the number of cases heard by the tribunals, let alone adjudicated, was only a tiny fraction of the total number of people displaced. The inability of the tribunals to effectively adjudicate disputes reinforced the segregation. Further, to speed up the processes, the central government recommended swapping properties between Liberals and Conservatives, with the aim of explicitly ratifying the partisan homogeneity to secure peace. The Tribunal of Valle reports anguish that the "country is divided into untouchable and closed zones." Acknowledging "the inadvisability of facilitating the formation of homogenous political nuclei," the Rehabilitation Commission "endorsed a plan [to arrange for property swaps]" (Karl 2011, 24). *Bolsas de finca raíz*—real estate exchanges—were also created to facilitate land swaps, which effectively made the political homogenization permanent.

The Liberal-communist allied armed groups also engaged in informal land swaps in areas where they had expelled conservatives. One account was the following, told to Molano (1994, 61):

> There was a debate within the group about what to do with the land and property of the conservatives who left. Marulanda wanted to bring in people to take over the property of what "was being cleansed." In the beginning, his view won out. "We were situating people who recently arrived in La Herrera, El Cambrín, El Davis, La Acción, La Gallera, Alto Saldaña. From there, all of conservatism left, just as all of liberalism had to leave the Cordillera Occidental, El Dovio, La Primavera, Betania. People arrived fleeing and we told them "go over there if you like that farm, put yourself over there where that tent is, grab that *cafetal*." As word started to get out that we gave land, well all of those that had to abandon it in other regions came over to our side. That's how the territory grew and grew. We were depopulating the *godos* [Conservatives] and populating it with Liberals.

The main difference, though, between the government's ratification of the new status quo following the displacement and resettlement and the Liberal-communist armed groups' activities was the location. The armed groups were operating in peripheral communities with little state presence. This type of resettlement became known as "armed colonization" (Ramírez Tobón 2001).

Colonization   The displaced civilians moving to far-flung areas of the country during La Violencia were not the first to arrive. Refugees from the Thousand Days' War had already settled in many of the areas (Steiner 2000), and further colonization by was led by peasants involved in agrarian movements during the 1930s and 1940s (Marulanda 1991).[19] The new

---

19. Indeed, some scholars link La Violencia to processes of colonization dating back to the nineteenth century (LeGrand 1992; Bergquist 1992).

waves of displacement sped the growth of frontier areas to an extreme. By one estimate, more than one-quarter of the total displaced population chose this path. Adams (1969, 528, cited in Gutiérrez Sanín, Acevedo, and Viatela [2007, 21n51]) estimated that six hundred thousand people moved into new colonization areas between 1951 and 1964. One town on the frontier, San José, the capital of Guaviare, tripled or quadrupled in size between 1958 and 1959 (Molano 1987, 34).[20] One guerrilla leader said, "People supported us because they saw that we weren't talking bullshit. The old people worked and the young ones were in the Liberal rank-and-file. We worked and we fought. We had 600 guerrillas and more than 3,000 families. The army didn't even cross through our territory" (Molano 1994, 61). As an indication of how distant these territories were from the reach of the state, they were not incorporated as fully recognized political units until the 1990s.[21]

The rehabilitation program of 1959 was followed by the Social Agrarian Reform of 1961, which "legitimized the occupation of territory" (Molano 1987, 46). Land reform, with its promises to redistribute and to provide land titles to hundreds of thousands of acres of public lands, might have stemmed the radicalization of displaced Liberals. But even from within the committee overseeing the program, its aims were redirected. Albertus and Kaplan (2013) write that "landed elites were able to shape the land reform process by (1) influencing the intensity of reform; (2) shifting its emphasis from expropriation and redistribution of latifundias to legalization and titling; and (3) determining the geographical targeting of reform." Regional elites, including some newcomers to the *gente bien* class, who had taken advantage of the violence to advance their own landholdings (Ortiz Sarmiento 1985), proved too powerful. In the Llanos, reform was blocked in San Luis de Cubarral, Guamal, and Acacías because they were dominated by Conservatives, who "impeded it" (Molano 1987, 46). These areas were able to block reforms partly by mobilizing

---

20. The Liberal-communist groups were not the only armed actors in the region: leaders dubbed "bandits" because they did not have a political affiliation, like Dumar Aljure, were also operating in the area and hated the communists (Molano 1987, 45).

21. Putumayo, Arauca, and Casanare were *intendencias*, while Amazonas, Guainía, Guaviare, Vaupés, and Vichada were *comisarías*. Guaviare is so remote that in 1988 an indigenous nomadic tribe had its "first contact" with the Colombian population, in what was then the *corregimiento* of Calamar (*Semana* 1988). Interestingly, governors were appointed for the former *comisarías* until 1997 because of "the influence of the mafias of narcotraffickers and the guerrillas" (*El Tiempo* 1991).

former guerrillas to engage in political banditry (Sánchez and Meertens 1983). President Lleras recognized the challenge and created the National Association of Peasants (ANUC) to help organize campesinos into an interest group that could serve as a counterweight to the powerful elites, and in 1958 Lleras formed the more formal Communal Action Committees (Juntas de Acción Communal, or JACs) based in the rural hamlets. But although the ANUC succeeded in mobilizing peasants, it was not enough to secure effective land reform.

The main areas where land reform was implemented were areas of new colonization, like the Magdalena Medio and the Llanos, where armed groups were already making inroads (Albertus and Kaplan 2013). Though some land was granted, no state services followed. The guerrillas were the only organized group in some areas throughout the 1970s. As Gutiérrez Sanín, Acevedo, and Viatela (2007, 21) note, "the triumph of colonization over reform activated the unoccupied territories, and strengthened them demographically while maintaining a complete state vacuum."

In addition to creating new communities on the periphery that depended on the order imposed and protection offered by the armed groups, the process of displacement also created a new sense of identity among the residents of these far-flung enclaves. As Mayor Lister, the early FARC leader, recounts,

> From the beginning we had to organize everything very well: managing so many people isn't easy. It helped us to be threatened by the troops [army] and identified as communists by the liberals. That made us feel closer to each other and to transform authority and discipline. Without that we wouldn't have survived given all that we needed and the ongoing siege. (Molano 1994, 27)

This view resonates with political and social psychology findings about collective identity formation (Flores 2014, 14).[22] These pockets transformed

---

22. The identities created during this process appear to have endured. In 1998, one resident of Calamar municipality in Guaviare (nicknamed CalaFARC by the military) told a *New York Times* reporter, "This is a town of people who have already been displaced from other areas. Nobody is about to run again" (Schemo 1998).

into the bases of the insurgency following another round of assaults by the government.

After 1958, violence began to increase again throughout the country. There were two types of groups that emerged during this time: those that became known as bandits and those that were regarded as revolutionary. Sánchez and Meertens (1983) argue that at least some of the bandits were specifically activated by local elites to protect what they had acquired during the earlier period of the war, while some of the armed groups previously associated with political elites became more independent. The bandits had begun to "tax" the landowners and to kidnap for ransom (Sánchez 1992). Other early fighters adopted new motives: Hobsbawm (1963b, 17) observes, "The men who fought for the parties, transferred their justification to the poor." For Manuel Marulanda, one of the defining moments toward rebellion was when "clean" Liberals killed his friend and comrade, Charro Negro (Karl 2017). Another key event was the army's attack on the autonomous republic of Marquetalia.

The autonomous republics were initially ignored by the government, partly because they were orderly: "Communist areas are armed, organized, disciplined, with a regular system of administration, education, and law, and are invariably recognizable because, even in the middle areas of bloodshed, they are free from *violencia*" (Hobsbawm 1963a, 254). Until 1960, Gilhodés (2007, 304) finds, the military did not view the communist enclaves as a threat. Instead, they characterized them as self-defense groups interested in managing their communities with some autonomy. Nevertheless, demands from regional elites to break up the enclaves (whose armed members they accused of cattle rustling beyond their borders), as well as assistance from the United States, eventually transformed the military's approach to the enclaves.[23]

The military attacked the autonomous republics in 1964. Most famously, it attacked Marquetalia, in southern Tolima, which was led by Manuel Marulanda. This turn to confronting the communist enclaves, as they were by 1964, marks the beginning of a new phase of political conflict and violence. The communists—armed and civilian—relocated to

---

23. The counterinsurgency Plan Lazo was adopted in 1959. The Colombian government legalized the counterinsurgency militias in 1965 under Decreto Legislativo 3398 of 1965, which became Law 48 in 1968 (Jaramillo 2005, 59).

Rio Chiquito and waited. According to LeGrand (2003, cited by Flores 2014, 22), "The state's violence against the peasant republics permanently transformed many refugees' attitudes towards the Colombian state and many now saw the government as an inveterate enemy." Eventually, the group decided to form a new insurgency following Marquetalia; in 1966 they officially adopted the name Revolutionary Armed Forces of Colombia (Fuerzas Armadas Revolucionarias de Colombia, or FARC).

The Insurgents and the Displaced

The segregation and colonization fueled by displacement were crucial for the development of the insurgency. The FARC's commitment to the settler communities was captured by the Liberal politician quoted in Bushnell (1993, 256), who characterized the group as "the rearguard of the *colono* [peasant settler]," rather than the vanguard of the proletariat. Even the CIA reported in 1967 that the Communist Party of Colombia (PCC) was committed to pacifism (CIA 1967). The FARC was only one insurgent group of many, though. Though each had a connection to displaced civilians, they had divergent approaches to rebellion, as well as different trajectories over time.

Other insurgents, for instance, did aim to engage the proletariat. The Marxist-Leninist Communist Party (PC-ML) emerged in 1964 as a result of frustration with the PCC, which seemed focused on local struggle and was generally war-averse (Pizarro Leongómez 1992, [1986] 2007). The ideological conflict was also reinforced from abroad; the debate between Maoists and Soviets was reflected within Colombia between the PC-ML and the PCC, respectively (in spite of the former's name).[24] The PC-ML created its own armed branch, the Popular Liberation Army (Ejército Popular de Liberación, or EPL) in 1967. The EPL and PC-ML tapped into urban student networks much more than the FARC. After more than two decades, the EPL demobilized in 1991.

A third insurgency followed Cuba's *foco* (enclave) path and created the National Liberation Army (Ejército de Liberación Nacional, or ELN)

---

24. Interview with Mario Agudelo, Bogotá, April 19, 2007; interview with William, Bogotá, August 6, 2007.

(Pizarro Leongómez [1986] 2007). The ELN drew its leadership from students and radical priests like the famed Camilo Torres, who died in battle shortly after joining a combat unit. The ELN remains active today, mostly in regions that feature extractive industries, particularly oil. On October 27, 2016, however, formal peace talks began in Quito between the Santos administration and the armed group, which may pave the way for its demobilization.

In 1974, a split over strategy within the FARC led Jaime Bateman to break off and launch the M-19, a group that opted for daring, urban attacks and propaganda campaigns.[25] The M-19 modeled itself after Uruguay's Tupamaros (Chernick 1988, 59). The group expanded quickly but never recovered from a disastrous attempt to hold Supreme Court justices hostage in 1985, which ended with the deaths of twelve justices and several top-ranking insurgent leaders. The M-19 demobilized in 1989 and formed a political party.

The FARC, of course, did not remain the rearguard. Rather, the organization drew on its deep ties to settler communities and experiences regulating economic, political, and social life to become a sophisticated insurgent army that spread to more than half of Colombia's territory by the 1990s.

Developing Loyalties in the Colonized Regions

Each insurgent group operated in a variety of regions and differed in their approaches to the communities. While the M-19 specialized in urban supporters and actions, it also had a presence in some rural areas, especially in the south. The EPL, ELN, and the FARC prioritized peripheral areas of the country, especially those that were recently settled. These areas—both rural hamlets and growing towns—were the most in need of organization and were the easiest to penetrate by offering order and public goods. Arjona (2016) describes and analyzes the social order armed groups were able to impose on communities, particularly those that were weakly organized, a trait new communities tend to share.

Displacement from La Violencia led not only to the settlement of frontier areas, but also to burgeoning towns in regions where cash crops—

---

25. The M-19 introduced itself with a flashy ad campaign followed by the heist of Simon Bolívar's sword in Bogotá (Fattal 2014). It took its name from the 1970 election that was allegedly rigged in favor of the National Front against opposition party ANAPO.

primarily bananas—and natural resource extraction—of oil, emeralds, and gold—were taking off. Regions in the first group include the Guaviare, the Macarena in the Llanos, and some undeveloped pockets in Urabá in the northwest. Towns with an insurgent presence included Turbo and Apartadó in Urabá, where the banana industry was booming, and Barrancabermeja, where the oil industry was developing. In each type of frontier—remote areas and growing towns—insurgent groups established early ties to the population by regulating economic actors on their behalf. Sánchez (2001, 6) identifies the areas as either having land issues, labor issues, or tributary extraction. Eventually, the insurgents would build off of their presence in these areas to expand into regions where the state traditionally had more of a presence, such as the coffee regions (Sánchez 2001, 6).

Rural Communities   In his study of the Guaviare region, Alfredo Molano (1987) documents two types of colonization: armed and spontaneous.[26] "However, little by little the hostility of the jungle, the privations and shared obstacles tended to dissolve the disparities and to give preeminence to the armed colonization over the spontaneous, given that in the former, forms of collective organization existed that acted as local power" (74). The "local power" was further reinforced by past experience: "The armed groups gained legitimacy because they protected the displaced from Conservative bands, from the army, during the Great March, and were now defending them against large landholders and companies" (49).

The arrival of coca in the region changed the dynamic, briefly. Initially, the FARC did not engage in the market. The first coca boom was followed shortly by a bust when the supply saturated the market and drove down the price (Molano 1987, 70–76). After the coca bonanza, only the old *colonos* managed to stick it out. They went back to planting regular crops—harvests called "*suertes*," or "luck" because they were so unreliable. "This moment, incredibly important in the colonization, was taken advantage of with astuteness and intelligence by the armed colonization . . . to advance in the organization of peasants who survived the avalanche, to create a solid local power" (77). In other words, the respite between periods of the coca market in the region allowed the guerrillas

---

26. This section draws from Molano (1987).

to organize the peasants, and when the coca market (and the accompanying drug-trafficking organizations) returned, the FARC was ready to regulate them.

To accompany its new regulatory role, the guerrillas also developed a tax system. Based on interviews of residents of the region in the mid-1980s, Molano (1987, 79) observed that

> the settlers [*colonos*] did not have—and do not currently have—a homogeneous opinion about the nature of the "economic norms" nor about the participation of the guerrillas in the bonanza [of coca]. For many, said participation, which oscillates between 8 and 10 percent of the market price, constitutes a voluntary and legitimate contribution and equates to what a union, Junta de Acción Communal, or political party calls the "membership dues or sustaining fees," which is to say, a determined proportion of the earnings or salary that is destined for the organization. For others, not a few, [the participation] is a cash loan in exchange for which they obtain personal security and order for business. For the rest, finally, the participation in the utilities is a war tax that is abusive and unjustifiable because it hurts profits. . . . Those most hostile to the taxes are the *grandes capos* [drug traffickers], who have to bribe the police and pay the tax.[27]

For years, the government would not or could not gain ground. Molano (1987, 61) writes, "For its part, the state was incapable of matching the efforts and sacrifice of the settler, and in the 1980s would lament this absence and pay a high price for it."[28] Even successful strikes by the military did not translate to the sole presence of the state.

Towns In contrast to the Macarena, Urabá in the northwest encompassed not only rural colonization in areas like Mutatá and the small mountain range that separated Antioquia and neighboring Córdoba department, but also a burgeoning agricultural export industry. The settlement and growth of towns in regions that held promise for commercial

---

27. The hostility of the last group would turn out to haunt the guerrillas.

28. Molano (1987, 61) cites a story in *El Tiempo* (Bogotá's largest daily) from 1986 on an agreement reached by the Barco administration and demonstrating peasants: There were also supposed to be "commissions to title the land, provide credit, technical training, and to guarantee the prices of products like corn and cocoa to eradicate coca." These promises are remarkably similar to those of the National Policy for Territorial and Regional Consolidation (PNCRT), adopted by the Santos administration in 2011.

crops and natural resource exploitation required a different form of engagement by the armed groups. In Urabá, the banana industry exploded in the 1960s, and in the region along the Magdalena River (Colombia's longest) between the Caribbean coast and Bogotá, known as the Magdalena Medio, oil refineries were established in the 1970s. In both cases, the challenge was not to protect and organize peasants, but rather to mobilize laborers. The efforts the armed groups undertook to do so in Urabá were emblematic of the approach.[29]

The FARC arrived in Urabá in the 1960s, led by Alberto Martínez, who formed what would become the powerful 5th Front.[30] Soon after, in 1968, the Communist Party (PCC) formed the union SINTRABANANO and began to organize the laborers on the banana plantations that lined the east side of the Gulf of Urabá. Angela organized for SINTRABANANO in the late 1970s and was fired for her organizing in 1977. "We worked from 4 a.m. to 11 p.m.," she told me, "but we were only paid for 7 a.m. to 5 p.m."[31]

The Marxist-Leninist Communist Party (PC-ML), along with its armed branch, the EPL, arrived a couple of years after the PCC and the FARC, in 1973 or 1974.[32] The head of the PC-ML political organizing in the region, Mario Agudelo, told me that one reason they decided to begin operations in the area was because, in contrast to peasants, "Workers were easier to organize and more active."[33] Agudelo arrived with his wife from Medellín, where they had been university students. In 1980 they began to work as laborers at a plantain plantation owned by Coldesa, a Dutch company. Working with his wife and one other organizer, they eventually created fifteen to twenty groups of twenty to twenty-five members each for SINTAGRO, the clandestine union the PC-ML created.[34] A former SINTAGRO organizer told me, "Kids didn't know their dad and vice versa. . . . The work days were so long that I would leave before they were awake,

---

29. Chapter 5 includes a detailed history of the Urabá region.
30. Interview with William, Bogotá, August 6, 2007.
31. Interview with the author, Apartadó, July 2, 2007.
32. Interview with Mario Agudelo, Bogotá, April 19, 2007.
33. Interview with the author, Bogotá, April 20, 2007. He added, "Peasants were not a source of resources, but rather information."
34. Interview with the author, Bogotá, April 20, 2007. The ELN also launched a union in the region, SINTRAJORNALERO, but it was much smaller.

and arrive after they were sleeping again." (The wife of another worker chimed in: "There was only enough time to make more children!")[35]

Some owners acknowledge that the working conditions were awful. Gabriel Harry, a plantation owner and member of AUGURA, the banana producers' organization (*gremio*), told me that in 1979 or 1980 his brother called him to tell him that the plantation workers were sleeping on the ground on the plantations he owned. Their response was to send a truckload of mattresses and materials to make shelters. They also enlisted someone from the welfare agency (then Bienestar Social) to provide services and advice to the families living on the farms. Harry said, "In 1986 [when the owners had a collective meeting under Barco], many owners of banana farms were learning about labor law for the first time."[36] Laborers and union organizers in the region might find this difficult to believe. Between 1975 and 1985, workers went on strike thirteen times in the banana region of Urabá. Five of those strikes spanned multiple municipalities, according to data collected by the Centro de Investigación y Educación Popular (CINEP) in Bogotá.

The adversarial relationship between unions and owners extended to the unions themselves. SINTRABANANO and SINTAGRO accused each other of being too sympathetic to the plantation owners.[37] Most union members, though, joined the union they did because each plantation required union membership to enter the job, and by the mid-1980s each was already dominated by one union or the other. The competition between unions led to violence between the groups in the 1980s, in what became known as the "union wars." The unions eventually jointly called a civic strike against the military's attempt to require identity cards for every resident of the banana zone in 1988. The unions united permanently in 1990 after the state withdrew their legal standing; the new union was named SINTRAINAGRO and its first action was to call a strike to protest the state's action. The strike lasted for thirty-three days.

In addition to union membership, another factor played a role in people's attachment to their identities and support for the armed groups in the

---

35. Interview with the author, Apartadó, June 29, 2007.
36. Interview with the author, Medellín, June 23, 2007.
37. Angela, interview, Apartadó, July 2, 2007; Álvaro, interview, Apartadó, June 25, 2007.

banana region: land "invasions." The goal of the invasions was to reclaim unused public or private lands to create housing for the banana workers, many of whom remained in camps on the plantations through the 1980s.

The EPL launched its first invasion in 1982, and three years later it created a coordinating committee. Two members of the community made up the lists and tried to help legalize the properties.[38] The main coordinator of the PC-ML-led invasions, Miguel Dario Osorio, known as El Condorito, said that they did not keep anyone off of the lists; they were based more on need. "Even liberals received land!" he exclaimed, but everyone knew the EPL was behind them. He imposed rules like prohibiting the sale of plots, regulated who could come in, and marked the plot for the family. The EPL led more than fifty invasions over the years, claiming more than ten thousand hectares in total for three thousand families, roughly ten to fifteen thousand people.[39] As with the unions, the invasions also became a source of competition between the EPL and the FARC, and neighborhoods were associated with one union or the other (and by extension, one armed group or the other). The FARC created its first neighborhoods—Policarpa Salvarrieta and El Concejo—in 1982 as well.

As in the Macarena, the organization of the workers and the armed groups' involvement in regulating the economy created strong loyalties among the population. In spite of the eventual union merge, even decades later people are still connected to their original union. The "pleasure in agency" they enjoyed while fighting for their labor rights might be linked to this connection (Wood 2003). Indeed, the unions, backed by the armed groups, were largely successful in securing higher wages and restricted working hours. It is possible that the successes supported closer identification with the organization that secured the improvements in people's material and working conditions.

Though the paths and nature of insurgents' presence in rural areas and towns differed, they shared deeply entwined connections to the residents of each place, as the examples from Guaviare and Urabá show. Further, the residents shared their experiences of forging these new communities and neighborhoods. Gloria Ocampo (2003, 251–52) writes, "The shared experience of the invasion is so intense that it defines the limits of the

---

38. Miguel Dario Osorio, El Condorito, interview, Apartadó, June 20, 2008.
39. Mario Agudelo, interview, Bogotá, April 27, 2007.

community by constructing an 'us' that excludes any circumstance beyond the community. The invasion, territorially and historically defined, is that which establishes the borders of the neighborhoods." Gould (1991, 716) observed, in turn, that "organizational networks maintained solidarity [in the Paris Commune] because they were structured along neighborhood lines." Once formed, the neighborhoods in Urabá town centers retained their ties to the armed groups that backed their formation. These loyalties would prove important for the violence and displacement that unfolded in the contemporary war.

Repression and Resistance

The development of the armed groups' ties to the population was nearly disrupted by an aggressive repression campaign by the government in the 1970s. Sánchez and Chacón (2005) find evidence that the FARC and the ELN were active in ninety-one municipalities between 1974 and 1978; in response, the state announced the Security Statute in September 1978, which introduced a "state of siege" that allowed government agents to arrest anyone participating in mass demonstrations.

The two main state forces dedicated to internal security were the army and the national police, both of which fell under the Ministry of Defense. (The CNP—the national police—were finally nationalized in practice in the 1960s [Llorente 2005].) The division of labor was primarily geographical: typically the army served in rural areas and the police in urban ones, though eventually the police were also posted to the municipal capitals, which were sometimes quite small towns. Later, the CNP would add the narcotics trade to its purview, while the army remained focused on the insurgency. Following Rojas's coup and his removal, the army formed a tacit agreement with the political elite not to interfere in political affairs and in exchange took substantial leeway over the security policies it pursued. The state of siege gave it even more.

To some extent, the repression kept the rebel groups restricted in their activities such as clandestine organizing for unions, and it nearly decimated the ELN and EPL in particular (Pizarro Leongómez [1986] 2007, 329). But it backfired in general (Restrepo 1992, 278) and helped the insurgents gain recruits (Reyes Posada [1991] 2007, 356).

The repression tipped some sympathizers into full-time membership in the insurgency (Esguerra 2009, 57). One former member of the EPL told me that she joined full time in 1982 after her university in Medellín had been closed for one year. Before that, she had attended meetings with a boyfriend but had not committed.[40] El Condorito, who eventually became the coordinator of land invasions in Urabá, told me he was arrested in the late 1970s (he couldn't remember the exact year) for putting up fliers in Medellín "in support of unionizing and the armed fight." After he spent a week in jail, where he was beaten and kept in the dark with little water, the authorities said they had arrested his parents too and were torturing them as well. Some of those arrested started to talk, but he truly was not involved with any group at that point. Then they finally released him. Two weeks after he was out of jail, some members of the PC-ML approached him and told him he had handled himself well. He agreed to join, but only the political organization, not the military wing. He relocated to Urabá in 1979.[41]

In addition, the repression of popular protest led peasants who had been members of independent social movements, such as ANUC, to join the guerrillas (Reyes Posada [1991] 2007, 355). While the insurgents were militarily weak, they were poised to take advantage of opportunities that arose in the early 1980s.[42]

Paramilitaries, Narcotraffickers, and Renegade Soldiers: The Counterinsurgency Alliance

Though the FARC developed strong ties to the population in areas it helped colonize, it created enemies too. The policies of the state of siege not only led to additional recruits for the FARC; it also prompted a change in how the FARC interacted with its civilian base in some areas. In the Magdalena

---

40. Interview with the author, Apartadó, June 24, 2008. She told me she did not find it difficult to commit, because the organization was "highly disciplined like my family . . . we couldn't go out anymore, because they took photos of the participants. But I couldn't go out anyway!" She became the leader of a group of ten tasked with robbing banks around Medellín and eventually in the greater region.

41. Interview with the author, Apartadó, June 20, 2008.

42. This seems especially true of the smaller EPL and ELN, which barely survived the 1970s.

Medio, the FARC managed to weather the crackdown by increasing its extortion (euphemistically referred to as a "vaccine" because it protected against possible violence) in areas it controlled (Ronderos 2014, 32–33). Locals—many of whom were not especially wealthy—grew tired of the payments and the threat of kidnapping. In addition to the increased pressure, new FARC leaders took command of the region's Fourth Front in 1979, and they did not command the same respect from residents as did the previous leader (Duncan 2006, 241). Henry Pérez, a former supporter of the FARC and rancher of modest means, is credited with founding the first "self-defense" force (*autodefensas*) in the Magdalena Medio region around this time (Ronderos 2014, 33).

The involvement of civilian militias in the conflict was not new. Such groups' roots reached back to the *pájaros* and *chulavitas* of La Violencia (Roldán 2002; Duncan 2006; Tate 2001). Following La Violencia and the founding of the FARC, the ELN, and the EPL, the military's counterinsurgency plans included arming the civil population for self-defense. The military then formed Civil Defense Units (Juntas de Defensa Civil) to "embolden" the peasants (*El Espectador* 2015). It was not until the repression of the Turbay administration, however, and the reaction in the Magdalena Medio, that self-defense forces formed that would have an enduring impact on the conflict. These are the groups that would come to employ political cleansing, and use the tactic to gain territory through the country.

The new self-defense forces formed independently of the military. Pérez organized a few neighboring ranchers in Puerto Boyacá; eventually they launched an organization called ACDEGAM, a cattle rancher association (Duncan 2006, 248). The organization created "health brigades" that involved civilian members of the "self-defense group" and traveled through four municipalities in the region (Puerto Boyacá, Puerto Berrío, Puerto Nare, and Puerto Triunfo). According to an investigation into paramilitary origins conducted by the Internal Security Administration (DAS) during Barco's presidency (1986–1990), these groups offered services in *veredas* (rural hamlet communities), which became "an opportunity to establish contact with the peasants, to hear about their concerns, and to locate those who were associated with the FARC, and which, in contrast, were tired of the guerrilla organization" (*Semana* 1989). Soon, the practice spread as "landowners, businessmen, and miners in regions like Urabá, Meta, northeast Antioquia and all of the Magdalena Medio, began to patronize the health brigades that preceded the so-called 'cleansing operations,' and the first massacres that occurred at that time in the country" (*Semana* 1989).

Fidel Castaño, a narcotrafficker and large landowner who transformed himself into a paramilitary leader, said in a 1995 interview,

> From there emerged, without anyone having taught us, one of the best mechanisms that we have used in the counter-guerrilla fight: if we couldn't combat [the guerrillas] where they were, we could neutralize the people that took them food, drugs, messages, aguardiente [liquor], prostitutes, and all of those types of things that they take to their camps. We realized that we were able to isolate them and saw that it was a strategy that gave very good results. Incredible. No one taught us that. I'm talking about the year 1982 and today we still apply that same mechanism [in Urabá], where in this moment we are combating the 5th Front of the FARC, with the same excellent results that we produced during that time. (Castro Caycedo 1996, 155)

But this effort was expensive, and the money started to run short. It was difficult to ask more of the landowners, because the self-defense forces did not want their patrons to find the requested support "more onerous" than the extortion of the guerrillas (*Semana* 1989). However, the self-defense forces soon got the infusion of financing and training it needed.

The self-defense forces gained powerful allies from two sectors: narcotraffickers and the military.[43] Narcotraffickers were attractive targets for guerrillas to extort, in two ways. First, they could pay much higher ransoms than peasants, so kidnapping was a tactic that some groups used. The most consequential occurred in 1981, when the M-19 nabbed Marta Ochoa, the daughter of powerful Medellín-based drug lord Jorge Luis Ochoa, and demanded a $1 million ransom for her release. In reaction, Ochoa called a meeting of narcotraffickers, where each "reportedly contributed $7.5 million" to form the group MAS, "Death to Kidnappers"

---

43. Liberal senator Pablo Guarín was a key supporter of the early self-defense groups (Duncan 2006, 242), foreshadowing the widespread connections between paramilitaries and politicians, eventually reaching from the local to the national levels (Romero 2007; López Hernández 2010).

(Bagley 1988, 76).[44] MAS allied with the Pérez group in Puerto Boyacá soon after, and the members of the self-defense forces no longer had to trudge among the *veredas*; they were now equipped with jeeps and proper weapons.

The other vulnerability of the narcos to the guerrillas stemmed from the increasing practice of purchasing land to launder money, to create clandestine airstrips to transport drugs, and to grow coca.[45] As the narcos expanded their land purchases—in at least three hundred municipalities of the roughly one thousand that existed in 1990, according to Reyes Posada ([1991] 2007, 357)—they encroached on territories where the guerrillas enjoyed a dominant presence. In Meta, the FARC was organized enough to impose taxes on coca growers (Molano 1987). Narcos like Rodriguéz Gacha, nicknamed "El Mexicano" for his evident love of Mexican culture and *ranchera* music, initially established working relationships with the guerrillas (Bagley 1988, 84). Some narcos, most famously Pablo Escobar, even expressed an affinity for the insurgents' antistatist, nationalistic views.

But these alliances frayed as the FARC started to cut out the "Medellín middleman" by taking over coca growing and refining themselves. The Medellín cartel refused to buy coca paste from the FARC, which led to some clashes. But, as Bagley (1988, 84) noted, "Unlike the previous landowners, the traffickers have been unwilling to pay the guerrillas protection money. Instead, they have used their resources and firepower to create large private armies to protect themselves from the rebels." These "large private armies" did not restrict their activities to protecting the interests of the narcos; in many instances, they began to engage with the FARC in battle directly. They also allied with the self-defense forces. One reason the collaboration between the narcos and the self-defense groups was possible was the veneer of legitimacy that narcotraffickers achieved. Bagley (85) presciently wrote, "As landowners, the drug lords will inevitably gain a foothold in legitimate associations of farmers and cattlemen that wield significant influence in Colombia's political system. In this fashion they may ultimately attain through the side door the kind of political power

---

44. The organization of MAS, the first explicit collaboration among the narcos, would also lead to the formation of the Medellín cartel through an informal division of labor among the traffickers (Bagley 1988, 77).

45. I sometimes refer to narcotraffickers as "narcos."

they initially sought via party politics" (referring to the failed attempts of Carlos Lehder and Pablo Escobar in particular to create a new political party and to influence the Liberal party, respectively). As early as that same year, 1988, the government estimated that the paramilitaries were almost "exclusively" financed by narcos, "as the payments of non-narcotrafficker landowners seem to have almost a symbolic character, and it would be difficult to cover the gigantic expenditures that have increased not only as a result of weapons and transportation and communications infrastructure, but also the salaries that distinct employees of the organization receive" (*Semana* 1989).

The self-defense groups and their narco allies received further assistance from sectors of the military. The military's latitude to pursue a full-on assault against insurgents and "subversives" during the state of siege under Turbay was substantially curbed in 1982, when the new president, Conservative Belisario Betancur, organized a ceasefire with four of the active insurgent groups, the FARC, EPL, M-19, and ADO (a tiny urban insurgency) (Chernick 1988, 59). (The ELN engaged in talks, but never reached a ceasefire agreement.) Insurgents were granted amnesty, which included the release of political prisoners. The government also recognized the status of the groups as "belligerents," affording them rights under the Geneva Conventions, though the military rejected this recognition (Chernick 1988). Military officers, including Betancur's first minister of defense, rejected what they perceived to be a weak approach, and the military openly opposed the peace talks (Romero 2003, 18). A few officers started to support small regional militias operating in some areas of the country.[46]

The army battalion near Puerto Boyacá began to meet with Pérez and other leaders. On October 22, 1984, representatives of ACDEGAM and the military held a meeting in Puerto Boyacá to analyze the first one hundred days of the truce; "they declared it a failure and proclaimed Puerto Boyacá the anti-subversive fortress of Colombia" (Medina Gallego and Téllez Ardila 1994, 96). The paramilitaries received training from the Colombian military, but also from Israeli and British mercenaries (Dudley

---

46. Romero (2000, 92) states that the ranchers reached out to the military; Dudley (2006, 67) says that the military took the initiative. It seems reasonable, in any case, that both sectors "felt betrayed" by the peace talks (Romero 2000, 92).

1997; Ronderos 2014). International corporations, including the Texas Petroleum Company were also linked to the paramilitaries, dating to the 1982 meeting convened in Puerto Boyacá (Dudley 1997). In 1983, the *procurador general*, Carlos Jiménez Gómez, denounced an alliance between narcotraffickers, landowners, and the military (Jaramillo 2005, 59–60).[47] The report did not deter the alliance, which only morphed and grew more powerful over time. This alliance would prove consequential for all forms of displacement and for political cleansing in particular.

Following the end of La Violencia, the nature of the conflict and violence in Colombia shifted. Rather than a competition over which political party would dominate the existing political system (and which partisans would reap the local benefits), the shape of the entire political system was challenged by new insurgent groups. This chapter traces the emergence of the multiple armed groups that claimed to have the best vision for what that political system should be and how to achieve it. It also describes the actors that fought back against the revolutionaries in favor of the status quo. The clash motivated by lofty ideas led to a much more profane, protracted war and large-scale violence.

Displacement during La Violencia accompanied and even precipitated the shift in the war, partly because the state failed to incorporate the millions of migrants into well-ordered communities. Though the National Front government took steps to address the loss of land by promoting colonization, it ultimately secured political segregation. Further policies aimed at justice through the Tribunals of Land Conciliation and, more broadly, at establishing a more fair distribution of land, or at least access to land for the displaced and poor, were ineffective, diluted, or abandoned before their intended effects could take hold. In the meantime, the nascent insurgencies remained active in areas of new colonization while the state withdrew.

The colonization of new territories, and the state's abandonment of the process, was essential for the formation of the FARC. Without the displaced families, there would be no community to govern, no one to mobilize, and no resources to procure. The FARC provided order in the new frontier

---

47. In Colombia, the *procurador general* is an inspector general who is charged with investigating and prosecuting public officials who break the law. The *fiscal general* is the equivalent of the attorney general.

communities. Other insurgencies also took advantage of the new settlements on the periphery of the country to forge deep ties to the residents.

Over time, the FARC became more assertive in response to government repression and the arrival of the drug trade in regions where it operated. The FARC took advantage of a ceasefire and peace talks with the government in the 1980s to expand its political base and enhance its military capacity. By the 1990s, the FARC was a powerful military force engaging in offensive action in more than half of Colombia's municipalities. The group's biggest, bloodiest challenge emerged from aggrieved peasants themselves, who united with powerful narcotraffickers and disgruntled military members to create paramilitary groups that countered the FARC's influence with brutal violence. Meanwhile, the state wavered in its strategy, moving from repression to engagement to collusion with paramilitaries. The overlap among these approaches led to the adoption of democratic reforms and the simultaneous failure to protect citizens as they exercised their new rights. As a result, they were exposed to a wave of political cleansing.

Civilian displacement connects La Violencia to the contemporary civil war. But as the war shifted, so did the predominant modes of displacement. Three factors differed between the two wars and the ways displacement emerged. First, La Violencia is an example of what Kalyvas and Balcells (2010) and Kalyvas (2005) call a "symmetric non-conventional" (SNC) war. This type of warfare is characterized by armed groups that are relatively weak but of equal strength, which is fundamentally different from insurgencies, or what they call irregular wars. The violence produced by these weak armed groups can be quite intense, but the groups are typically not strong enough to control territory. As a result, they do not face the same incentives I outlined in chapter 1 to expel people as a tactic to gain control. Rather, the violence tends to be more sporadic, which again does not make it any less vicious. At the same time, the second factor that distinguished the two wars relates to the cleavage of the war: In La Violencia, the fighting began along partisan lines and fanned out quickly throughout the country (except in communities like Urrao that resisted polarization and rejected outside armed groups, as Roldán [2002] describes). Neighbors knew each other's partisan views, and once violence arrived they could not prevent armed groups from targeting their neighbors, and in some cases took advantage of it for their own private gain. Third,

Conservatives and Liberals were much more evenly spread throughout the country than the pockets of support that developed around the contemporary insurgent groups. This led to a widespread pattern of separating from one another—as described in this chapter—even when there was not a specific armed group engaging in political cleansing per se. It was also mobilized by civilians themselves. At the same time, collective targeting against Liberals and Conservatives does seem to have been an important factor in the displacement.

The next chapter traces the collision between the insurgents, the paramilitaries, and the state from the mid-1980s until 2012, which led to another round of widespread displacement.

3

THE CONTEMPORARY CIVIL WAR
IN COLOMBIA, 1986–2012

The previous chapter introduced the actors that became the main protagonists in the contemporary war: the insurgents, the paramilitaries, the
state armed forces, and the civilians living in newly settled areas. This
chapter describes the escalation of the clash among these groups and the
implications it had for violence and displacement. Ironically, the intensification of the war followed Latin America's first serious peace talks, led by
the Betancur administration beginning in 1982. The talks tipped disgruntled military officials into an alliance with civilian self-defense groups,
which remained beyond the control of the state and the rule of law. The
talks also launched institutional changes that had devastating and unfore-
seen effects on the violence. After the talks fell apart in 1986, the war
moved from isolated pockets of struggle to generalized violence that eventually affected every department in the country.

The war since 1986 can roughly be divided into three periods. First, the
FARC improved its military capacity and expanded its presence during the
1980s and 1990s. The ELN, the other major insurgent group, also rebuilt

a strong presence in extractive zones of the country. Second, the paramilitaries followed by expanding their presence after successfully defeating the FARC in some of its strongholds. This led to the intensification and spread of the violence in the years from 1996 until 2002. Finally, the state began to retake the initiative, organizing the demobilization of paramilitary groups and attacking the FARC's leadership beginning in 2003.[1] This chapter describes each phase in turn.

One key characteristic of the war was that even when the insurgents were powerful, they were never as powerful as the state forces (especially in combination with their informal allies, the paramilitaries). This power imbalance creates a situation known as "irregular" or "guerrilla" warfare: the insurgents avoid direct confrontation with state forces because they would lose (Kalyvas 2005; Kalyvas and Balcells 2010).[2] Instead, insurgents rely on clandestine activity and on the civilian population for resources, information, and camouflage. Civilian communities become the battlegrounds, then, where noncombatants are exposed to and targets of violence.[3] The final section of the chapter describes what this meant for Colombian communities in terms of the lethal violence and civilian displacement they witnessed. The history raises central questions about the origins, modes, and scale of civilian displacement over the past thirty years and across Colombia's regions, which the rest of the book sets out to answer.

FARC Ascendancy

Over the course of the ten years following the peace talks with the government, the FARC expanded its presence from roughly 173 municipalities in 1985 to more than half of the municipalities in the country (622) by 1995 (Chernick 1999, 167). The peace talks and ceasefire with the Betancur administration allowed the insurgent groups some room to organize

---

1. For a similar periodization, see Comisión Nacional de Reparación y Reconciliación (Colombia), Grupo de Memoria Histórica 2013, 33.

2. In a few cases, the insurgents did launch attacks on posts like the FARC did in Mitú, the capital of Vaupés department. But they did not have sufficient manpower to hold the conquered territory.

3. For more on irregular civil wars, see chapter 1.

publicly and more generally raised the profile of the FARC, largely unknown to urban residents (Chernick 1988, 62–63), who were much more familiar with the M-19.

As part of the negotiations, the FARC and the PCC created a political party in 1985 called the Unión Patriótica (UP) and embraced the strategy of a "combination of all forms of the struggle" (*todas formas de la lucha*). The framework under Betancur set in motion a series of institutional reforms to address insurgents' grievances. Betancur agreed to expand political competition by permitting the entry of the UP into electoral politics. Further, elections were extended to the municipal level in 1988. The creation of the UP and the local elections were key changes in Colombian politics that led to shifts in the war as well (Gutiérrez Sanín, Acevedo, and Viatela 2007).

The FARC ended the ceasefire with the government in 1986, and with the EPL, ELN, and M-19 formed the Simón Bolívar Guerrilla Coordination Group (Coordinadora Guerrillera Simón Bolívar, or CGSB), a formal alliance among the groups. The M-19, though, never recovered from its attempted occupation of the Supreme Court in Bogotá in 1985 and negotiated a demobilization with the Barco administration in 1989.

Other groups followed the M-19. With the collapse of the Soviet Union and the offer of a constitutional assembly for which insurgent groups could win representation in a special election, the EPL and several smaller groups, the PRT (Partido Revolucionario de Trabajadores), CRS (Corriente de Renovación Socialista, a splinter of the ELN), and the indigenous group Quintín Lame agreed to demobilize (Chernick 1999, 180).[4] The election for the Constituent Assembly that would write the

---

4. The decision of the EPL is interesting; it had been considered the most radical of the insurgent groups until that point. The reversal required an internal coup: Even though twenty of the twenty-eight members of the Central Committee were in favor of demobilization, stalwarts were in control of the nine-member Executive Committee, which had the authority to call meetings for votes. Because seven of the nine did not favor demobilization, but the majority of the rest did, they refused to call a meeting. As a result, the other nineteen had to circumvent them and hold a meeting with the government directly (Fajardo Landaeta 2009, 46). In May 1990, dialogue between the EPL and the state began, and in February 1991 the peace agreement was signed. On March 1, 1991, roughly twenty-five hundred EPL combatants demobilized from several camps where they assembled. Within six months, dissidents began to rearm (Reyes Posada and Correa 1992, 41). The largest group formed under the leadership of Francisco Caraballo, the former commander of the EPL's armed wing. They became known as the EPL-D, or the Caraballistas. Caraballo was captured in 1994 and imprisoned, leading to the dissolution of the group. One small faction of the original EPL remains active

new constitution marked the first time the traditional parties did not have a majority of the seats. The M-19's list won the highest proportion of votes, at 27 percent (Shugart 1992). The new assembly also revoked the mandate of the Congress elected in 1990 and called for a new election in 1991, attempting to restrain the traditional parties' influence in order to approve the new constitution (Bejarano 2001, 56).

The government tried to entice the FARC and the ELN (the remaining components of the CGSB) to participate by offering another round of peace talks with favorable terms. The talks would "recognize the territorial domains of the guerrillas and contemplate their transformation in organizations of local power, subject to democratic rules. Another aspect of the negotiation announced publicly is the partial, not total, disarmament of the insurgents, with the government accepting the existence of 'civic guards' and local police whose ranks the ex-guerrillas would fill" (Reyes Posada [1991] 2007, 360). President Gaviria reportedly offered to cede sixty municipalities to the CGSB, but the group was apparently demanding ninety-six municipalities (Sánchez 2001, 15).[5]

Two factors explain the FARC's refusal to negotiate. First, since 1986 leaders of the UP had been systematically assassinated by right-wing and narco groups in what some term a "politicide" (e.g., Gutiérrez Sanín, Acevedo, and Viatela 2007) and what others refer to as a "genocide" (e.g., López Hernández 2010). More than three thousand UP members are estimated to have been killed since 1986. This "dirty war" seems to have radicalized the FARC leadership: How could they demobilize and participate in electoral politics if their members and candidates are ruthlessly killed off?[6] The targeting of the UP will be outlined in greater depth in the next chapter.

---

in Santander. Noted historian Gonzalo Sánchez (2001, 25–26) observed, "Partial negotiations, the Colombian experience seems to indicate, do not arrest the magnitude of the overall conflict, but simply serve as space for the repositioning of the principal actors in the war. Moreover, the demonstrable tendency or norm is that after every negotiation, new divisions and radicalizations are produced."

5. In retrospect, the offer of sixty municipalities appears to be the best that the FARC and ELN would ever receive. In the 1998 peace talks with the Pastrana administration, the FARC secured six. In the current agreement, combatants are disarming and demobilizing in twenty-six regions, but they do not have the autonomy that the Gaviria administration was offering.

6. As I discuss in the next chapter, the UP broke away from the FARC in 1989 under the leadership of Bernardo Jaramillo, largely as a rejection of the FARC's war on all fronts.

Second, in 1990, as elections were held for the constitutional assembly, the army took the FARC's de facto headquarters in La Uribe. This attack apparently humiliated the FARC and increased its leaders' resolve. The FARC responded with a massive wave of violence, cementing their unwillingness to negotiate and exposing the military's inability to stop the attacks (Reyes Posada [1991] 2007, 360).

At its 1993 conference, the FARC adopted a plan for its military expansion and formed regional blocs of at least five fronts each. These blocs would be powerful enough to engage in large-scale military operations. One of the first large-scale military moves the FARC made was a 1993 attack on northeastern Dabeiba, an attempt to isolate the Urabá region from the rest of the country. Each municipality is supposed to have at least one police post in the municipal capital; in the 1990s, these posts were frequent targets of the FARC's crude mortars, and police officers were also routinely kidnapped and held for many years. The state's military and police forces proved unable to fend off the advances of the FARC, and by 1996 the FARC had established a military advantage, dominating the south of the country and delivering several defeats to the military (Echandía 2006, 134). The FARC had an estimated 10,500 combatants with 105 fronts in 1994, up from 7,700 combatants and 80 fronts in 1991 (Sánchez 2001, 15). The fronts were grouped into seven blocs that eventually covered the majority of the country's territory (Ferro Medina and Uribe Ramón 2002, 43–45). Marks (2003) estimated that by 2003, in addition to approximately 16,500 combatants, another 8,000 to 10,000 were active in local militias.

The trade-off for the FARC's military expansion was that it would no longer develop the sort of deep ties within the communities that it had over the previous two decades. As a result, where FARC had expanded in the 1990s it focused on economic extraction rather than building networks (Echandía 2006, 39). William, a former combatant, explained that they were successful militarily but not with the population. The failure to establish more enduring ties to the population may have contributed to the spectacular spread of the FARC's rivals: the paramilitaries. In 2001, the FARC leadership reversed its strategy and told front commanders to revert to their old formation and build new ties to communities, especially in territories they once controlled.[7] By that time, though, the organization was already facing a much more powerful paramilitary foe.

---

7. William, interview, Bogotá, August 6, 2007.

Paramilitary Expansion

The paramilitaries transformed from isolated self-defense groups in the 1970s to well-equipped and trained counterinsurgent forces with powerful fronts across the country by the 1990s (Romero 2003).[8] But the expansion occurred in fits and starts. Until 1986, the paramilitary movement was confined to pockets in the country, the epicenter of which was Puerto Boyacá. From there, in March 1988, combatants were sent to Urabá. Roughly twenty of them stayed for about ten months in hotels in Apartadó and were easily identifiable to the population.[9] The paramilitaries ultimately committed two massacres of workers living on the banana farms Honduras and La Negra, apparently in the service of "clients" in the banana region (*Semana* 1989).

The violence, though, attracted the attention of the government. Under the Barco administration (1986–1990), the state security agency, the DAS, investigated two paramilitary groups following massacres they perpetrated in 1988. One group was associated with El Mexicano ("Los Justicieros"), which was allegedly killing members of the UP; the other was associated with Escobar, and was accused of assassinating peasants and protecting Escobar's properties and drug laboratories (*Semana* 1989). The army was ordered to attack both groups. The Barco administration then outlawed the paramilitaries in 1989, overturning Law 48 of 1968, which had permitted the military to create militias (Reyes Posada [1991] 2007, 359). Barco adopted Decree 1194, which established penalties to whoever financed or promoted paramilitaries.

In addition, Barco ordered the beginning of the war against "narco-terrorism" following the assassination of presidential candidate Luis Carlos Galán in 1989. The war strained the alliance between Escobar and other narcotraffickers. Escobar had united the narcos to form the "non-extraditables" to fight the possibility of extradition to the United States for drug trafficking (where they knew they would not enjoy the same privileges and leniency as they would in Colombia through threats and bribes). Escobar envisioned a war against the state, but the Cali cartel leaders (and the smaller Norte de

---

8. Romero (2003) makes a distinction between *autodefensas*, or self-defense forces, and paramilitaries. The former typically remained local and defensive, while paramilitaries branched out and eventually engaged in an aggressive counterinsurgent campaign. Many groups that started out as *autodefensas* morphed into paramilitary groups.

9. Mario Agudelo, interview with the author, Bogotá, April 27, 2007.

Valle cartel) opted go to war against Escobar to maintain their independence (Duncan 2006, 221, 223). After years of bombings and assassinations in Medellín, Cali, and Bogotá, Escobar negotiated to turn himself in after a prohibition on extradition was written into the constitution of 1991. He was held in La Catedral in Antioquia, where he continued to run his empire and live comfortably. When the state decided to move him to an actual prison in 1992, Escobar was tipped off and escaped right before they arrived.

Soon the Cali cartel and narcos formerly allied with the Medellín cartel joined forces to hunt Escobar (Douglas 1999). They formed Los Pepes ("The Persecuted by Pablo Escobar") and joined the Colombian police, military, and US DEA to track Escobar. In December 1993, Escobar was killed, effectively terminating the Medellín cartel.

A key leader of the Pepes, Fidel Castaño, a narcotrafficker with a private army and vast landholdings in northern Córdoba, had demobilized his paramilitary group when the EPL signed peace accords in 1991.[10] He also announced the creation of a foundation (Funpazcor) to distribute some of his own land to displaced peasants in the region, a foundation that turned out to be a fraud, because most of the land remained in control of the Castaño family.

The Castaño family, headed by Fidel until his brothers Carlos and Vicente had him killed, led the "new generation of paramilitaries" (Ronderos 2014). Fidel downplayed his criminal past and emphasized a narrative of personal revenge instead (Reyes Posada [1991] 2007; Ronderos 2014). In 1980, the FARC kidnapped the patriarch of the Castaño family near Segovia in the Magdalena Medio region. When he was killed after the third ransom request (the first two of which had apparently been paid), Fidel supposedly organized his younger siblings to fight the FARC. By 1997, the Castaño brothers would form the most powerful paramilitary bloc the country had seen, and they would play a key role in the escalation of the war.

Once Escobar was killed, Castaño turned his attention to the dissident group of the demobilized EPL that had rearmed in Urabá near the Castaños' base in Córdoba (and became known as the EPL-D, for dissidents).

---

10. By 1987, Fidel Castaño had purchased vast tracts of land with proceeds from the narcotics trade in Córdoba (Bushnell 1993, 65). There he formed a new group known as the Tangueros, based in the municipality of Valencia (Romero 2000, 93).

To combat the group, Fidel and younger brother Carlos organized a new paramilitary group that would become the Peasant Self-Defense Forces of Córdoba and Urabá (Autodefensas Campesinas de Córdoba y Urabá, or ACCU). The initial target was the EPL-D, in the north of Urabá. But the FARC allied with the EPL-D, and both groups pressured the demobilized members of the EPL who were still living in the area to rearm. They accused those who refused of betraying the revolution and, more to the point, of providing intelligence to the state. The targeted former EPL members, particularly the rank and file, were exposed to the violence. They decided to form protection groups, known as Popular Commands (Comandos Populares, or CPs), which went after FARC and EPL-D members.

Soon, Urabá became the epicenter of an all-out war. The ACCU broadened its war to include the FARC and entered the municipality of Turbo from the north. They recruited HH (an alias), who had been a militia member of the FARC, and they formed a new group. Until then, Agudelo told me, the ACCU "did not have tentacles in the region. They of course had supporters, but not enough to really enter."[11]

The group also found support in AUGURA, the banana producers' organization. AUGURA members represented the elites of the region: the plantation owners, many of whom were also politicians, like Jaime Enríquez Gallo. AUGURA members were fed up with the lack of security in the region; many of them were exiled in Medellín (though many never lived in the region to begin with). Gabriel Harry, the onetime AUGURA president, told me the army could have been tougher: "they have been missing a fierceness [*berraquera*]" (though he also sympathized with them, since "human rights problems could end a career").[12] The banana industry paid protection money to the paramilitaries (VerdadAbierta.com 2010; ElEspectador.com 2009; VerdadAbierta.com 2009; National Security Archives 2011). A member of the Fiscalía of Medellín told me that AUGURA hired Jazbún, himself a banana plantation owner, to "look after their interests."[13] Chiquita Brands International acknowledged years of payments to both guerrillas and paramilitaries in the Urabá region when it agreed to a plea deal in the United States in 2007; as both groups

---

11. Interview with the author, Medellín, May 14, 2008.
12. Interview with the author, Medellín, June 26, 2007.
13. Interview with the author, Medellín, May 25, 2013.

were classified as terrorist organizations, US companies were prohibited from providing them resources of any kind.[14]

Another source of support were the CPs. Even though the EPL had formerly been the primary rival of Castaño's groups, many of the members switched sides to join their former enemy. One example is Rafael Emilio García, alias El Viejo (the Old Man), who revealed in his confession (*"versión libre"*) to the special attorneys appointed to investigate paramilitary leaders that it was during this period of demobilization that he joined the paramilitaries. He testified that he was recruited by Mario Agudelo in Urabá, the PC-ML organizer, into the study groups they formed. He received two bodyguards following his demobilization with the EPL, but he could not return to Apartadó because he was targeted by former comrades. He helped to form the CPs. According to El Viejo's testimony, Carlos Castaño recruited him to join the ACCU in 1992 by arranging a meeting between him and one of his lieutenants in Medellín. Castaño took over the financing of the CPs in 1993, according to El Viejo, though they were formed earlier and depended on community support for survival. Afterwards, Castaño told him that "the political part is missing" and appointed him to organize a political wing to compete with the guerrillas.[15]

Urabá soon experienced by far the highest levels of violence in the country. Public outcry forced the paramilitaries to adjust, and they began to argue that they were a political organization on equal footing with the insurgents (Reyes Posada [1991] 2007, 359). They made political pronouncements throughout the 1990s, mostly as a justification for their existence and actions (Cubides 2001, 139) and to hide their connections with organized crime (Echandía 2006, 33). Reporter Steven Dudley observed, "[Carlos] Castaño himself symbolizes paramilitary legitimacy. He regularly meets with the press and human-rights groups to speak of his private war against the guerrillas" (Dudley 1997).

---

14. Chiquita paid a $25 million fine meant to compensate Colombian victims. See the clearinghouse at the National Security Archives (NSA), http://nsarchive.gwu.edu/NSAEBB/NSAEBB340/, for more than fifty-five hundred internal Chiquita documents from the Department of Justice and the Federal Bureau of Investigation. The NSA argues that these documents prove that Chiquita directly benefited from these payments in the form of security provision in the Urabá region. In the 2007 settlement, Chiquita claimed that the payments were extortion (National Security Archives 2011).

15. Versión Libre, Rafael Emilio Garcia. Primera Vez que Aparece Bloque Bananero. July 17, 2008. Fiscalia 17.

The proliferation of paramilitary groups took off when Gaviria issued an order to legalize self-defense forces again in 1994, which became the Convivir under President Samper. Paramilitary groups were still active in Puerto Boyacá, and in the Boyacá department, where the "emerald czar" Victor Carranza also mounted a powerful private army. The legalization allowed the nascent groups to flourish and, importantly, to form open ties to sympathetic organizations such as the banana *gremio*, AUGURA. The legal opening was brief but important. The Convivir groups were declared constitutional but prohibited by the Constitutional Court from receiving military-grade weapons (Tate 2001, 167), which effectively disbanded them in November 1997.[16]

Meanwhile, the Castaños had organized the Magdalena Medio and Llanos paramilitary groups into a federation known as the United Self-Defense Forces of Colombia (Autodefensas Unidas de Colombia, or AUC) earlier the same year.[17] It was the first national-level counterinsurgency project (Sánchez 2001, 24). Soon after, the AUC expanded into César, Bolívar, and Magdalena (Echandía 2006, 35). By 2002, there were thirty-two blocs across the country. In addition to their increasing military power, the paramilitaries also engaged in political and economic activities.

Castaño estimated that by 2002, 70 percent of the finances for paramilitaries came from the drug trade (Dudley 2002). Gutiérrez Sanín (2004, 270) documents that while paramilitary groups paid their recruits a salary and allowed fighters to individually profit from war via looting, insurgents in the FARC "carry on a hard and dull life." He goes on to argue that desertion from the FARC is driven by its organizational structure and incentive systems, noting that right-wing paramilitary organizations have attempted to lure FARC fighters with combat skills by offering material rewards (see also Oppenheim et al. 2015).

The paramilitaries' political activities included penetration of the local community councils (Juntas de Accion Comunales, or JACs). For example, the investigative journalism organization VerdadAbierta.com reported that "El Alemán" ("the German") "worked from the [JACs] to construct a social base that would allow them to consolidate their

---

16. See the court decision at http://www.corteconstitucional.gov.co/relatoria/1997/C-572-97.htm.

17. Carlos took over leadership of the paramilitaries after Fidel was killed in 1994, apparently by his own men on orders from his brothers.

political movement." El Alemán created "Promoters of Social Development" (PDS), mobile units of injured combatants who visited communities to recruit candidates for municipal office and to spread the word about which candidates to support in the departmental and congressional races (VerdadAbierta.com 2014; Ronderos 2014, 274–75). The PDS units were the earliest form of political mobilization by a paramilitary group, and other blocs followed suit with their own forays into politics. A unifying factor across blocs, regardless of how much they were invested in local politics, was mobilization for congressional and presidential elections beginning in 2002.

State Resurgence

The paramilitaries' eventual shift from local to national politics was precipitated in part by institutional changes the state implemented. Paradoxically, reforms associated with decentralization and democratization, which solidified the "municipalization" of political life (Gutiérrez Sanín, Acevedo, and Viatela 2007), ultimately facilitated the spread of violence across the country (Chacón 2013). The measures were adopted because reformers believed they would mitigate the conflict and help end the war (Eaton 2006). Following Betancur's extension of elections to the local level, the Barco (1986–1990) and Gaviria (1990–1994) administrations devolved fiscal authority and budgetary responsibility to the municipalities for several public goods (such as education, health, and road upkeep). Unfortunately, the reforms had the opposite of their intended effect: rather than dampen the violence, they fueled it. Municipalities became attractive targets for armed groups because of the transfers and royalties they received and because the state was unable to provide security to them. Referring to the failure of the 1991 constitution to lead to the end of the war, Bejarano (2001, 69) observed, "It was necessary to recognize that behind a weak and incomplete Colombian democracy lurked a precarious State unable to back up and enforce basic democratic institutions, freedoms, and rights."

With the new constitution, the military and the Colombian National Police (CNP) fell under the command of a civilian defense minister for the first time. But as the armed groups took advantage of the new resources available in the municipalities, the new civilian-led ministry could not exercise authority or effective military force against either the insurgents or paramilitaries.

The CNP's primary focus on countering the narcotics trade and on urban areas shifted with reforms adopted in 1993, which expanded its official role in the counterinsurgency. Every city with more than fifty thousand inhabitants would have an urban police force "trained to respond to public demands and the security challenges that appear in that kind of environment" (Llorente 2005, 194). In rural areas, a "strike force" of *carabineros* would be formed to focus on public order. The reforms were not enough to effectively confront the increasing violence: "Between 1996 and 2002, the police abandoned more than 70 rural posts as a consequence of guerrilla harassment. In contrast, during the 10 previous years, only a little more than 30 posts were abandoned" (Llorente 2005, 42).

The government was hobbled by the overwhelming profits of the cocaine trade, which the cartels used to penetrate many institutions of the state, including its security forces. The Medellín cartel famously used *plata o plomo* (silver or lead—i.e., money or bullets) to get its way. The administration of Ernesto Samper (1994–1998) was handicapped by the scandal of the Proceso 8,000, an investigation into the campaign funding of the president that found substantial financing from the Cali cartel. The scandal led the United States to cut off foreign aid to Colombia.

One law the Samper administration managed to adopt, which arguably had an impact on the war over the long term, established a demobilization process for insurgents. Law 418 of 1997 provided amnesty to members of politically motivated groups who turned themselves in, as long as they were not guilty of crimes against humanity. Also in 1997, the government adopted a law to register the internally displaced following a court order to provide humanitarian assistance to IDPs. I return to this below.

The following year, Conservative Andrés Pastrana was elected in 1998 on a platform that promised to secure the demobilization not just of individual fighters but of the entire insurgency. His administration began talks with the FARC and as a gesture of good faith ceded a large territory southwest of Bogotá—the size of Switzerland—known as the *despeje*. Another territory in southern Bolívar was possibly going to be ceded to the ELN to start peace talks as well. The approach of granting the armed groups territory was met with incredulity by political elites who favored a military response to the insurgency, and according to Martínez (2010), it pushed some politicians to seek out more explicit alliances with paramilitaries.

At the same time, Pastrana began reforms of the police and military. One issue that plagued the military was that few of its troops were professional, or trained for combat (Sweig 2002). Of 133,000 soldiers in 1998, only 40,000 were dedicated to combat (Gottwald 2003, 3), and there was not enough funding to recruit more (Marks 2003, 47). By early 2002 only 35,000 soldiers could be deployed for combat (Sweig 2002). This fraction of the military force was not large enough to implement the counterinsurgency plans the military had created, which "recognized the need to dominate local areas by providing a security umbrella under which the normal functions of the state could be exercised" (Marks 2003, 47).

To help with funding and training, Pastrana turned to assistance from the United States, which was once again willing to pledge aid. In a plan designed in DC but known as Plan Colombia, the United States approved a package of military assistance to the army that included training for special forces and helicopters to accompany coca fumigations (the CNP was primarily seen as in charge of coca eradication and interdiction). The overall plan was envisioned as assistance for the improvement of justice and civil institutions and for development assistance, but it was never fully funded. The EU balked because the funding approved by the United States was overwhelmingly for the military (Sweig 2002). Human rights advocates in the United States successfully lobbied for the inclusion of the Leahy amendment to the package, which required that each military unit set to receive US assistance be cleared of any past charges of collusion with paramilitary groups. The units rarely met this standard, which required the secretary of state to issue an exception to the amendment on national security grounds. There is evidence that paramilitaries increased their activity in areas surrounding military units that received assistance, indicating a tacit joint counterinsurgency effort (Dube and Naidu 2015). The United States also trained three new special forces units. Though the military does appear to have professionalized (Sánchez and Chacón 2005), several generals I interviewed in the early 2000s betrayed disconcerting views. All complained about the influence of NGOs, which they said were fronts for the insurgents, and explained that civilians were often actually insurgents.[18] One even seemed to suggest that the human rights violations were a fabrication by Miguel Vivanco, the head of the Americas division of the international advocacy group Human Rights Watch, because without them "he would not have a way to eat."[19]

Even as the reforms and US assistance were fortifying the military with equipment and training, the peace talks and the absence of the police and military from the *despeje* gave the FARC time to consolidate and expand its capacity. The Eastern Bloc—based in the *despeje*—became a powerful military unit led by Mono Jojoy and funded by its unimpeded drug trafficking. After a series of humiliations at the negotiating table for Pastrana, and as the FARC encroached on Bogotá, the final blow to the peace process came in February 2002, when the FARC hijacked an airplane in Cali. Pastrana ordered the invasion of the *despeje*. At this stage, the military still relied on paramilitaries to a troubling degree (Isacson and Steele 2001).

The public's dismay at the failure of the talks and the lack of good faith demonstrated by the FARC catapulted previously unpopular presidential candidate Álvaro Uribe to a lead in the polls. A Liberal from Antioquia who was previously governor of that state and mayor of Medellín, Uribe was a strong supporter of the Convivir groups in Antioquia in the 1990s as violence skyrocketed, especially in Urabá.

Once elected, Uribe implemented the military plan "Democratic Security" (Seguridad Democrática), raised a tax on the wealthy to pay for an expansion of the military, and secured renewed US financial assistance for the military (Marks 2003, 47). Though the new tax was billed as a "one-time" levy, it was renewed in subsequent years, and Rodríguez-Franco (2016) argues that it was an important state-building step because it constituted elite buy-in to the state.

Elites' willingness to ante up helped to fund Democratic Security, which led to structural changes in both the CNP and the military. In 2002, 15 percent of rural Colombian municipalities had no police force (Llorente 2005, 186). Democratic Security aimed to increase the number of

---

18. Interviews with the author, Bogotá, May 8, 2007. These comments about NGOs came without prompting.

19. Interview with the author, Bogotá, May 8, 2007.

carabineros and to create new "police assistants" (*auxiliares de policía*). Over 2002 and 2003, twenty thousand more police officers were recruited. This time, the majority were deployed in rural areas and along highways rather than in the cities (sixteen thousand went to rural areas, and four thousand to cities). To deploy so quickly, training was cut from one year to six months and only three months for the police assistants. By 2004, all municipalities had a police post "and the number of police personnel assigned there had increased to at least 30 percent of the force" (Llorente 2005, 204).

The new police deployment was accompanied by a new military force called Soldados de mi Pueblo ("soldiers from my hometown"). Marks (2003, 48) describes this as the "missing link" in an effective counterinsurgency policy:

> These were indispensable to establishing state presence in affected areas and neatly sidestepped legal objections (and fierce opposition from international human rights organizations) by utilizing a forgotten law, discovered still on the books, that allowed a portion of the national draft levy to opt for service in hometown defense units. These 40-man units were constituted as regular platoons assigned to complement regular battalions stationed nearby.

The Uribe administration was plagued by the ties of its political allies to paramilitaries and by accusations of widespread human rights violations. The worst was the "false positives" scandal, in which the military was found to be kidnapping young men from urban neighborhoods, assassinating them, and counting them as dead insurgents. The prosecutor general's office estimated that nearly forty-five hundred civilians were killed in this way and that thousands of army officers and soldiers were involved (Gill 2016).

Demobilization, Reintegration, and Peace Attempts

In addition to shoring up the military, Uribe immediately began to negotiate favorable terms for the demobilization of the paramilitaries. His effort was supported by more than one hundred members of Congress who signed the Santa Fe de Ralito pact in July 2001 and who were elected with the support of paramilitary blocs (Romero 2007; López

Hernández 2010). Acemoglu, Robinson, and Santos (2013) find evidence that these legislators supported the lenient terms of the demobilization package. The scandal, which became known as "parapolítica," was uncovered in 2005 by investigative reporter Claudia López, herself elected to the Senate in 2014. Former paramilitary leaders have also testified that they ordered their subordinates to mobilize votes for then-candidate Uribe as well. Paramilitary units had been tinkering with local and regional politics since at least 1997 (Romero 2007; López Hernández 2010). The parapolitics scandal was the culmination of a long dance between the paramilitaries and the central state: occasionally the state would punish, investigate, and attack them, and occasionally it would legalize and laud them.[20] Sometimes both approaches were embraced simultaneously, even by the same leader.[21] Ronderos (2014, 52) speculates that electoral calculations were the key to understanding the apparent contradictions: "The cerebral hemisphere that Colombian politicians use to calculate electoral math is not in communication with the other hemisphere, the one that designs the large-scale policies for the state." In other words, electoral calculations lead Bogotá politicians to ignore paramilitaries, or to support them, which in turn undercuts those same politicians' state-building efforts.

As mentioned above, the 1997 Law 418 granted amnesty to all fighters in politically motivated groups. At this time, the guerrillas were recognized as eligible for the amnesty, while the paramilitaries were not. The law guaranteed that insurgents who turned themselves in would not have to serve jail time, as long as they were not responsible for human rights violations. Since that time, this approach has proven successful at attracting combatants to demobilize (though less so, apparently, in preventing new recruitment). The military has a special program dedicated to demobilization (the Program for Humanitarian Assistance to the Demobilized), which uses tactics like radio broadcasts of commercials and testimonials from the demobilized, airdropped fliers, and bold Christmas season messages to persuade combatants to give up arms. Between 1997 and 2012,

---

20. By "state" I mean the Bogotá-based administration.

21. Betancur pursued a peace deal with guerrillas but traveled to Puerto Boyacá to congratulate the leaders of self-defense forces there in 1985 (Ronderos 2014, 51); Samper favored peace talks with the insurgents but legalized the Convivir.

approximately eighteen thousand combatants demobilized from insurgent groups. Decree 128 in 2003 extended benefits to the demobilized, which probably accounts for the increase in demobilization following that date.

In 2002, Law 782 extended Law 418 to recognize paramilitaries' political status and make them eligible for the amnesty (the AUC had called a ceasefire with the government after Uribe took office). Demobilized paramilitaries would also be eligible for the social assistance offered under the following year's Decree 128. Once these legal protections were in place, the AUC and the government reached the Santa Fé de Ralito agreement in 2003 (so named because it was signed in the same Córdoba ranch where the secret Santa Fé de Ralito pact was signed with the corrupt politicians). The pact set a timeline for ending all paramilitary bloc demobilizations by 2005 and set a framework for negotiations between each AUC subgroup (*bloque*) and the government. Commanders were supposed to gather all their fighters in one location and list all combatants and weapons. Government agencies were supposed to collect and verify everything, in the process determining who qualified for amnesty and who did not.

The Justice and Peace Law (Law 975) was the result of further negotiations with paramilitary leaders. The leaders were not eligible for amnesty because they had committed crimes against humanity, so they required a different framework (the law also applied to demobilized insurgents who also committed crimes against humanity). It was roundly criticized as an extremely lenient law because it mandated maximum sentences of five to eight years in exchange for commanders' confessions of the crimes they committed. The next year, the Colombian Constitutional Court demanded changes to the Justice and Peace Law. The court ordered the state to fully investigate the confessions given by armed group leaders, and if it was determined that the former combatants did not confess the whole truth, they would be excluded from the program and entered into the normal criminal justice system. Based on this modification, Uribe extradited fourteen paramilitary commanders to the United States to face narcotrafficking charges, accusing them of not cooperating with investigators. Many observers and the extradited paramilitaries alleged that Uribe extradited the leaders to protect himself from allegations of collusion with the groups. More than thirty-two thousand combatants demobilized between 2003 and 2006, a number much higher (nearly double) than any wartime estimate of the paramilitary groups; allegedly the gap was due to many narcotraffickers fraudulently participating to gain the benefits of demobilization packages and lenient judicial processes. The link is unsurprising given the important role of narcotraffickers in the origins of the paramilitaries. Since demobilization, several groups have reformed and others have morphed into other types of organizations such as NGOs.[22] Those that remained armed or reconstituted themselves are now called "criminal bands," known as BACRIM for "bandas criminales." Some, like the so-called Black Eagles or ERPAC (Colombian Revolutionary Popular Antiterrorist Army), engage in political activity, such as threatening human rights activists and those demanding land restitution, while others seem more exclusively dedicated to narcotrafficking, such as the Urabeños and the Rastrojos (McDermott 2014). Uribe successfully changed the constitution to run for a second term (and unsuccessfully attempted a third). His second administration saw the assassination of several of the FARC's top leaders, including Raúl Reyes, Alfonso Cano, and Mono Jojoy. In 2008, the military also launched a daring rescue of kidnapping victims held by the FARC, including former presidential candidate Ingrid Betancourt, held for six years, and three US contractors.

These high-profile maneuvers were led by Uribe's minister of defense, Juan Manuel Santos. Santos capitalized on his success and, with the endorsement of Uribe, won the 2010 election. Soon after, Santos began secret talks with the FARC to create the terms for official peace talks. News of the discussions leaked to the press, and in October 2011 Santos acknowledged the talks. The same year, Congress approved the Victims' and Land Restitution Law, which increased the scope and conditions for reparations for victims (including victims of state forces, for instance) and land restitution for the displaced. The law also labeled the conflict as an internal war, which acknowledged that all parties, including state forces, were subject to international humanitarian law. This was an important step to continue the peace talks with the FARC. In spite of Uribe's vocal condemnation (mostly via Twitter) of the Victims' Law, the acknowledgment of an internal conflict, and the peace talks, Santos was reelected in 2014, and the talks continued in Havana. The government and the FARC announced

---

22. See Daly 2016 for a detailed study of these trajectories, which she explains as the product of the paramilitary blocs' recruitment base (from the area of operation or far away) and the proximity to rival armed organizations.

the completion of the agreement in August 2016 and formally signed the accords on September 26, 2016, in Cartagena. Less than a week later, on October 2, 2016, the Colombian public dealt a blow to the process by narrowly defeating a referendum that would have ratified the agreement and paved the way for its legal adoption and implementation (the margin was less than 1 percent, or fifty thousand votes of more than six million cast). Nevertheless, President Santos was awarded the Nobel Peace Prize the following week, and university students organized several large-scale marches to urge the leaders of the No campaign (including former presidents Uribe and Pastrana) and the government and the FARC to quickly come to a new solution for peace. The government received more than four hundred proposed modifications to the agreement in October, and returned to Havana with the FARC to try to negotiate a new package. The negotiators were able to modify the original agreement and announced a new one on November 12. Congress ratified the agreement in a vote on November 28, and on December 13, the Constitutional Court upheld "fast track" power for Congress to pass the laws necessary to implement the agreement more quickly than usually mandated. The agreement (which reached over three hundred pages) includes six sections—agrarian reform, political participation, the illicit economy, transitional justice and victim reparation, demobilization, and ceasefire—and commits the government to large-scale reforms and investment. On the FARC's side, the agreement incorporates many concessions, including the acceptance of the country's economic and political structure as fundamentally legitimate.

Violence and Displacement

The guerrillas, paramilitaries, narcotraffickers, and the state engaged each other for decades, producing hundreds of thousands of deaths. The impact of all these armed groups fighting one another, often indirectly through the civilian population, has been devastating. In 2012, a group commissioned by the Colombian government to study the war, the Historical Memory Group (Grupo de Memoria Histórica, or GMH), released its report on victims of the war.[23] The report compares estimates

---

23. Since La Violencia, the Colombian government has supported efforts to study the sources and consequences of war.

of lives lost from various sources and concludes that there have been 220,000 victims of lethal violence dating back to 1958 through 2012. Of those, approximately 81.5 percent have been civilians (about 180,000), and 18.5 percent combatants (roughly 40,000) (Comisión Nacional de Reparación y Reconciliación [Colombia], Grupo de Memoria Histórica 2013, 32). In other words, for each combatant killed, four civilians have died.

The patterns of violence—in terms of lethal and nonlethal forms and the scale of each—have varied over time and across the country. Gutiérrez Sanín and Wood (2017) show that these "repertoires" of violence also vary by armed group. For instance, paramilitaries were much more likely to commit massacres than the FARC, while the FARC was much more likely to kidnap. The next sections describe how death and displacement have shifted.

Patterns of Violence

The GMH organized datasets on different forms of violence in Colombia through 2012, which form the basis of the report that the group produced, *Basta Ya*. The sources are a mix of human rights reports and press, and the datasets vary in their completeness and biases. Colombian government data are not included in these datasets. Further, data on sexual violence, disappearances, and child recruitment are not available publicly in order to protect privacy.

The Colombian government's Unique Registry of Victims (Registro Único de Víctimas, or RUV; formerly the Sistema Único de Registro, or SUR) includes victims of violence, predominantly internally displaced persons (IDPs). The GMH compared a random sample of its data on selective assassinations to the victims in the RUV and found that only 13.7 percent of the cases appear in the RUV (Comisión Nacional de Reparación y Reconciliación [Colombia], Grupo de Memoria Histórica 2013, 33n7). The Colombian police also recorded data on victims, mostly in terms of the number of victims for each violent event reported. The police dataset also includes other types of violent events, such as highway blockades and military clashes. A comparison of victims recorded by the GMH and the government follows in the charts below.

Figure 3.1 shows trends in the GMH and Colombian government (GoC) data on selective assassinations. The comparison categories are

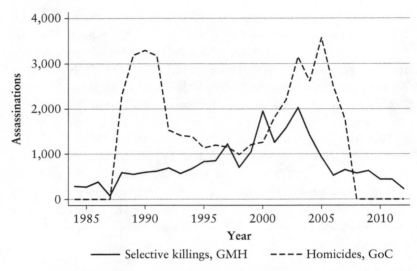

Figure 3.1. Selective killings in Colombia, 1984–2012. Total GMH victims during this time period: 22,566; total GoC homocide victims: 40,832. Data from GMH and GoC.

imperfect: the GoC data is more general because it includes homicides that could be unrelated to political violence. As a result, the GoC data includes higher numbers, especially in the early 1990s when the narco war was particularly intense. Since the peaks in 2004–2005, both murders and selective assassinations have declined in both datasets.

Figure 3.2 plots the total number of massacre victims recorded by the GMH and GoC over time. Here the GMH datasets record many more victims than the GoC database, though both decline following peaks around 2000.

Kidnapping victims data resembles the massacre victims data: the GMH records much higher numbers than the GoC. Figure 3.3 compares the datasets over time.[24] Since around 2001, the numbers have declined substantially.

Additional, nonlethal forms of violence unavailable in a disaggregated way are incidents of sexual violence and disappearances. So far, more than 1,100 cases of sexual violence have been reported in Colombia, according

---

24. The GMH report accompanying the datasets only notes 27,023 kidnappings since 1970, whereas the datasets indicate 38,202 kidnappings. I cannot account for the discrepancy.

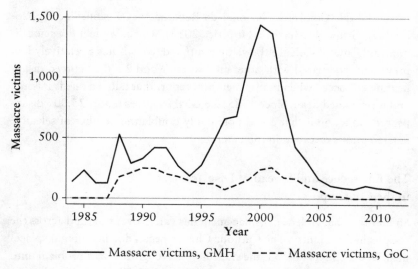

Figure 3.2. Massacre victims in Colombia, 1984–2012. Total GMH victims 1984–2012: 11,380; total GoC victims: 3,048. Data from GMH and GoC.

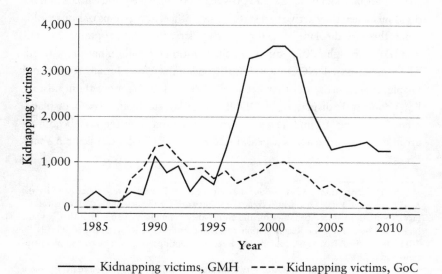

Figure 3.3. Kidnapping victims in Colombia, 1984–2012. Total GMH victims 1984–2012: 38,202; total GoC victims: 15,471. Data from GMH and GoC.

to the GMH (Comisión Nacional de Reparación y Reconciliación [Colombia], Grupo de Memoria Histórica 2013), which, while it does not diminish the awful violence the victims suffered, constitutes a relatively low prevalence compared with other civil wars (Wood 2006). "Forced disappearances" occur when family members report that a loved one is missing and is presumed dead. Since 1985, the GMH sources report 25,007 disappeared, an amount that could potentially double the number of selective assassinations recorded in the dataset.

The Emergence and Spread of Displacement in the Contemporary War

Similar to lethal violence, displacement has varied over time and across the regions in the country. The Catholic Church began documenting displacement in the mid-1980s, but the state did not recognize it as a problem until a decade later, when it adopted Law 387 in 1997. The law offered emergency assistance for the displaced, as well as guidelines for reparations and restitution (though neither was fully implemented systematically).[25]

The Unit for Attention and Integral Reparation for Victims—previously Acción Social (Social Action, or AS)—registers displaced households and individuals when they arrive to a state agency office, and groups of households when they are displaced together.[26] Its registry, the RUV, contains 2.6 million IDPs through 2007,[27] and since then, another 2 million have registered. The Bogotá-based NGO CODHES (Consultancy for Human Rights and Displacement) estimates that between 1986 and 2007, more than 3.8 million people were displaced.[28] CODHES records a steady increase in displacement beginning around 1994, which increases at a faster rate beginning around 1996 and reaches a peak in 2002. The RUV data indicate a sharp

---

25. The reparations and restitution measures within Law 387 were superseded by the 2005 Justice and Peace Law, which created a framework for the demobilization of paramilitary groups and reduced penalties for the crimes they committed. Also within that law, the National Commission for Reconciliation and Reparation (CNRR) was created. Finally, in 2011, the Victims' Law was adopted, which replaced both previous frameworks for reparations and restitution.

26. Groups of ten households or fifty individuals constitute "mass displacement," and a state representative is supposed to attend to them.

27. The registry was previously called the Sistema Unica de Registro, or SUR. The last year for which I have disaggregated data is 2007.

28. I discuss the differences in greater depth in the next chapter.

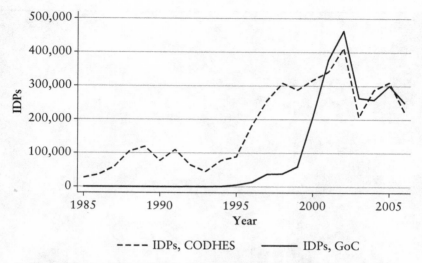

Figure 3.4. Internally displaced persons in Colombia, 1985–2006. Total IDPs, CODHES: 3,942,066; total IDPs, GoC: 2,277,030. In GoC data, 233,943 IDPs were recorded with missing or incorrect year. Data from CODHES, GoC (RUV).

increase beginning in 2000, which may be an effect of better monitoring rather than a new wave of displacement. These data also indicate a peak in 2002, the year paramilitaries began to negotiate demobilization with the incoming Uribe administration. Figure 3.4 compares the scale of displacement as registered by AS and CODHES between 1985 and 2006.

Displacement did not occur everywhere in the country with the same intensity, though it has affected all thirty-two of the country's departments. Aggregating the number of registered IDPs by municipality, it becomes obvious how much displacement has affected the country: only 33 municipalities of 1,136 did not experience any displacement; only 88 have received no IDPs. The average number of people expelled from a municipality between 1998 and 2006 was roughly 2,200, with a maximum of 59,000 (RUV).

Figure 3.5 shows the proportion of the population (recorded in the 1993 census) displaced in each municipality between 1998 and 2006. Substantial variation across regions and even across municipalities is evident. And, as chapter 5 shows, variation also exists within municipalities.

The RUV also tracks where IDPs resettle. Figure 3.6 shows the variation in destinations (again by proportion of the population) across

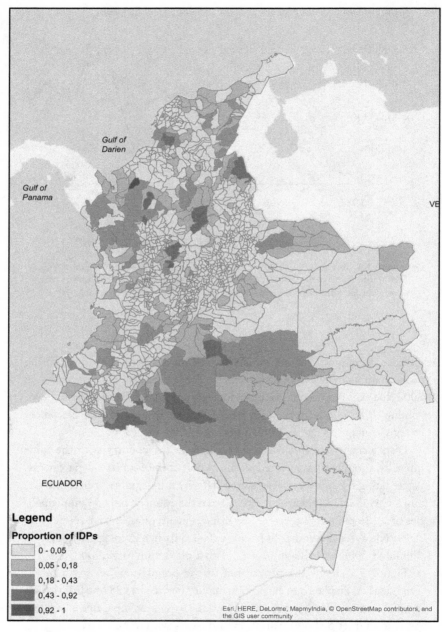

Figure 3.5. IDPs as a proportion of 1993 population across municipalities in Colombia, 1998–2006. Categories created by natural breaks. RUV displacement data; DANE census data. Map by Jessica Di Salvatore.

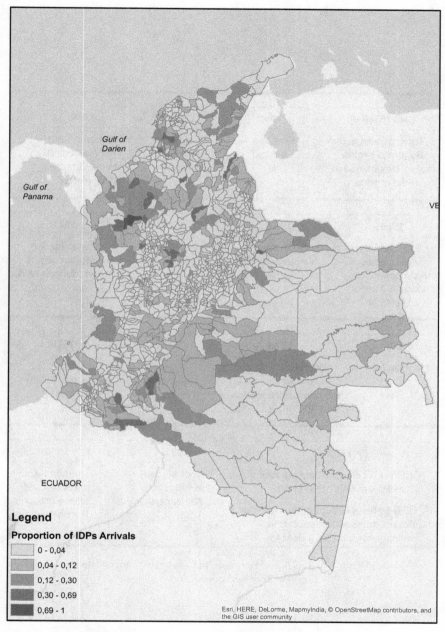

Figure 3.6. IDP arrivals as a proportion of 1993 population across municipalities in Colombia, 1998–2006. Categories created by natural breaks. RUV displacement data; DANE census data. Map by Jessica Di Salvatore.

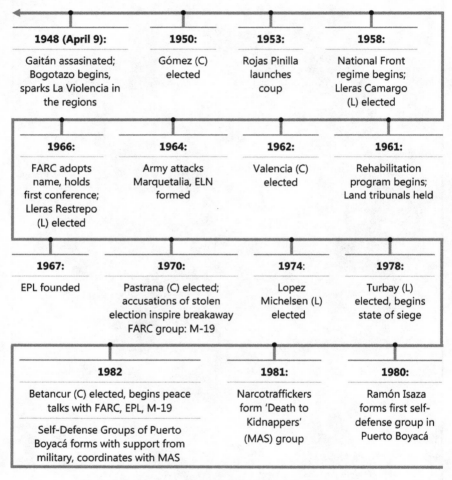

1948 (April 9):

Gaitán assasinated;
Bogotazo begins,
sparks La Violencia in
the regions

1950:

Gómez (C)
elected

1953:

Rojas Pinilla
launches
coup

1958:

National Front
regime begins;
Lleras Camargo
(L) elected

1966:

FARC adopts
name, holds
first conference;
Lleras Restrepo
(L) elected

1964:

Army attacks
Marquetalia, ELN
formed

1962:

Valencia (C)
elected

1961:

Rehabilitation
program begins;
Land tribunals held

1967:

EPL founded

1970:

Pastrana (C) elected;
accusations of stolen
election inspire breakaway
FARC group: M-19

1974:

Lopez
Michelsen (L)
elected

1978:

Turbay (L)
elected, begins
state of siege

1982

Betancur (C) elected, begins peace
talks with FARC, EPL, M-19

Self-Defense Groups of Puerto
Boyacá forms with support from
military, coordinates with MAS

1981:

Narcotraffickers
form 'Death to
Kidnappers'
(MAS) group

1980:

Ramón Isaza
forms first self-
defense group in
Puerto Boyacá

Figure 3.7. Timeline of key events in Colombian history. Figure
by Nicole Martinez Moore.

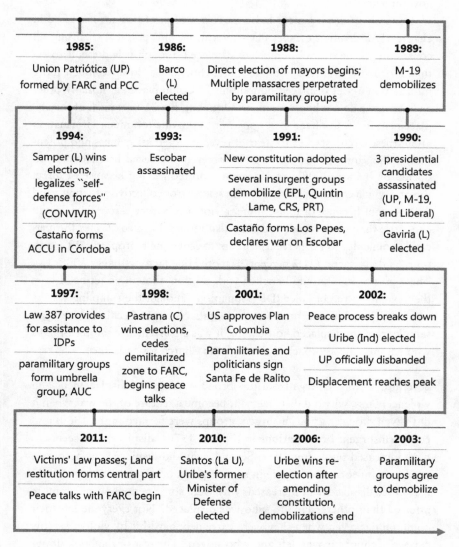

1985:
Union Patriótica (UP) formed by FARC and PCC

1986:
Barco (L) elected

1988:
Direct election of mayors begins; Multiple massacres perpetrated by paramilitary groups

1989:
M-19 demobilizes

1994:
Samper (L) wins elections, legalizes ``self-defense forces'' (CONVIVIR)

Castaño forms ACCU in Córdoba

1993:
Escobar assassinated

1991:
New constitution adopted

Several insurgent groups demobilize (EPL, Quintin Lame, CRS, PRT)

Castaño forms Los Pepes, declares war on Escobar

1990:
3 presidential candidates assassinated (UP, M-19, and Liberal)

Gaviria (L) elected

1997:
Law 387 provides for assistance to IDPs

paramilitary groups form umbrella group, AUC

1998:
Pastrana (C) wins elections, cedes demilitarized zone to FARC, begins peace talks

2001:
US approves Plan Colombia

Paramilitaries and politicians sign Santa Fe de Ralito

2002:
Peace process breaks down

Uribe (Ind) elected

UP officially disbanded

Displacement reaches peak

2011:
Victims' Law passes; Land restitution forms central part

Peace talks with FARC begin

2010:
Santos (La U), Uribe's former Minister of Defense elected

2006:
Uribe wins re-election after amending constitution, demobilizations end

2003:
Paramilitary groups agree to demobilize

Figure 3.7. Continued

119

Colombia. These locations may not be the final or first destination of the IDPs; they reflect where they are when they register as displaced with the government.

The scale of displacement hides the forms of displacement discussed in chapter 1. Individual escape, mass relocation, and political cleansing all contribute to the overall number of displaced, though it is difficult to estimate proportions well. For one thing, though we do have much more information about displaced households in Colombia than in many other civil wars, we do not know many details about the circumstances of the displacement itself. Civilians may not want to provide too much information about these circumstances for fear of revealing their allegiances and potentially falling into danger again. In a survey of displaced households conducted by Ibáñez (2008), 54.5 percent reported leaving because of direct threats (which could be consistent with selective or collective targeting), and 39.1 percent because of indiscriminate violence. Survey respondents could cite more than one reason, and they also reported armed clashes (36 percent), homicides (34.5 percent), orders to leave their property (29.6 percent), and massacres (21.2 percent) as motivating factors (Ibáñez 2008, 13). These proportions should be taken with caution, though, in terms of how they extend to the broader IDP population. Though the sampling was as careful as possible to capture a representative sample, because there is no sample frame of displaced households, it was a convenience sample of IDPs who had initially approached the Catholic Church for assistance.

Several questions emerge from this broad overview of displacement and violence. First, why did displacement become a feature of the war when it did? Even though various insurgent groups were formed in the 1960s and counterinsurgent organizations in the late 1970s, displacement seems to have increased only after 1986. Second, why did displacement become a predominant form of violence in some regions of the country before others? Once displacement increased, why were some regions so much more affected than others? Finally, who was displaced? Not everyone left their communities, even when they were extremely hard-hit by violence. How can we account for who left and who stayed? The rest of the book draws on the theory outlined in chapter 1 to explain why displacement began when it did and where it was most severe, and to illustrate how it took place within a municipality.

4

DEMOCRATIC REFORMS AND THE EMERGENCE OF POLITICAL CLEANSING IN COLOMBIA

Despite the formation of the FARC and other insurgencies in the 1960s with the support of displaced people, displacement did not demand concerted attention again until two decades later, when it increased substantially. The Colombian government responded to UN and NGO pressure and passed Law 387 in 1997, which guaranteed humanitarian assistance to internally displaced persons (IDPs). In contrast to the state's lag, the Catholic Church began documenting displacement as early as 1986. How can we account for the onset of displacement two decades after the beginning of the contemporary civil war? Existing explanations suggest that violence must have increased prior to or parallel with displacement. This chapter shows that this formulation misses a key part of the story. Displacement did not increase as a by-product of the violence; violence increased because armed groups sought to displace civilians and engage in political cleansing.

The onset of displacement as a massive feature of the contemporary Colombian civil war is linked to democratic reforms. The book argues

that political cleansing is likely when an armed group (especially counterinsurgents) pursues territorial conquest and where it has information
about civilians' loyalties. This chapter illustrates this argument and shows
that the revelation of loyalties can also facilitate campaigns of conquest.
The introduction of elections at the local level in Colombia and the participation of the leftist insurgent political party had two effects: they provided information about civilians' loyalties to outsiders directly, and they
generated incentives for local political elites to form alliances with outside armed groups. The FARC-backed political party, the Patriotic Union
(Unión Patriótica, or UP), contested elections for the first time in 1986;
reports of displacement increased soon after. Tragically, as democracy improved, violence against civilians increased and the war intensified.

This chapter also illustrates how the extension of elections to the local
level enabled regionally based paramilitary groups to spread to other areas
of the country. Elections provided the opportunities to do so through two
channels: first, they revealed information about civilians' loyalties that
allowed armed groups to determine who to expel to improve the chances
of conquest; second, elections prompted local elites whose political power
was threatened by the new democratic inroads to ally with armed groups
in an effort to beat back insurgent electoral victories. Political cleansing can benefit contesting armed groups because it enables them to gain
control of an area; it can also benefit the local political opposition by
changing the constituency in their favor. The abilities to target civilians
collectively and to form new alliances were key factors in the expansion
of the paramilitaries.

The next section describes the process of democratization that Colombia experienced in the 1980s, highlighting the expansion of competition
with the introduction of local-level elections and the introduction of a
legal party that represented a new challenge to the traditional Liberal and
Conservative dominance.[1] Both measures enhanced two pillars of democratic governance: representation and participation. The third section of

---

1. Third parties existed in the past, most famously ANAPO, which was created and led
by former coup leader Rojas Pinilla. The party garnered substantial support in the 1970
presidential elections, but the results favored Liberal candidate López Michelsen. Allegations
of fraud were widespread and partly inspired the leaders of the M-19 when they formed their
insurgent group. The name M-19 refers to the date of the allegedly stolen election.

the chapter, however, documents how edging closer to these ideals also facilitated an increase in violence and political cleansing in two ways. First, it allowed the FARC's rivals to target unprotected civilian political leaders in what became known as the "dirty war." Second, and less well known, is that it also allowed counterinsurgents to target civilian supporters of the UP for political cleansing and to ally with political elites who sought to protect their local power against democratization. The fourth section describes early patterns of displacement that are consistent with political cleansing by counterinsurgents. The fifth section concludes.

Representation and Participation

The almost simultaneous emergence of the FARC and other insurgencies, and the creation of the National Front consociational regime between Liberals and Conservatives, led many observers to speculate that the limited nature of Colombia's democracy fueled rebellion (e.g., Pécaut 1989). Romero (2000, 84) observed that that dynamic became compounded over time, because the "lack of recognition by the center of these regional, radical identities has left them excluded from the political community." This reading of the conflict, as well as the FARC's explicit demands, led to efforts to reform democratic institutions to be more inclusive and representative of local interests, beginning with the Betancur administration. The first step was to allow the FARC to create a political party that would contest elections; the next was to extend elections to the local executive, the mayor of the municipality.

The Unión Patriótica

The Unión Patriótica was created by the FARC during the peace process that began with secret talks with the Betancur administration in 1982.[2] The party would be the legal political arm of the FARC, while the Communist Party of Colombia (PCC) would continue to operate clandestinely. FARC leader Jacobo Arenas conceived of the UP as filling a gap in the *"todas formas de la lucha"* (all forms of the fight) approach, which called for the FARC and PCC

---

2. The negotiation and the agreement that resulted (discussed below) was the first of its type in Latin America (Chernick 1999).

to pursue revolution by confronting the state using all available violent and nonviolent means. This would be the first time the rebels would use electoral institutions to do so. Previously, the FARC and PCC had rejected participation in such institutions to avoid inherently legitimizing them, but Arenas made the case that contesting elections was an opportunity to appeal to a broader segment of the population.[3] The ELN and the EPL, however, opted not to participate in elections at this stage.[4] They believed that legal channels were futile and that the *lucha armada* (armed fight) was the only way to achieve their goals (Villarraga Sarmiento 1996, 54).

The Uribe Accords were signed between the government and the FARC in 1984 and began a two-year ceasefire.[5] The announcement of the UP's creation followed one year later, in May 1985 (Esguerra 2009, 63). Six months later, the party held its first congress in Bogotá, and a twenty-point platform was adopted that emphasized social justice. The meeting report states, "Our great historical responsibility is to unite in one single torrent all the democratic and progressive tendencies and all those who are for peace so that with a new base of political forces a democratic opening becomes possible, a fundamental base to progress toward an advanced democracy" (Esguerra 2009, 69).

From the beginning, FARC combatants and PCC militants formed the core of the UP. Its leaders were Braulio Herrera and Iván Márquez, members of the *estado mayor* of the FARC, who like Arenas both joined the ranks of the armed group after membership in the PCC (Giraldo 2001, 21).[6] Beginning in May 1985, all fronts of the FARC were ordered to organize the UP in their area through "Juntas Patrióticas" (JPs) (Dudley 2006, 60);

---

3. Jacobo Arenas was a nom de guerre. After initially joining the ranks of the Communist Party years before La Violencia began, he formally entered the FARC in the 1960s. The PCC tried to maintain control over the FARC but was not always successful. Another leader of the FARC, Alfonso Cano, and the main interlocutor for the group before his death in 2008, Raúl Reyes, were both sent from the party to gain more control over the armed group. Instead, they began to work decidedly on behalf of the guerrillas (Dudley 2006, 53).

4. The EPL introduced the Frente Popular in 1988, and A Luchar was the ELN's political vehicle. Both were more radical than the UP and did not initially participate in elections (Pizarro Leongómez [1986] 2007, 334). Many members of the Frente Popular were also targeted and killed (Esguerra 2009, 124).

5. The accords were named for the municipality where the delegations met, La Uribe, Meta.

6. Iván Marquéz was the lead negotiator for the FARC in the peace talks with the Santos administration between 2012 and 2016 that resulted in a signed agreement between the FARC and the government.

there were about eleven fronts and a thousand members at the time. Not all JPs were organized by the FARC, however. Many emerged spontaneously, and by 1986 there were four thousand JPs (Dudley 2006, 60, 51, 64).

The UP was presented to the public as a mechanism for the guerrillas to demobilize altogether, and an important aspect of its success was the party's appeal to citizens who hoped that the UP would lead to peace (Dudley 2006, 28, 61). Álvaro Salazar, a FARC member who became a UP spokesperson and the head of the party's international relations, explained that the UP was mostly a centralized organization.[7] At the same time, "In some regions, joining the UP was done knowing that it was a political force that had military support" (Giraldo 2001, 22).

The first elections the party contested were in 1986. It won 3 senate seats (with 3 alternates), 6 congressional posts (with 3 alternates), 19 departmental assembly seats, and 351 local council seats in 187 cities (Giraldo 2001, 23). The presidential race was contested by Jaime Pardo Leal, a former lawyer, magistrate, and union leader. He won 4.5 percent of the vote—more than three hundred thousand votes—an unprecedented amount for the Left in Colombia (Bushnell 1993; Giraldo 2001, 258).

Local Elections

A constitutional amendment, enacted in 1985, was the second main achievement of the peace talks. It introduced the popular election of mayors, rather than their appointment by the department governors. Bushnell (1993, 258) argues that though such a reform had been under discussion between the two traditional parties, the timing of its adoption can be explained by the need to demonstrate a "democratic opening," a key, if vague, demand by the FARC.

Until 1988, mayors were appointed by governors, who were in turn appointed by the president. The turn to local elections was particularly important for the FARC, given its pockets of isolated support that would not amount to much clout at the national level (Shugart 1992, 136). Indeed, even as the UP won a surprising share of the vote during the 1986 presidential elections, it was more successful in municipal contests. The UP won 15 mayoral posts and had representation in 105 more municipalities in local

---

7. Interview with the author, Bogotá, May 27, 2013.

coalitions of opposition groups (Giraldo 2001, 25), meaning that the UP enjoyed some share of political power in more than a tenth of the municipalities of the country. The party also won more than 400 local council seats (*concejales*) (Cepeda Castro 2006).

These victories represented the first time third-party mayors were elected. As a result, those who had traditionally relied on the old system of clientelism and patronage were suddenly challenged. As with many processes of democratization, these regional elites were "sore losers" (Przeworski 1991) who sought to disrupt and resist the new competition. The traditional party elites based outside Bogotá opposed the "democratic opening" from the start. In 1986, as a transition to the forthcoming mayoral elections, the Barco administration ordered governors to appoint mayors from the UP for each municipality with a majority of municipal council members elected from the UP. For the department of Antioquia, the total would be five mayors; the governor delayed appointment until October of that year (Reiniciar 2006, 73). Worse, because the state did not have a monopoly on violence and even tolerated paramilitary groups, these regional elites could resort to violence to try to retain their previous positions of power, a tradition in Colombia that dates back decades (Robinson 2013).

The situation became even more tense because by 1987, talks between the FARC and the Barco administration—Betancur's successor—fell apart (the truce was effectively already broken by the FARC in 1986). Herrera and Marquéz—two of the UP congressional representatives, the first and only active insurgents elected to Congress—were called back to the FARC's ranks in April 1987 (Giraldo 2001, 24). As a result, the FARC was officially at war with the state again, but this time with a political arm competing in elections as well.

Violent Reaction

Democratic reforms facilitated two forms of violence: the dirty war and political cleansing. Both types were perpetrated by paramilitaries with the collaboration of some members of the armed forces, including the military, the national police, and the DAS (the state intelligence agency). Between 1986 and 1988, selective assassinations of UP candidates for office terrorized party members, from the presidential candidate in 1986 down to local municipal council candidates. After 1988, when the first elections for municipal mayors (*alcaldes*) were held, the violence shifted to collective targeting against UP supporters. As a result, those supporters frequently fled their homes in the peripheral regions of the country for the relative safety of larger cities. Less scholarly and popular attention has been given to the displacement that accompanied the "dirty war," which a handful of nongovernmental organizations (NGOs) documented. They characterize early displacement as targeted against leftists in general and UP supporters in particular.

The Dirty War

The *guerra sucia* (dirty war) against party leaders and candidates started soon after the party's creation (Cepeda Castro 2006; Cepeda Castro and Girón Ortiz 2005; Giraldo 2001). The first killing of a UP member that appears to have been politically motivated was on September 28, 1985 (Dudley 2006, 80). In its first resolution, the first congress of the UP denounced the detention of a party activist from Chaparral, Tolima, who later disappeared (Esguerra 2009, 79). An organization founded by UP members in 1993, Reiniciar, reported that during this period "various paramilitary groups characterized by their bloodthirst, began to operate in Tolima, and assassinated, tortured, threatened and displaced a considerable number of social leaders, among them various militants of the Unión Patriótica" (Esguerra 2009, 83). In January 1986, the party held its second congress and issued the following statement: "This cohesive, reactionary escalation has not been exclusive to military repression and attacks and hostilities against FARC Fronts in the truce, but also has the support of numerous congress members and the censorship provoked by the monopolies of mass media over information" (quoted in Esguerra 2009, 84).

The first wave of violence seems to have been initiated by an alliance between narcotraffickers and paramilitaries.[8] Rodríguez Gacha, known as El Mexicano, had a dispute with the FARC, apparently over coca taxation.

---

8. Many drug traffickers were allied with, funded, or formed their own paramilitary groups by 1986.

El Mexicano was a supplier of coca from the Llanos (the eastern plains region) and had coexisted with the FARC until this time.[9] Jacobo Arenas of the FARC apparently refused to negotiate with El Mexicano. It is unclear why, because the FARC "worked with others, like Carlos Lehder [a narco tied to the Medellín cartel]."[10] In the north, different narcos, like Fidel Castaño, invited confrontation by buying lands in areas of guerrilla influence and refusing to pay extortion.[11] Whatever the fallout's origins, Rodríguez Gacha decided to address his grievances by killing UP politicians and leaders, who were easy, unarmed targets. To do so, according to Salazar, "El Mexicano strengthened paramilitaries that already existed but did not have a lot of money. It was an alliance of landowners, all over. Like in the Magdalena Medio, in El Dorado and Puerto Boyacá, and the Llanos Orientales."[12]

Between 1986 and 1988, an estimated 550 UP militants were reported killed, including its director, two senators, two congressmen, and forty-five local councilmen and mayors (Giraldo 2001). Jaime Pardo Leal, the head of the UP and its first presidential candidate, was assassinated in October 1987, allegedly on the orders of Rodríguez Gacha. At this point, the UP had already created self-defense forces that the military itself trained and armed. The DAS also provided security guards to high-profile UP leaders (Dudley 2006, 130–31). In addition, the Barco administration commissioned an investigation into paramilitary groups that condemned them harshly. These measures reveal how disjointed the state's response was to paramilitary violence. On the one hand, official policy was to train and arm the UP forces, protect its leaders, and investigate the threats to its security, while on the other, some military and police officers, politicians, and DAS members trained, supported, and collaborated with the paramilitaries that were targeting the UP. Some in the military even openly harassed UP leaders (Dudley 2006, 80).

---

9. Previous to the early 1980s, the drug trade in Colombia was focused mainly on coca processing. But after coca eradication began in Peru, the drug traffickers began to cultivate coca in Colombia. The need to grow coca in ungoverned spaces brought the cultivators into contact with rural insurgents like the FARC.

10. Álvaro Salazar, interview, Bogotá, November 11, 2010.

11. According to Salazar, the FARC charged a 10 percent "tax" on coca, "the same as for any other crop" (interview with the author, November 11, 2010, Bogotá).

12. Álvaro Salazar, interview, Bogotá, November 11, 2010.

In 1989, Medellín cartel leader Pablo Escobar asked for a meeting with Bernardo Jaramillo Ossa, who had taken over the leadership of the UP after Pardo was killed, but Jaramillo sent Salazar instead. Escobar wanted to broker a truce to avoid fighting a war on two fronts against both the state and the guerrillas. There, Escobar warned Salazar that El Mexicano was not a threat compared to paramilitary leader Fidel Castaño and that he doubted he would be able to get Castaño to commit to a truce.[13] This meeting, and the subsequent assassination of Rodríguez Gacha by Colombian security forces in December of that year, ended the period of narco involvement in the dirty war. However, paramilitaries continued to pursue the UP in alliance with local political elites around the country.

The UP officially broke from the FARC in February 1989 in a meeting in Ibagué, Tolima (Giraldo 2001, 19). The party did not denounce the guerrillas, but also rejected the notion that it was the "spokesman" for them (50). After 1989, some took the collapse of the Soviet Union as an indication that democratic socialism was a more reasonable goal than revolution. In addition, after the violence began, leaders of the party began to question—in private—the wisdom of the "all forms of the fight" approach, given that followers were dying and they were left unprotected by the FARC (19, 47).[14] This debate mirrored internal divisions within the PCC between the "Perestroikans" and the "orthodox" over the question of whether to fully engage in democratic institutions (Dudley 2006; Giraldo 2001). To outsiders, however, the official separation between the FARC and UP, and the internal debates, were not sufficient to divorce members from association with the FARC. Salazar recounted, "For the military and paramilitaries, the FARC and the UP were the same. They didn't care about or understand the internal debate." Nonetheless, the partnership between the FARC and the UP was over: "There was no reconciling—there was no way [to overcome it]. After perestroika in the USSR and fall of the Berlin wall, people started to think that violence was not the way forward."[15]

---

13. Álvaro Salazar, interview, Bogotá, November 11, 2010.

14. At the same time, in public, party leaders questioned how the FARC could logically demobilize, given the violence perpetrated against the party members (Giraldo 2001).

15. Salazar, interview, Bogotá, November 11, 2010. UP leaders took two actions that estranged it from the FARC: (1) They supported the M-19 peace process, and (2) they joined the International Socialists (the Union of Democratic Socialists in Europe), which represented an "effort to locate the UP in the center left" (Salazar, interview, Bogotá, November 11, 2010).

Jaramillo was assassinated by Castaño's men while campaigning for the presidency in 1990, as Escobar had predicted.[16] It was a final blow to the moderates within the UP, an estimated one-tenth of whom left the party only a month after he was killed (Giraldo 2001, 13, 27, 55).[17] Only one year later, the UP was deflated. The peace project "died with Jaramillo," according to Salazar, and the central party effectively died as well.[18] Yet it continued to be an important political force in regional pockets like Urabá and Meta, which drew the ire of local competitors and motivated them to ally with paramilitaries.

The dirty war assassinations were selectively targeted against leaders and political candidates from the Unión Patriótica. Many fled into exile or hid in the larger cities. Ivan Cépeda writes that the goal of the paramilitaries was "to end the political group, or at least, to expel its survivors from public life and social bases that resisted the wave of violence" (Cepeda Castro 2006, 102).[19] He calls the violence against the UP a "political genocide" in which the state was complicit. The Commission on Human Rights (CIDH) of the Organization of American States agreed to investigate state complicity in the violence against UP members in response to a petition brought by family members of the victims.[20] The relatively well-documented murders overshadow the displacement that began during this period.

---

16. Carlos Castaño, involved in the killings of both Jaramillo and the M-19 presidential candidate at the time, Carlos Pizarro, acknowledged that it was a mistake to kill Jaramillo because he might have helped legalize the opposition and defeat the FARC more quickly from the inside (Molina 2001). Jaramillo initially supported the hard-liners within the PCC, but he shifted and by 1989 denounced the FARC's actions, particularly kidnapping. Jaramillo was celebrated in death by the UP, though the FARC never named a front in his honor, as they did with Jaime Pardo Leal (Dudley 2006, 166).

17. Dudley (2006, 171) also claims that former UP militants joined the FARC as a result of the violence. In other words, the violence had a polarizing effect. The relative proportions of UP members who had actively participated in leftist politics and then joined the FARC are unknown.

18. Salazar, interview, Bogotá, May 27, 2013.

19. Cépeda's father, Manuel, was a senator and the last UP elected representative. He was killed in 1994 by members of a military intelligence unit in collaboration with paramilitaries.

20. In its decision (case number 11,227), the CIDH concluded that the case was admissible, but that the crimes against the UP (allowed but not directed by the state) did not constitute genocide (Comisión Interamericana de Derechos Humanos 1997).

Collective Targeting and Political Cleansing

In addition to brutally assassinating UP leaders and politicians, counterinsurgents also targeted UP supporters in an effort to conquer areas where the FARC was influential.

Identifying the Disloyal   Fidel Castaño was a crucial link between the dirty war against party leaders and the broader effort to target UP followers collectively. He made an agreement with Henry Pérez, the leader of a paramilitary group in the Magdalena Medio region, to follow the "Puerto Boyacá model" (Medina Gallego and Téllez Ardila 1994, 115): "The typical mode of action consisted of penetrating regions by force where the guerrillas had influence and committing selective massacres that terrorized the population and provoked forced displacement" (Reyes Posada 2009, 88). This "model" was initially used to target Communist Party sympathizers where they were visible and known, as in Puerto Boyacá in the early 1980s. After the start of local mayoral elections, it evolved and expanded. A brutal example took place in the Magdalena Medio municipality of Segovia in 1988. Despite years of selective killing around Segovia, guerrillas still retained a presence in the municipality. A group of paramilitaries, organized by the Puerto Boyacá leaders, arrived in Segovia, where "names of people were replaced by names of city blocks" that displayed yellow and green banners, the colors of the UP (Dudley 2006, 123–24). Pamphlets were circulated that warned citizens to leave or die. Targeting known areas where UP sympathizers gathered or lived, paramilitaries lobbed grenades and opened fire, killing forty-three people (124). It was the first massive targeting of UP supporters, not just leaders or candidates. Again, for the perpetrators of violence, the internal divisions and debates among the UP, the PCC, and the FARC were irrelevant; each was synonymous with the other.[21]

Alliances   Local elections and broader representation (in terms of political parties) not only helped counterinsurgents identify supporters of the

---

21. As a result of the violence against the party and the systematic elimination of the moderate wing described below, the PCC and the orthodox group regained dominance of the UP, officially at the XIII Plenum in 1991 (Giraldo 2001, 28). Álvaro Salazar claims, however, that by then the party was only a shell (interview with the author, Bogotá, May 27, 2013).

guerrillas, but they also raised the stakes for local elites. In turn, these leaders allied with paramilitaries and provided additional local information and expanded displacement beyond regions where paramilitaries were already operating.

Local elites anticipated the electoral threat early on. In the first UP congress in November 1985, the party denounced an effort in the Senate by "official" Liberals to prevent UP participation in the elections or to "annul its vote," and a military presence in areas of influence meant to "repress the thousands of Colombians from joining the new political project" (Esguerra 2009, 68). The southeast of Tolima was "completely militarized" for the 1986 vote in an attempt to "sabotage" the work of the UP and its coalition partners (Esguerra 2009, 165). Despite the implication that the military was involved, Alejandro Reyes ([1991] 2007, 355) highlights the role of state weakness:

> Regional elite movements tend to use violence when they perceive that the democratic transferral of the conflict would substantially alter their institutional privilege, derived from the structure of property and the control of public resources. The rejection of mass participation is inspired by the fear of losing elite exclusivity in basic decision-making. The first condition of the surge in paramilitarism is, then, the structural weakness of the Colombian state to impose on regional elites a system [*marco*] of democratic behavior to resolve social conflicts.[22]

Importantly, this observation outlines regional elites' motivations to organize violence to protect their power, and their ability to do so. During this period, as the paramilitaries increased their capacity with financing from the narcotics trade, they also expanded their reach by allying with elites in regions where paramilitary groups had not yet emerged.

Álvaro Salazar recalls that the true violence against the UP began only after the first elections.[23] The UP noted immediately following the first election in 1986 that "a plan of extermination against militants, their families, and sympathizers was consolidated" (Esguerra 2009, 99). The plan of "extermination" was not attributed to narcotraffickers, but to

---

22. This situation persists more than two decades later, according to James Robinson, who characterizes the governance of Colombian regions as indirect rule (Robinson 2013).

23. Interview with the author, Bogotá, May 27, 2013.

paramilitary groups allied with traditional Liberal elites in the departments. For example, in Tolima, politician Santofimio was alleged to have formed a paramilitary organization in 1983 known as Rojo Atá (Esguerra 2009, 115). Pablo Guarín and Jorge Perico Cárdenas provided political cover to the paramilitaries in Puerto Boyacá in the early 1980s and received electoral support for Senate campaigns in exchange, according to the paramilitary leader Iván Roberto Duque, alias Ernesto Báez de la Serna (Ronderos 2014, 48–53). In some regions, in other words, the alliance between paramilitaries and political candidates was established before the UP contested local elections; but once it did, such alliances spread.

Romero (2003, 20) writes, "The growing political competition in the local sphere led to a real bloodbath." "When the UP and Frente Popular started to compete in elections, it was too much for paramilitaries" (142).[24] A UP report in Urabá notes, "The [UP's] imminent invasion of local power, to the detriment of the traditional parties' political bosses [*gamonales*] who consider the mayoral posts their personal turf, unleashes the ire of the *politiqueros* who believe that the time has come in which Communism will snatch their perks from them" (Reiniciar 2006, 73). Carroll (2011, 43) argues that where an armed insurgency had a presence and a social movement existed, democratic reforms led to electoral gains for such movements, which provoked an elite backlash "sponsored and largely carried out by politically displaced elites" and the military. This backlash included the expulsion and killing of rivals and their purported supporters; in other words, political cleansing.

Political Cleansing   The confluence of the paramilitaries' and elites' interests led to a model replicated across regions. When Reyes asked Carlos Castaño in 1999 the political and military purpose of the massacres he committed, Castaño responded as follows:

> Not everyone is a military objective. There exists group A, where you find those who are obligated to work for the guerrillas; they are prohibited from collaborating from the guerrilla. In group B are the voluntary collaborators, who are told to leave the region. And in group C are the guerrillas that act like civilians and they are military objectives for us. (Reyes Posada 2009, 105)

---

24. The Frente Popular, the EPL's legal party, was active primarily in Urabá.

A demobilized paramilitary gave me a similar description: "We killed the people who were guerrillas, and we told the ones who sort of helped them, or sometimes helped them, to leave. Those were the displaced."[25]

Local political leaders invited paramilitary groups to combat the new political threat. One witness to the massacre in Segovia said,

> Segovia was a very Liberal town, too Liberal, and when the Unión Patriótica won, the Liberals were very resentful, too much so. First the majority of the Unión Patriótica was young; however, the older people—parents— became aware and started becoming part of the Unión Patriótica. The big Liberals did not accept this: for example, this hurt César Pérez García for the rest of his life, because he had manipulated the town his whole life. There were even pamphlets threatening the town before the massacre, in his name: "Soon we will be in Segovia. We will take the town of Segovia by force [*a sangre*]." (Reiniciar 2009, 168)

Although initially investigated and absolved of the crime, Pérez García was recently retried and convicted based on testimonies of paramilitaries. *El Tiempo* reports: "The Court found that the massacre was the punishment imposed by Pérez for the triumph of the UP in the first popular elections for mayor in Segovia, where he had been in charge for years, and where, as a result of the crime, he continued to be the electoral 'baron'" (*El Tiempo* 2013).

In Meta, the Unión Patriótica, in an alliance with the Communist Party, won the mayoral election in Villavicencio, the departmental capital, and several other municipalities; in many more, party candidates came in second. Medina Gallego and Téllez Ardila (1994, 169) write, "From then on, a campaign of extermination and terror was initiated, directed at stopping the influence of the sectors of the Left led by the Unión Patriótica and to recuperate the political control that the traditional parties had exercised in the region." The political elites of the department held a meeting in Villa de Leyva (Boyacá) to discuss the growth of the Unión Patriótica in 1990. They later met with the VII Brigade of the army and the governor, who approved the campaign against the UP. "With the aim of producing panic, disorganization, and the obligation to abandon the region," paramilitaries

---

25. Jefferson, interview with the author, Bogotá, April 27, 2007.

started to assassinate political leaders, "as well as committing a series of indiscriminate massacres in zones of political influence of the UP and the Communist Party, accompanied by detentions and disappearances, torture, and assassinations" (171).

Interestingly, an exception to the pattern emerged in northern Tolima, where local UP chapters formed an alliance with traditional elites. As a result, the Liberals intervened on their behalf to prevent violence against them (Esguerra 2009, 157). Not all municipalities in Tolima were spared, however, as the Puerto Boyacá model was applied to most of them (160).

The military could have intervened, but instead did nothing. "The army justified their inability to protect the electoral participation of [the UP and Frente Popular], by alleging that if their comrades were kidnapping and undertaking extortion, they should pay the consequences, since they were only the 'unarmed arm of subversion'" (Romero 2000, 94). Romero (94) argues that this position "validated all types of attacks against members of these political groups." These groups

are represented as "extremists" or, in the case of peasants and land colonizers, as part of the "floating" population open to "revolutionary adventures" and to "agitators," and therefore, lacking values associated with morals and progress. This way of representing resistance to projects from the center as anarchical and irrational makes it easy to propose a solution—the pacifying, order-bringing and rational presence of the central state. (86)

Bombings by the military in 1989 and 1990 in municipalities such as Yondó—a base of UP support in the Magdalena Medio—were denounced by the displaced; the military captain responded that the mayor of the municipality supported the guerrillas (Pastoral Social 2001a, 17). The state did not intervene. Future president César Gaviria, as minister of government, made a statement in May 1988: "the government is incapable of eradicating the violence in the zones of recent colonization such as Urabá, Magdalena Medio, Arauca, and Caquetá" (Medina Gallego and Téllez Ardila 1994, 131).

As more and more local elites invited paramilitary groups into their communities, the conflict intensified. The emergence of paramilitaries in some areas—especially in the very beginning—can be traced to the overreach of guerrilla groups, which generated sufficient resentment among sectors of communities tired of "revolutionary" taxes and kidnapping (Gutiérrez Sanín 2003). But the *expansion* of the paramilitaries in the late 1980s was facilitated by an alliance between traditional party leaders and the paramilitary groups in order to stave off the UP or win back local political seats. Further, new local allies allowed the paramilitaries to establish a presence in the communities (Gutiérrez Sanín 2003), rather than just launch targeted strikes against visible leaders.

Selective targeting effectively shifted the tactics of the UP and its ability to participate in legal channels, but it did not affect the FARC's strength. Political cleansing was required. For example, Pastoral Social, a social service organization of the Catholic Church, documented that in Puerto Nare, in the Magdalena Medio, paramilitaries targeted the leaders of unions, most of whom were also UP members. The organization observed, "Even as [the assassinations] facilitated control over Puerto Nare by [paramilitary] groups, it has not been sufficient to prevent incursions by fronts of the FARC and the ELN" (Pastoral Social 2001a, 12). Vargas (2009, 19) notes that even though the paramilitaries had successfully killed leaders in the area, it was not until they entered Yondó between December 1996 and January 1997 and killed seven people and gave a deadline for others to abandon the area that they were able to neutralize the FARC.

Neutralization came through displacement. Medina Gallego and Téllez Ardila (1994, 165) observe that "displacement became the only option" in response to paramilitary violence, and that assassinations and "collective killing" were the most frequent forms of such violence. In turn, the political cleansing of UP areas led many of the displaced to go to the headquarters of the UP in Bogotá for help, Salazar told me.[26] Their arrival "made the importance of humanitarian assistance clear." The party created a foundation, Ceda Vida, to offer assistance beginning in April 1988. Another reaction by those targeted was similar to what happened following the repression: they joined the FARC for protection. Salazar put it in stark terms: "The UP was a sacrificial battalion for the FARC."[27] This is one reason why even as the paramilitaries successfully conquered FARC territories, the FARC continued to survive and retain substantial military capacity.

---

26. Interview with the author, Bogotá, November 11, 2010.
27. Interview with the author, Bogotá, November 11, 2010.

The danger voters faced in retaliation for their open support of the UP, and the inability of the FARC to protect them, raises the question of why supporters would vote in such a high-risk environment. Here, the sequence of events and the spread of the violence were important. The violence was confined to regions at the outset because the counterinsurgency was not yet operational in many areas of the country in the late 1980s. Voters in the south of the country did not feel threatened even as UP supporters in the north received threats and faced displacement and execution. But once northern paramilitaries joined forces with local politicians in the south and relocated and expanded there, UP supporters in the south were targeted as well. Once violence began in a particular region, UP support there dropped substantially. Overall voter turnout in Apartadó, for instance, declined from 60 percent in 1988 to lower than 25 percent in 1994, and reached only 30 percent in 2000, several years after the highest waves of cleansing took place. Once the national-level reach of the paramilitaries became apparent, it was not long until even the FARC barred UP supporters from voting, in 1997 (FARC-EP 1997).

Implications and Tests

If paramilitaries engaged in collective targeting of UP supporters and alliance formation with local elites, then communities and neighborhoods that supported the UP would have been among the first to experience political cleansing and displacement. The aggregate data on registered IDPs in Colombia can help test this implication. Though the Colombian government did not begin to collect systematic data on the displaced until 1997, following the adoption of Law 387, IDPs can register as displaced dating back to 1985.[28] Of the people who have registered as displaced prior to 1998, a higher percentage were displaced where the UP won any electoral support at the local level. This indicates that municipalities with UP support were more likely to be targeted early on in the escalation of the war. Figure 4.1 shows that people from UP municipalities were displaced earlier, and on a higher scale, than people from non-UP municipalities.

---

28. The Victims Law of 2011 limits eligibility for any reparations and restitution to 1985, a decision that was criticized by some for limiting access to justice for earlier victims of violence.

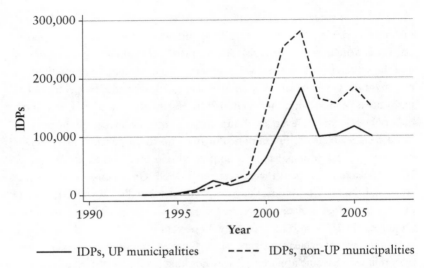

Figure 4.1. Displacement from municipalities with UP support and without, 1993–2006. Data from the Registraduría Nacional and the RUV.

We also have an additional indicator that UP municipalities—and supporters—were among the earliest victims of displacement. Over the course of local elections in the 1990s, 205 municipalities registered votes for the UP. Through 1997, 144 of those, or 70 percent, had already registered some level of displacement. Nearly three-fourths of all UP municipalities experienced displacement at a time when about half of all municipalities in the country had. Another indicator is that of the overall level of registered displacement, the scale of displacement from UP municipalities was much higher than from municipalities where the UP had no support. Table 4.1 shows that among those 66,217 registered from 582 municipalities through 1997,[29] 58 percent (38,174) were from 144 municipalities that had UP vote support.

In other words, UP municipalities make up roughly 25 percent of all municipalities that registered IDPs, but together they account for the majority of IDP households before 1997. Of a total of 2,505,598 internally displaced people registered in Colombia between 1998 and 2006,

---

29. Individuals could register at some locations in 1997, but most of these registrations are retroactive; pre-1997 displacement occurred after 2002.

TABLE 4.1. UP presence and displacement

Period	Total municipalities that registered UP votes	Proportion of UP municipalities that registered displacement (%)	Proportion of overall displacement that UP municipalities produced (%)
Pre-1998	144	25	58
1998–2006	205	18.5	44

1,104,885 left municipalities that had UP electoral presence between 1990 and 1998. These 205 municipalities (18.5 percent of the 1,103 total) account for a disproportionate 44 percent of the displacement in Colombia. I analyze this variation further in chapter 6.

Another indicator of the massive nature of expulsion early on is the proportion of the population targeted by paramilitaries. CODHES, the Bogotá-based advocacy organization, estimates that approximately 1,247,000 people were displaced between 1986 and 1997. This estimate is much higher than the government's recorded registrations, as would be expected given that registrations did not begin until 1997. Police data indicate paramilitary activities in 66 municipalities before 1997, with a total population of roughly 12,300,000 people, of which 10 percent were displaced from those regions. In contrast, between 1998 and 2006, paramilitary activities were recorded in 728 municipalities, covering a total population of roughly 38,000,000. CODHES estimates that in the same period, there were 2,650,000 displaced people, or 7 percent of the total population in those areas. The proportion displaced of the potential population affected in the two time periods decreased by 30 percent, even as the overall levels increased. (This conclusion must be taken with some caution, however, as there are good reasons to believe that paramilitary activity was not adequately reported by the police, either in the earlier or later period.) While the attention usually focuses on the years for which the government data improves, and when the scale of displacement seems to increase substantially (in 2002), this work points to the relative proportion of populations affected, given where paramilitary groups operated before and after unification as the AUC.

The RUV data are necessarily incomplete, because they depend on the registration of the displaced with the government, which many were reluctant to do for fear they would be identified and targeted again (Comisión Inter-congregacional de Justicia y Paz, Instituto Latinoamericano de Servicios Legales Alternativos, and Instituto Interamericano de Derechos Humanos 1992). They are, however, supported by qualitative evidence. The first national conference on the issue of displacement in Colombia was orga-nized in 1991 by the groups Justicia y Paz, the Instituto Latinoamericano de Servicios Legales Alternativos (Latin American Institute of Alternative Law and Society, or ILSA), and Instituto Interamericano de Derechos Hu-manos (Inter-American Institute of Human Rights). Representatives from Meta, Córdoba, the Magdalena Medio, Sucre, Antioquia (Bajo Cauca and Urabá), and Putumayo reported on displacement in their regions, dating to 1986 for all besides the Magdalena Medio. The earliest reports for the latter region began around the same time that paramilitary groups were founded in 1982 (Comisión Intercongregacional de Justicia y Paz, Instituto Latinoamericano de Servicios Legales Alternativos, and Instituto Interamericano de Derechos Humanos 1992). Pastoral Social reported that this early displacement involved "the peasant populations that lived in zones of influence of the Communist Party in *veredas* of Puerto Ber-río and Puerto Triunfo toward the periphery of Yondó" (Pastoral Social 2001a, 20). Paramilitaries relied on locals' information and guerrilla de-serters to identify civilians who collaborated with the FARC, particularly "Black Vladimir" (Medina Gallego and Téllez Ardila 1994, 97).[30] The tactics of the first paramilitary groups in the early 1980s—targeting union members, community organizers, and Communist Party members—are consistent with this process as well; those groups' members were stig-matized as guerrilla sympathizers. The formation of the UP allowed the paramilitaries to target a new group and expand their reach. The descrip-tions of displacement beginning in 1986 linked it to collective targeting of the UP and those accused of being collaborators of the guerrillas (Pastoral

---

30. Black Vladimir then became a commander of the Autodefensas del Magdalena Medio. He recently confessed to assassinating fourteen members of the UP between 1986 and 1989, including in San José de Apartadó and Yondó (*Semana* 2008).

Social 2001a, 15).[31] They all describe displacement as a reaction to terror and collective assassinations directed against UP-associated neighborhoods and communities. In Putumayo, for example, the report states, "The majority [of the displaced] have left from Puerto Asís and Valle del Guamuez—exactly the municipalities that have suffered the most from the dirty war" (Comisión Intercongregacional de Justicia y Paz, Instituto Latinoamericano de Servicios Legales Alternativos, and Instituto Interamericano de Derechos Humanos 1992, 67).

By 1994, internal displacement received attention in scholarly work on the increasing presence of paramilitaries (e.g., Reyes Posada 1994; Medina Gallego and Téllez Ardila 1994) and from the UN, which sent its special rapporteur on internal displacement, Francis Deng, to investigate its extent, causes, and government response. He cites an estimate of three hundred thousand IDPs through 1994, though he also notes that the displaced avoid identification, preferring to try to blend in where they resettle (Deng 1994, 10). Deng writes that displacement occured as a result of "fleeing from counterinsurgency" (61) and identified paramilitaries as the "primary source of violence and related displacement" (56–57). The weekly *Semana* covered the "crisis" of displacement for the first time in July 1998. At that point, at least half of the entire displaced population was from Urabá (*Semana* 1998). The article notes, "The terror and the operations of cleansing against the presumed popular bases of support [of the guerrillas] were converted into the counterinsurgency plan of the paramilitaries" (*Semana* 1998). The paramilitaries expanded next into the northern departments of César, Bolívar, and Magdalena, following the Boyacá/Castaño model (Echandía 2006, 35). In one of the few systematic studies of early displacement (1995–1999), Pérez Murcia finds that the presence of paramilitaries is the strongest predictor that a municipality would register displacement (Pérez Murcia 2001, 226–27). Additionally, the tactics of the paramilitaries were consistent with an intent to expel people from their homes. One UP organizer recalls, "Many arrived to Bogotá; there were massive displacements. The para[militaries] would arrive

---

31. The report mistakenly states that the UP was targeted between 1977 and 1983 in the Magdalena Medio, though it was not formed until 1985 (Pastoral Social 2001a, 15). Most likely it was referring to the PCC, which was active in these regions.

and say, this entire *vereda* has to be evacuated by tomorrow."[32] Echandía (2006, 142–43) also points out that between 1997 and 2002, massacres were a feature of paramilitary expansion. Massacres were the most effective way to generate displacement.[33]

By 1995, the government began to study displacement under the Samper administration; in 1997, it adopted a public policy response to it, Law 387. That year marked the beginning of the largest increase in displacement the country had seen, according to CODHES. The group estimated that the number of the displaced tripled in 1997 (Human Rights Watch 1998).

Without the creation of the UP or the extension of elections to the local level, collective targeting and political cleansing would not have emerged as a tactic in Colombia's war. Indeed, if the UP had never been formed and elections had never been held at the local level, it is unclear when displacement would have started, on what scale, and even the direction the war might have taken. In other words, precisely when participation and representation improved, citizens became more endangered and the war intensified. This chapter showed that the common impression that violence causes displacement is incomplete. Rather, it is often the case that because displacement is the goal, violence increases. In Colombia, the increase in violence in order to politically cleanse territories was possible through the identification of insurgents' supporters through political party affiliation. Further, the chapter indicates that identification was a necessary but not sufficient element for territorial conquest. Only after counterinsurgents gained local allies seeking to oust rivals were they able to secure footholds into new regions. Elections were the mechanism that both changed the stakes for local and regional elites and provided a way for counterinsurgents to initiate a campaign of conquest. Political cleansing spread across the country, starting in areas where the insurgent political party enjoyed high levels of local support and facilitated by the paramilitary-politician alliance.

While I cannot eliminate alternative explanations or mechanisms for each particular instance of displacement, my explanation better accounts for the onset and spread of displacement than do the alternatives. For

---

32. María, interview with the author, Bogotá, May 17, 2011.
33. Alejandro Reyes, interview with the author, Bogotá, May 27, 2013.

instance, narcos were already expanding their landholdings, and violence was increasing in the mid-1980s, but neither on its own can account for the onset or spread of displacement.

Additionally, it is possible that even in non-UP municipalities, similar mechanisms related to loyalties and territorial competition produced displacement eventually. For example, in Barrancabermeja during the paramilitary incursion of the city in 2001, neighborhoods historically associated with the ELN were targeted with collective violence for political cleansing, even though they were not associated with a political party.

Part of the reason we would expect displacement to shift is because civilians are rational actors; if they are being targeted for their electoral participation, we would expect them to stop participating. Voter turnout did decline, both overall and for the UP specifically. In 1997, the FARC prevented electoral participation in areas it controlled, at least partly to "prevent the incursion of paramilitaries" (Echandía 2006, 44). After a decade of a steady drop in voter support, the UP officially disbanded in 2002. That same year, paramilitaries initiated demobilization negotiations with the Uribe administration. Displacement substantially declined in the following years.[34]

In addition, humanitarian and human rights organizations encouraged the "depoliticization" of the issue to reduce the targeting of civilians (Deng 1994, 80). Depoliticization became the mantra of domestic NGOs (as it already was for international NGOs). And for good reason: the displaced arriving to cities such as Medellín, accused of being guerrillas, faced ongoing violence and discrimination.[35] Yet the call to depoliticize also led to studies that avoided the topic of politics altogether, perhaps because it was too difficult to raise the issue of political association without implying that the displaced had been affiliated with the leftist insurgency and were therefore responsible for their own circumstances.

---

34. My argument does not suggest that as voting declines so should displacement. Rather, political cleavages tend to be longer lasting than one or two election cycles, and this knowledge should be locally retained. Paramilitaries can discover who within a community voted for the UP in the past and therefore is likely to be a sympathizer of the rival insurgent group.

35. This move also unwittingly allows the government to make two claims: that it is not responsible and that it cannot "do" anything. Deng himself pointed to the Colombian government's "emphasis on complexity as a 'rationalization for the helplessness'" (Deng 1994). This evasion continued until the government yielded to international pressure in 1997.

5

POLITICAL CLEANSING AND RESISTANCE IN APARTADÓ

Urabá, the northwest region settled in part by families displaced by La Violencia and later by the FARC and the EPL, was also the region earliest affected by paramilitary conquest in the 1990s. I went to the region to investigate whether or not political cleansing was part of the campaign and, if so, whether or not it unfolded the way my theory would expect. The region would allow me to make comparisons between rural communities and towns, residents with differing political loyalties, and periods of contestation and control between armed groups. It was also possible to conduct fieldwork there in 2007, when I first visited the region, because the situation was relatively calm. Fieldwork was essential to gather information on political identities and the tactics employed by armed groups, and to find out if there was any relationship between political loyalties and the likelihood of political cleansing.

Based on the interviews and archival materials I was able to collect, I show that residents associated with the UP were indeed targeted for political cleansing by the paramilitaries. An additional, intriguing finding emerged from the qualitative work in Apartadó. Members of a rural community that turned out overwhelming support for the UP were less likely to leave the municipality than were their urban counterparts. I explore why and propose possible explanations for their resilience, based on interviews in the area. The next chapter provides evidence that this pattern repeated itself in the country, something I could investigate only after my fieldwork in Urabá.

Urabá and Apartadó

Apartadó is the de facto capital of a region known as the *eje bananero*, or banana belt, where the bulk of the country's bananas are harvested and exported. The municipality is situated near the gulf of Urabá and in the heart of the region of the same name, in the department of Antioquia. The region is about one-tenth the land mass of Colombia and contains about one-tenth the population. Figure 5.1 shows the region of Urabá. Apartadó's six hundred square kilometers include flatlands and mountains, anchored by one midsize city surrounded by three rural districts and two indigenous reservations (*resguardos*).[1] Even though it is only twelve kilometers away, it takes about an hour by jeep to reach San José de Apartadó, the mountain town, from the city. Figure 5.2 is a map of the municipality. Its variation in terrain and socioeconomic base, combined with variation in the presence of armed groups over time and across communities, makes Apartadó a basis for comparison with other types of communities within Colombia, and it allows me to test key implications of the argument.

Sparsely settled, the region was mostly inhabited by indigenous communities and subsistence farmers until the mid-twentieth century. Between 1951 and 1964, the population exploded to five times its initial level (Parsons 1968). It was officially founded in 1968 and grew from 22,325 inhabitants in 1973 to 48,969 in 1985. By 1993, there were 67,591 people living in the municipality, and according to the 2005 census, the population had nearly doubled to 131,405 (Departamento Administrativo Nacional de Estadística [DANE] 2010b).

---

1. The city and the municipality share the same name.

Figure 5.1. Urabá region of Colombia and the municipality of Apartadó (shaded).
Map by Joseph W. Stoll, Syracuse University.

Three developments transformed the region: the completion of the road
linking Medellín to Turbo (and to the sea);[2] the ensuing expansion of the
nascent banana industry;[3] and the arrival of Colombians from the interior

2. The first car made it to Turbo from Medellín in 1954; construction started on the road
in 1926 (Parsons 1967, 60, 52). Regular flights from Medellín began in 1966. It is about a
twenty-minute flight but an eight-hour drive (67).

3. The first banana concession was given to a German company south of Turbo in 1909
(Parsons 1967, 49).

Figure 5.2. Apartadó city and surrounding rural districts. Map by Joseph W. Stoll, Syracuse University.

escaping the partisan violence of La Violencia. The first wave of settlers were predominantly Liberals, and some Liberal guerrillas accompanied them (Reiniciar 2006, 19). Parsons (1967, 101) estimates that Liberals outnumbered Conservatives two to one and suggested that this shaped in-migration to the area.[4] The displaced from La Violencia may have encountered patches of settlers themselves displaced from the Guerra de los Mil Días (the Thousand Days' War) at the turn of the twentieth century (Steiner 2000, 10). They would have also encountered descendants of escaped slaves who first settled the west coast of the gulf and defended

4. To the point, Parsons, a political geographer, wonders, "What person in his right mind from Marinilla [in Eastern Antioquia], where in a recent election Conservative votes outnumbered Liberal ones 3,925 to 60, would voluntarily pull up stakes for Urabá where, in the same election, Liberals outnumbered Conservative votes in the four *municipios* of Turbo, Chigorodó, Mutatá, and Arboletes [municipalities of Urabá] by a crushing 28 to 1 ratio?" (Parsons 1967, 101).

it from Spanish encroachment with militias (Steiner 2000). Of the three largest indigenous groups, one, the Cuna, was originally from the region. Two others, the Sinu and Embera-Katío, sought refuge in the area during the Thousand Days' War.

The second set of migrants arrived with the completion of the road to Medellín (referred to as a highway but which is a two-lane road that remains unpaved in some parts of Urabá). The road saved hours of travel from the interior and linked the region commercially to the industrial center. Previously, the region's economy depended on trade with Quibdó, the Pacific coast capital of the Chocó, reached by river, and Cartagena, the Atlantic coast capital of Bolívar, reached by the sea (Steiner 2000, 10). The first banana shipment left Turbo, the port city of the region, for European markets in 1964 (Parsons 1967, 77).[5] The work on the plantations represented opportunity for men from the Pacific and Atlantic coasts, who were otherwise dedicated to subsistence farming. Already in 1967, wages were "substantially higher than elsewhere in the country" (Parsons 1967, 103), though living costs were also higher. By 1965, labor disputes emerged over living conditions and hours worked (Parsons 1967, 81). Labor laws were unknown to either the new entrepreneurs or to the laborers,[6] and the men worked fourteen hours a day.

With the sudden growth came many social problems. Parsons found that there was a substantial housing shortage and referred to a survey that "classified 70 percent of the houses of Turbo and 85 percent of those of Apartadó as 'chozas' or 'turgurios,' that is, slum dwellings." Some of the banana farms and palm plantations created workers' housing (Parsons 1967, 103). Parsons (97) observes,

> In 1960 Apartadó had less than one hundred houses; today [1967] it is a vast, swollen slum of muddy streets and rough, palm-thatched houses without running water, or latrines. But Apartadó has three banks, a bull-ring, a radio station (*Voz de Urabá*), a newspaper (*Vanguardia de Urabá*), a modern "subdivision," and dozens of noisy cantinas (taverns).

---

5. United Fruit Company created an "associate producer program," in which it did not own the plantations but offered low-interest loans for start-ups and created incentives for growers to sell only to them (Parsons 1967, 77, 108). The company was eager to avoid another catastrophe after the banana massacre of 1928 in Magdalena, farther up the Atlantic coast (immortalized in García Márquez's *Cien Años de Soledad*).

6. Mario Agudelo, interview with the author, Apartadó, June 2007.

The state is portrayed as indifferent to Urabá, but also incapable: "In Urabá the responsibility for the provision of these services has overnight been thrown onto the shoulders of public authorities without the resources or the experience to handle it" (108, 109). In other words, even if state officials wanted to enforce existing laws or organize the settlement process, they could not.

It was in this context that insurgent groups cultivated long-term relationships with residents of the region.

Insurgency and Political Loyalties

As described in chapter 2, leftist armed groups developed networks in several peripheral areas of the country like Urabá. The Communist Party helped organize the settlement of refugees from La Violencia, followed shortly by the FARC around 1965, which founded its powerful 5th Front in the Serranía de Abibe, the mountains outside the boomtown of Apartadó (Reiniciar 2006). The Popular Liberation Army (Ejercito Popular de Liberación, or EPL), established a presence in Urabá by the 1970s.[7] The 1970s was generally a quiet decade for both guerrilla movements in the region. The EPL's clandestine political party, the Marxist-Leninist Communist Party (Partido Comunista–Marxista Leninista, or PC-ML), sent Mario Agudelo and his wife to the region to establish the party together in 1978. He told me it was impossible to make inroads among the peasants in the region. "Everyone was fine without us—they had land. They didn't want anything else."[8]

In the banana belt, the guerrillas found a more receptive audience. The FARC and the EPL organized banana workers through their clandestine political parties. The PC-ML and the political party of the FARC, the Communist Party of Colombia (Partido Comunista de Colombia, or PCC), competed at night for union members on the banana plantations.[9] The FARC backed SINTRABANANO, and the EPL supported SINTAGRO. Union members and party organizers I interviewed explained that union membership (and, by extension, association with either of the clandestine

---

7. Another group—the ELN—also had a slight presence in the area, but it was mostly confined to small areas of the region and never came to have a significant influence.

8. Interview with the author, Bogotá, April 19, 2007.

9. The EPL emerged from the PC-ML after it broke off from the PCC in the 1960s.

political parties) was determined by the plantation where they worked rather than by an ex ante political preference. Over the course of the 1980s, strong identities formed among the civilians and workers (Suárez 2007). Agudelo told me that by the early 1990s, "People had really strong identities. They had a sense of belonging. . . . People would say, 'I am a communist, I am an *esperanzado*.'[10] And in Apartadó, even if they didn't, if they lived in 'X' neighborhood, they became associated with the identity of that neighborhood."[11]

When the UP contested elections for the first time in 1986, the clandestine political organizing by the FARC formed a natural basis for a transition to legal political competition. The announcement of the UP was welcomed by five thousand supporters in Apartadó from the Urabá region (Reiniciar 2006, 54). When elections were extended to the mayoral level in 1988, UP candidates won mayoral posts in three Urabá municipalities: Apartadó, Mutatá, and Riosucio.[12]

Policarpa, a neighborhood in Apartadó that PCC leaders helped create through an invasion of private land in 1982, was a stronghold of the UP. By 1986, the Catholic Church's social service branch observed that it was there "where the leaders of the Unión Patriótica were able to meet collective necessities and create community action and solidarity related to the construction of the neighborhood and the strengthening of local initiatives" (Pastoral Social 2001b, 84). Alfonso López, the neighboring barrio, was similarly influenced by the UP. Both neighborhoods were in Comuna 1 in Apartadó.[13] The *comuna* is now named for Bernardo Jaramillo, the UP presidential candidate assassinated in 1990, who got his

---

10. When the EPL demobilized, it formed a political party known as Esperanza, Paz, y Libertad (EPL) or Hope, Peace, and Liberty. Its supporters became known as *esperanzados*.

11. Interview with the author, Medellín, May 14, 2008. He added that residents of Turbo were also strongly identified with the party, but were more dispersed throughout the city rather than concentrated in specific neighborhoods.

12. The EPL and PC-ML contested local *alcalde* elections beginning in 1988 as well through its party, the Popular Front (Frente Popular). According to Agudelo, however, there was no electoral strategy comparable to that of the UP (interview with the author, Medellín, May 14, 2008). The EPL preferred to organize through the unions.

13. Colombian cities are organized by *comunas*, or districts, which generally comprise several *barrios*, or neighborhoods. Each neighborhood has its own community council, the Junta de Acción Comunal, and *comunas* elect Juntas de Administradoras Locales (JALs).

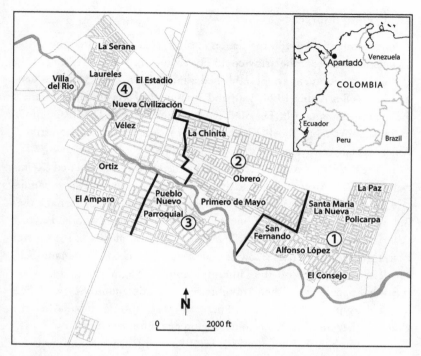

Figure 5.3. Apartadó city *comunas*. Map by Joseph W. Stoll, Syracuse University.

start as a municipal official in Apartadó. Figure 5.3 shows the *comunas* in the city of Apartadó. Comuna 2 was a stronghold of EPL supporters. In the mountains, the town of San José de Apartadó and the twenty-four surrounding hamlets were the historical stronghold of the powerful 5th Front of the FARC and the base of UP support.[14]

In 1988, local rivalries were subsumed under a coalition of the EPL, the FARC, and the ELN, called the Coordinadora Guerrillera Simón Bolívar (CGSB). Together, the guerrilla groups were too strong in Urabá for the military to combat or for the paramilitaries to penetrate.

---

14. The FARC is organized militarily by *bloques* (blocs) and *frentes* (fronts). The Bloque José María Córdoba, which includes the 5th Front, operates in Urabá, the northern Chocó, and parts of Córdoba.

The Counterinsurgency

Despite a military base in the region and the pleas of banana plantation owners to intervene, the army could not establish control over Urabá. In 1986, the government even established a military "mayor" (Medina Gallego and Téllez Ardila 1994, 130) and attempted to register all individuals living in the banana belt. The SINTRABANANO and SINTAGRO unions (with support from the PCC and PC-ML) organized a "civic strike," which halted the regional economy until the military backed down.

In 1987, the first council member from the UP was assassinated (Reiniciar 2006, 77). Around the same time, Fidel Castaño formed the paramilitary group Los Tangueros in Córdoba, across the mountains from Urabá. But even with the support of banana plantation owners (who had strong ties to or were themselves traditional political elites, mostly of the Liberal Party), the paramilitaries likewise found no inroads to the banana belt. The 1988 massacres on the Honduras and La Negra plantations were the only appearance of the paramilitaries at the time, and they were perpetrated by paramilitaries from Puerto Boyacá, not Córdoba. After the violence, they did not return to the region again for several years.

The demobilization of the EPL in 1992 marked a turning point for counterinsurgents. After an initial calm following the demobilization, the FARC accused demobilized EPL members of betraying the revolution and, more to the point, of denouncing FARC leaders and sympathizers to state intelligence and military forces. Together with a dissident group of the EPL that re-armed six months after demobilization, the FARC began targeting ex-EPL members. As a result, the former rank-and-file EPL members created the Popular Commands (Comandos Populares, or CPs). Each side began engaging in tit-for-tat assassinations and massacres, the largest of which was perpetrated in January 1994 by the FARC in an *esperanzado* neighborhood in Comuna 2 called La Chinita; thirty-four people were killed at a street party.

Castaño reactivated his paramilitaries after a brief hiatus and christened them the Peasant Self-Defense Forces of Córdoba and Urabá (Autodefensas Campesinas de Córdoba y Urabá, or ACCU). The ACCU allied with the CPs, who sought protection and had information, and set up payment schedules for *bananeros* and Chiquita Brands, the dominant banana exporter (National Security Archives 2011). The army battalion under Rito

Alejo del Río collaborated with the ACCU as well to round out the new counterinsurgent coalition. The ACCU entered Apartadó in 1994, and homicides surged. In 1995, the coroner's office recorded 265 deaths, for a homicide rate of nearly 400 per 100,000 residents. Local and regional officials and human rights advocates began reporting a surge in displacement (Actas 1995).

By 1998, the FARC was on its heels attempting to regain its historical presence in the region, but it was largely marginalized to remote areas. Paramilitaries controlled the towns. That year, the EPL mayoral candidate was elected, and the UP was decimated. I argue that these shifts were the product of political cleansing of UP supporters. The highest levels of displacement occurred prior to 1998, before the government registry was established.[15] In the next section, I show that the levels appear to be extremely high, consistent with my expectations, given the strong base of UP support. There is no evidence of collective targeting and political cleansing before elections and before the ACCU launched the attempted conquest of the region. The question for my argument is whether or not the counterinsurgent campaign specifically targeted some communities and UP areas more than others, and if displacement resulted.

Documenting and Explaining Political Cleansing in Apartadó

To get a sense for who was displaced and from where within Apartadó, I collected fine-grained quantitative and qualitative data for its nine communities. Support for the UP varied across city neighborhoods and rural communities. This variation allows me to test a central implication of my argument: civilians perceived to be disloyal are more likely to be targeted than other residents. Yet even if we see variation in displacement across political groups, it may be explained by dynamics other than armed groups' strategic behavior. To test whether or not the correlations are explained by my argument, I trace the behavior of the counterinsurgent forces in neighborhoods and communities in Apartadó using archival and

---

15. This explains why Apartadó is a surprising outlier in the cross-sectional analyses presented in the next chapter: contrary to how it appears in the data, displacement did occur in the municipality, but it occurred earlier than the creation of the government registry.

interview evidence. As I discuss below, this approach allows me to explore an unexpected outcome and develop insights into the conditions under which civilians are able to resist political cleansing.

According to my argument, armed groups attempting conquest of a territory should target the particular subsets of communities they associate with rival armed groups. If that is correct, we should observe those subsets losing relatively higher proportions of their populations than others. In the specific context of Apartadó, residents of neighborhoods and communities that supported the UP should be more likely to leave than residents of communities that did not have UP support.

As noted in chapter 1, it is difficult to test this implication with either qualitative or quantitative data. Individuals who believed they were targeted for displacement because of political loyalties would have strong reasons to hide them in their new communities and not to disclose them during interviews.[16] In the Apartadó municipal registry (*registraduría*), which is responsible for tracking births, deaths, voters, and election results, I found fine-grained data on individual residence and political affiliation that allow me to compare pre-paramilitary, local-level data linking individuals to groups—in this case to the UP—with comparable postconquest information to get a sense for patterns of targeting and political cleansing. In this way, I did not have to prod anyone to reveal sensitive information or to rely on recollections of the time, which can be inaccurate and incomplete. In 1991, electoral support for the UP varied across the neighborhoods and communities of the municipality. If the argument is correct, then residents of areas that supported the insurgent-backed political party should have been more likely to leave than their neighbors.

The Data

I was able to gather data on where voters resided within the municipality in both 1991 and 1998 through voter censuses. The two snapshots of residence spanned the period of the paramilitary conquest of the municipality, which allowed me to compare who lived in the municipality before and

---

16. I searched for individuals from neighborhoods and communities associated with the UP, but with little success. I gave up the search because I began to feel intrusive and wanted to respect those who preferred not to be found.

after the conquest. Each census listed individuals by their unique identification number (*cédula*) and the polling station where the individual was
registered. I found the data at the municipal registry. Even though individuals register to vote with their municipality, such censuses are not kept on
file as a matter of course; I discovered these in a rooftop attic area in un-
marked binders.[17] Each form of each census contained roughly four hundred individuals, indicated by their *cédula*. I photographed the forms, and
the data were transferred from 969 photos to Excel datasets.

The 1991 census provides a baseline of who lived where. In 1991,
24,627 individuals were listed in the census (excluding duplicates), and in
1998 there were 41,031. As I explain further below, the increase in population is the result of high in-migration to the municipality, often promoted
by the paramilitaries. To detect which individuals left, I matched individuals' identification numbers. Matched individuals were coded as "stayed,"
unmatched individuals from the 1991 census were coded as "left," and
unmatched individuals from the 1998 census were coded as "arrived." To
link the polling station and voters with the UP, I also collected data at the
local registry on voting patterns by polling station within the municipality, including turnout and number of votes for each candidate.[18] The most
complete electoral returns in terms of municipal coverage from 1991 are
those from the national congressional election in October. Because the
voter census listed identification numbers by polling station, I could link
voters to disaggregated electoral returns. Figure 5.4 shows the electoral
returns form.

I used the electoral returns to create a continuous variable of UP party
support by polling station in 1991 ("UP vote share"). The vote share for
the UP ranged from 10 to 90 percent, reflecting wide variation within
the municipality. I also coded each polling station as "urban" or "rural":
"rural" is a dummy coded as "1" if the vote location is not within the
city according to the Department of National Statistics (DANE). There

---

17. My attempts to find comparable data for neighboring municipalities were unsuccess-
ful. In nearby Turbo, for instance, the registrar told me that such documents were lost in a
flood and that the office had been relocated. Unfortunately, this level of precision is unavailable for the entire country.

18. Again, this level of disaggregation—contained in official E-24 forms—is not archived
regularly at the local level or maintained in the departmental or national registries, according
to interviews with officials in Medellín and Bogotá.

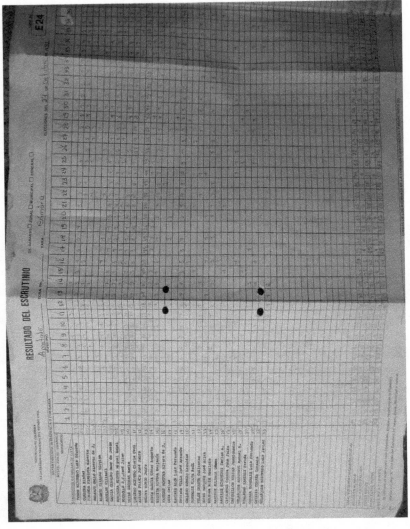

Figure 5.4. Apartadó electoral returns by polling station. Photo by author.

were 2,401 voters from the rural communities of Apartadó, across three polling stations. Of the three rural communities, one supported the UP with more than 90 percent of the vote, another with only 28 percent, and the third with 21 percent. The descriptive statistics of the variables are

TABLE 5.1. Descriptive statistics, Apartadó voter censuses, 1991 and 1998

	Obs.	Mean	Std. dev.	Min.	Max.
=1 if absent from Apartadó in 1998	24,627	0.34	0.47	0	1
=1 if in rural polling station	23,810	0.10	0.30	0	1
=1 if UP vote share > 50%	21,600	0.51	0.50	0	1
UP vote share 1991	21,600	0.50	0.19	0	0.90
N	24,627				

presented in Table 5.1. Again, "left" is a dummy variable coded as "1" if the individual's unique ID is not in the 1998 census.[19]

Comparisons

The first thing to note is the substantial proportion absent from Apartadó in 1998 across polling stations and communities; roughly one-third of those registered in 1991 no longer resided in the municipality. Further, this finding is consistent with the broader refugee and IDP literature. As violence increased with the arrival of the paramilitaries, so did displacement. Variation within the municipality, however, indicates that this story is incomplete.

Table 5.2 presents the tests of differences in the average proportions of displaced residents between polling stations with higher UP influence and those with lower influence. In each column, the differences between the proportions are significant at the 99 percent level. The 95 percent confidence intervals are also presented for each. In the entire sample, more displacement occurs in UP neighborhoods. Comparing all individuals in Apartadó in 1991 indicates that living in a UP-influenced area increased the likelihood that the individual would not appear in the 1998 census.

Disaggregating by rural and urban communities, however, reveals a different pattern. Residents of the rural community that was a UP stronghold were *less* likely to be absent from the 1998 census, as shown in the second and third columns.

---

19. Below I consider the possibility that this absence is due to factors other than displacement, such as death.

TABLE 5.2. Difference in means of proportion that left urban and rural UP and non-UP polling station areas in Apartadó, 1991–1998

Polling station	All	Urban	Rural
UP	0.353	0.365	0.267
	(.005)	(.005)	(.016)
95% C.I.	0.344–0.362	0.356–0.375	0.244–0.291
Non-UP	0.317	0.310	0.396
	(.005)	(.005)	(.012)
95% C.I.	0.308–0.326	0.300–0.319	0.365–0.428
Obs.	21,600	19,298	2,302

Note: Standard errors are in parentheses.

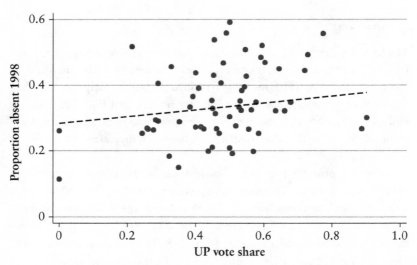

• Proportion absent in 1998 by polling station   – – – – Fitted line

Figure 5.5. Proportion of residents who left Apartadó between 1991 and 1998, by polling station and UP vote return. Data from Apartadó Registraduria.

To get a better sense of what these average proportions substantively mean, we can disaggregate by UP vote share and by rural and urban communities. Figure 5.5 shows the distribution of the proportion gone from the city in 1998, by UP electoral support. The figure indicates that while polling stations where the UP gained less than 20 percent of the vote were likely to lose about 20 percent of their residents, polling stations where urban residents supported the UP with 80 percent of the vote were likely to lose 40 percent of their residents. In other words, moving from the lowest level of UP support to the highest yielded twice as much population loss on average.

These data are consistent with my argument for the sixty polling stations in the city. Table 5.2, however, indicates that residents of the rural communities that overwhelmingly supported the UP were resilient relative to their urban counterparts.

Analysis

Despite the fine-grained nature of these comparisons, it would be ideal to rule out alternative explanations for the variation. One possibility is that class or socioeconomic status better explains who left Apartadó during this time. For one thing, leftist insurgents at least claimed to represent the interests of the working poor in the region. As a result, it is possible that counterinsurgents would target the working poor, who also happened to disproportionately support the UP. In other words, UP support is correlated with another factor that better accounts for who was most likely to leave. Another possibility is that those who left did so because of an increase in *indiscriminate* violence by armed groups in the area, not because of collective targeting directed against UP supporters. Such displacement would have been a byproduct of the violence between armed groups rather than an intended outcome, like political cleansing. I address each alternative in turn, the first with additional quantitative data and the second with qualitative process tracing.

In order to evaluate the first competing explanation, I consulted the Sisben (Sistema de Identificación de Potenciales Beneficiarios de Programas Sociales), which registers individuals and households in Colombia for potential inclusion in the welfare system throughout the thirty-two departments of the country. In 2007, the Sisben contained roughly thirty-two million records of individuals in the system, with their unique identification numbers. I matched individuals registered to vote in Apartadó in 1991 in the database using their ID numbers. An advantage with the Sisben, in addition to confirming a new place of residence in 2003, is that the database also includes information on sex, age, and class, which allows me to control for potential individual-level differences in the likelihood of displacement.

I was able to match 61.7 percent of the 1991 Apartadó voters, for a total of 15,986 individuals of the original 24,627. Of those, I was able to match 13,042 to a polling station. Factors such as wealth and access are likely to influence who is registered in the Sisben, but I do not expect them to vary systematically by polling station or political party affiliation.

Descriptive statistics are presented in Table 5.3. "Left" is a dummy variable coded as "1" if the individual no longer resided in Apartadó in 2003 according to the Sisben, and "rural" is a dummy coded as "1" if the vote location is not within the city. Here the proportion of the residents of Apartadó in 1991 who left Apartadó is much higher, roughly 60 percent. Again this is a substantially higher proportion than indicated in the government's registry.

I estimate linear probability and logit models with the individual-level data to test the likelihood that an individual will leave Apartadó, given the UP's vote share at the polling station where the individual was registered. Controlling for class, sex, and age, I find a statistically and substantively significant relationship between the likelihood of leaving the city and living in an area associated with the UP (robust standard errors clustered by polling station are reported in parentheses). Table 5.4 presents the results for urban residents.

TABLE 5.3. Descriptive statistics, Apartadó voter census, 1991, and Sisben database, 2003–2007

	Obs.	Mean	Std. dev.	Min.	Max.
=1 if absent from Apartadó in 2003	15,986	0.62	0.49	0	1
=1 if in rural polling station	14,646	0.10	0.30	0	1
=1 if UP vote share > 50%	13,042	0.52	0.50	0	1
UP vote share 1991	13,042	0.50	0.19	0	0.90
Sex	15,986	0.40	0.49	0	1
Age	15,986	43.18	15.79	0	99
Socioeconomic stratum (SES)	15,986	1.38	0.89	0	6
N	15,986				

TABLE 5.4. UP vote share in 1991 and absence from Apartadó urban neighborhoods in 2003

	OLS			Logit		
	(1)	(2)	(3)	(4)	(5)	(6)
UP vote share 1991	0.28***	0.34***		1.18***	1.63***	
	(0.07)	(0.06)		(0.29)	(0.31)	
UP influence			0.08***			0.39***
			(0.03)			(0.13)
Sex		−0.05*	−0.06**		−0.20	−0.23*
		(0.03)	(0.03)		(0.13)	(0.13)
Age		−0.01***	−0.01***		−0.04***	−0.04***
		(0.00)	(0.00)		(0.00)	(0.00)
SES		−0.01**	−0.01**		−0.07**	−0.07**
		(0.01)	(0.01)		(0.03)	(0.03)
Constant	0.48***	0.84***	0.95***	−0.10	1.59***	2.11***
	(0.04)	(0.04)	(0.03)	(0.15)	(0.21)	(0.19)
Observations	11,524	11,524	11,524	11,524	11,524	11,524
R^2	0.008	0.083	0.078			

* $p < 0.10$, ** $p < 0.05$, *** $p < 0.01$

Note: Standard errors in parentheses clustered at the polling station.

Figure 5.6 presents the predicted probability of leaving, depending on the UP vote share of an individual's polling station, holding sex, age, and class constant. As the vote share for the UP increases, the likelihood of leaving increases substantially. Residents of areas with the highest support for the UP were more than 30 percent more likely to leave than those living in areas that did not support the UP. These results undermine the argument that displacement is a byproduct of violence. If that were the case, we would expect to observe a more evenly distributed likelihood of leaving.

Interestingly, focusing on rural residents indicates that the pattern there was indeed distinct from in the city. Table 5.5 shows the results from estimating the same models as above, with data on rural residents only, again with robust standard errors clustered by polling station. Party vote is no longer a significant factor associated with the likelihood of leaving.

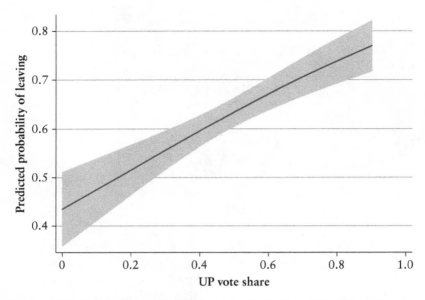

Figure 5.6. Predicted probability of leaving Apartadó city based on UP vote share of nearest polling station, 1991–2003. Predicted probabilities for a man to leave Apartadó city, with SES and age at means. Calculated with the MCP package for Stata 12, by Patrick Royston.

TABLE 5.5. UP vote share in 1991 and absence from Apartadó rural communities in 2003

	OLS			Logit		
	(1)	**(2)**	**(3)**	**(4)**	**(5)**	**(6)**
UP vote share 1991	−0.02	0.06		−0.09	0.33	
	(0.08)	(0.09)		(0.36)	(0.41)	
UP influence			0.04			0.24
			(0.05)			(0.25)
Sex		−0.03	−0.03		−0.13	−0.13*
		(0.01)	(0.01)		(0.08)	(0.08)
Age		−0.01***	−0.01***		−0.03***	−0.03***
		(0.00)	(0.00)		(0.00)	(0.00)
SES		0.11**	0.11**		0.55***	0.56***
		(0.02)	(0.02)		(0.10)	(0.09)
Constant	0.64**	0.76***	0.77***	0.57*	1.25***	1.33***
	(0.07)	(0.06)	(0.05)	(0.32)	(0.33)	(0.23)
Observations	1,518	1,518	1,518	1,518	1,518	1,518
R^2	0.000	0.097	0.098			

* $p < 0.10$, ** $p < 0.05$, *** $p < 0.01$

Note: Standard errors in parentheses clustered at the polling station.

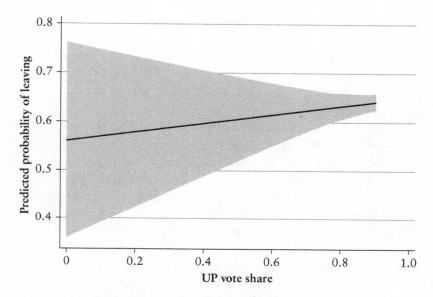

Figure 5.7. Predicted probability of leaving Apartadó rural areas based on UP vote share of nearest polling station, 1991–2003. Predicted probabilities for a man to leave a rural community in Apartadó, with SES and age at means. Calculated with the MCP package for Stata 12, by Patrick Royston.

The predicted probability of a rural resident leaving, given living in an area of UP support, is only slightly higher than those living in an area where the UP was not supported, as shown in Figure 5.7. In other words, the rural residents' behavior does not indicate political cleansing.

Caveats

While these data represent important advancements in precision over what types of individuals left the municipality, there are two potential concerns: missing data and the validity of the indicator for displacement (e.g., individuals may not appear in the 1998 census for many reasons). I address each in turn.

Perhaps the census data from 1991 is incomplete. Below, I compare the aggregate data available from Colombia's National Registry on registered voters for Apartadó. The figures indicate that the data I collected are roughly the same as the total at the national level. Table 5.6 presents the comparison.

TABLE 5.6. Aggregate census data and voter files for Apartadó

	1990	1997/98	2000
National registry	21,234	40,476	47,353
Apartadó census	24,627	43,141	52,814

In spite of the consistency with the national-level records in the data I collected, there was some unevenness in terms of which submunicipal areas were registered. Some individuals are registered to polling stations for which I could not find corresponding electoral returns. I do not have political affiliation for 1,802 individuals, 7 percent of the original population. In addition, 2,219 people registered in 1991, or 9 percent, were not linked to a polling station. In total, of the 24,627 individuals listed in the 1991 census, 84 percent (20,606 individuals) are linked to both a location and to the vote return. In addition, two polling stations do not have corresponding voters. This is potentially problematic because they are the polling stations with the highest UP vote share in the city. Polling station 75, for example, which the UP candidate won with 91 percent of the vote, has no recorded voters. Further, for polling station 6, which supported the UP with 90 percent of the vote, only sixteen individuals were recorded. The registrar of the municipality in 2008 could not offer any clues about where polling stations were located in 1991, so I cannot check likely outcomes in press or archival materials. They are, however, only two of sixty-one total polling stations, representing a very small percentage of the total.

I am more concerned that the available data underrepresent the number of people displaced from the municipality, rather than the other way around. Unless individuals register in a new municipality, they remain registered in their previous one. If my argument is correct and people are displaced as the result of a perceived association with an insurgent organization because of their inferred electoral behavior, I would expect them to be reluctant to register to vote in their new communities.

A more problematic objection might be made: I am inferring that those not appearing in the 1998 dataset or the Sisben have been displaced sometime between 1991 and 1998, or between 1991 and 2003. There are many possible reasons for why individuals who appear in 1991 do not appear in 1998 or 2003. One could be death. Mortality rates for Antioquia were higher than the national average: 7.58 between 1990 and 1995, and 7.14 between 1995 and 2000 (Departamento Administrativo Nacional de Estadística [DANE] 2010a). Based on the 1991 census population, deaths would have been expected to reach 1,461 for the period between 1991 and 1998. In other words, approximately 9 percent of the total missing from the 1998 census are potentially due to death, not displacement.[20]

Another possibility is migration unrelated to violence. Based on the migration rates estimated by the National Department of Statistics (DANE) for the Department of Antioquia (the lowest level of disaggregation for which I could obtain estimates), a net of roughly nine people would have been likely to migrate *into* the municipality during this period (Departamento Administrativo Nacional de Estadística [DANE] 2010a).[21] I have not uncovered any evidence in the archival materials why some neighborhoods and communities would be more likely than others to shrink during this period for reasons unrelated to the violence. While it is impossible to know with certainty the motivations of each individual or household, the job opportunities and wages available to manual laborers in this region were favorable relative to comparable sectors elsewhere in the country. In fact, the population of the region nearly doubled between 1991 and 2005 at least in part because wages in the banana industry were the highest in the country for blue-collar work, and demand for labor on the plantations remained high during this period.

Even with these caveats, the relationship between proportions absent in 1998 and 2003 and UP vote share is strong. In the next section, I use

---

20. Further, the mortality rate for the department is likely to be lower than for the municipality during this time period, because the homicide rate in Apartadó was quite high according to archival records of coroner's reports that I found (Actas 1995). The most violent year appears to have been in 1995, when 346 bodies were collected. An upper limit of potential additional deaths from the 1991 census, based on the 1995 homicide rate, would be 2,280 people. This estimate would represent 14 percent of the number of people who apparently left the municipality. Further, it is plausible—and in fact expected according to my argument—that nonnatural deaths were distributed unevenly throughout the municipality as well. But it is difficult to determine how much of each neighborhood's population loss was due to homicide rather than migration. At the same time, it is safe to say that the mortality and homicide rates are not attributable to deaths in only some parts of the municipality.

21. The migration rate for Antioquia was −0.46 over 1990–1995 and 0.89 for 1995–2000. This rate was lower than the national migration rate: −0.85 over 1991–1996 and −0.63 between 1992 and 1997 (Departamento Administrativo Nacional de Estadística [DANE] 2010a).

archival materials and interviews to evaluate if the urban pattern indicated by the data is accounted for by my argument—that the paramilitaries used collective targeting to produce political cleansing—or if instead the displacement was an unintended consequence of indiscriminate violence. I also explore why the rural pattern deviates from my expectations.

Collective Targeting, Political Cleansing, and Resistance

The previous section provided evidence that political cleansing took place in Apartadó city. With the data on residence in Apartadó and electoral patterns, I showed that the likelihood that individuals would leave between 1991 and 1998 and between 1991 and 2003 was linked to their neighborhoods' support for the UP. This association is consistent with my argument, but it is possible that the relationship is the result of a causal path other than the one laid out in my theory. Further, the comparison of voter censuses and regression analyses revealed a puzzling outcome: the urban pattern is consistent with the argument, while the rural one is not. In this section, I use qualitative evidence to evaluate if the processes that led to displacement from the city are consistent with my argument, and I also explore why the residents of the rural communities associated with the UP were less likely to leave.

The ideal evidence to show whether or not political cleansing was the goal, and if UP support was the basis for targeting, would be a paper trail of paramilitary strategy that explicitly refers to an effort to expel UP supporters. Unfortunately, such a record does not exist.[22] Instead, I draw on interviews with former and current residents of Apartadó, including armed group members, and archival materials to trace the extent to which the observed variation is due to a counterinsurgent strategy of displacement. I find that my argument accounts for the variation. First, the displacement was not a haphazard byproduct of other violence; it was strategic. Further,

---

22. Paramilitary commanders in the Justicia y Paz process are required to confess all their war crimes (including displacement) in *versiones libres* (roughly, testimonies) in order to be eligible for a substantially reduced prison sentence. While tens of thousands of murders have been claimed, however, only a meager amount of displacement has been conceded by these commanders, apparently to avoid returning ill-gotten lands.

paramilitaries behaved in ways that are consistent with a goal of displacement. There are two important mechanisms that stand out: direct threats to residents of UP-supporting neighborhoods and lethal violence targeted at group members *because* of their membership. This type of targeting is what I call collective; paramilitaries targeted members of neighborhoods associated with the UP (and not others) and—by extension—the FARC. Rather than indiscriminate, this violence was employed to generate a sensation of risk among a group of people they sought to expel.[23] In this sense, the expulsion of civilians based on political identities closely resembles ethnic cleansing: it is political cleansing.[24]

Second, the existing literature would expect collective targeting of individuals who were on one side of the macro-cleavage. But I show that this is not the case, based again on variation in the location of the reported activities of the paramilitaries. If class, or even ideology, were the primary basis for targeting, then Comuna 2 should have also been targeted, given its residents' socioeconomic profiles and sympathy with the leftist EPL. Yet Comuna 2 was not targeted by paramilitaries. Class might have been a determining factor for inferring loyalties, but the targeting was more nuanced. The demobilization of the EPL in the early 1990s and the formation of the paramilitary-allied CPs ended up protecting the EPL's former civilian base from violence perpetrated by the paramilitaries. At the same time, these civilians were not spared violence from the FARC in its attempt to hold on to its influence over the town in the face of the paramilitary incursion.

Finally, I explore the violence in San José de Apartadó to uncover why its residents were able to stay in spite of the mountain district's support for the UP. I find that counterinsurgents did attempt to displace the civilians in the area, but two different communities were able to resist, though they adopted different strategies to do so.

---

23. My theory allows for several possible mechanisms to ultimately generate displacement at the individual and household levels. I argue that it is advantageous for armed groups competing for control to employ a variety of tactics likely to trigger departure of members of the collectively targeted group.

24. In Colombia, political cleansing (*limpieza política*) is a term with meaning, but it tends to refer to lethal violence against particular people: political (or social, in the case of *limpieza social*) undesirables (e.g., Taussig 2005). The exception is Romero (2003), who characterizes the mid-1990s violence in Urabá as political cleansing as well.

Political Cleansing in the City

Among residents and leaders from Apartadó I interviewed, from those sympathetic to the UP and the FARC to those who sided with the EPL and paramilitaries, there was a consensus that UP supporters were targeted for displacement from Apartadó.[25] Gloria Cuartas, mayor of Apartadó during the period of the paramilitary incursion, told me that "displacement was a policy of the state. . . . [The military] called it a recuperation, Plan Return. It was an attempt by the state to reposition itself, through militarization [*via armada*]." Cuartas was elected following a pact among elites to put forward only one candidate in 1994 in an effort to avoid electoral violence. She had formerly been a health administrator in the municipality without ties to a political party, though many accused her of being sympathetic to the UP and the FARC. During the time she was in office, from 1995 to 1997, she believed there "was a policy of displacement to cleanse the area, as they called it. Displacement was directed at the UP."[26] A former FARC commander who was stationed in the region between 1997 and 2000, who now goes by William, said that the state launched an offensive "to take back the region from the UP."[27] Leonidas Moreno, a parish priest of the Catholic Church who has been in the region since the early 1980s, told me, "[The paramilitaries] wanted to push [the guerrillas] back so they would lose contact with the people, and lose their power. In order to carry out their strategy, the tactic they used was the perverse one of draining the sea [*quitarle el agua del pez*]. It was barbaric."[28]

Observable indicators also suggest paramilitary strategy, especially the location and type of lethal violence, and explicit threats. In August of 1995, Mayor Cuartas formed a group called the Committee for the Epidemiological Monitoring of Violence (Comité de Vigilancia Epidemiológica en Violencia, or CVEV), comprising representatives of the mayor's office, the local branch of the national coroner's office (Instituto de Medicina

---

25. Between April and August 2007 and March and July 2008, I conducted more than one hundred interviews with residents of Apartadó, displaced individuals in Medellín, ex-combatants who operated in the region, former politicians and state officials, and representatives of nongovernmental and intergovernmental organizations (NGOs and IGOs) operating in the region.

26. Interview with the author, Bogotá, June 13, 2008.

27. Interview with the author, Bogotá, August 6, 2007.

28. Interview with the author, Apartadó, June 29, 2007.

Legal), the police, the army, the Red Cross, and the local prosecutor's office. During these monthly meetings, a coroner presented a summary of the autopsies performed in the previous month and the causes of death.[29] The first several meetings report on a generalized sense of threats and fear in the municipality. In the second meeting, the committee makes reference to threat-related displacement: "Threats affect the population in general. The exodus [of people] isn't only a response to death, but also to diverse types of threats." (Actas 1995, vol. 2). The next year it recommends "that the Police remove the violent graffiti that there is in those parts, as those signs also terrorize and are a source of disturbance to citizens' tranquility" (Actas 1996, vol. 15). Menacing graffiti and threats would not have been employed if the counterinsurgents intended to avoid displacement.

Further, the tactics were directed toward members of political groups, especially UP supporters. Starting in 1996, the CVEV specifically and notably highlights that Policarpa and Alfonso López in Comuna 1 were experiencing high levels of violence. In three years of monthly meetings, no other neighborhoods or communities besides those in Comuna 1 and San José de Apartadó—UP-dominated areas—are mentioned in connection with paramilitary activity. In October 1996, the CVEV reports "an increase in the number of homicides on the way to Alfonso López. In that zone, there is no presence of the army" (Actas 1996, vol. 11). In December of 1996, the committee notes that the highest increase in violence has been in the Bernardo Jaramillo district—Comuna 1—"which makes it necessary to reinforce the security in that sector, including the possibility of establishing a military base" (Actas 1996, vol. 12). In March 1997, the CVEV records, "History has taught us that after any violent event there are always retaliations, something that is already evident with the presence of the [paramilitaries] in Alfonso López and San José de Apartadó, which caused what we foresaw in the previous Committee meeting: the increase in the displacement of people. . . . To this, add the calls received about the 'patrols of armed people' in Policarpa and Alfonso López" (Actas 1997,

---

29. These documents were collected at the municipal archives of the mayor's office in Apartadó. Minutes of the meetings were compiled by the head of the coroner's office, a medical doctor. The committee listed four objectives at the first meeting: to analyze the risk factors leading to violence in the municipality, to provide in a timely fashion an analysis of violence-related deaths, to distribute the analyses to the public, and to establish effective preventive measures, to be evaluated periodically (Actas 1995, vol. 1).

vol. 18). Arturo, a former resident of Alfonso López whom I interviewed in Medellín, told me that this was the reason he left the region: unrecognizable men and boys on motorcycles started riding through the neighborhood, intimidating and frightening residents.[30] Another former resident of Policarpa I interviewed in Medellín, Jorge, told me that the nickname for his former neighborhood was Poliplomo, a play on its name that incorporates a slang term for bullets.[31] Miguel, the head of a neighborhood council where the UP had support and who was a founding resident of the neighborhood in 1986, told me that paramilitaries "came in here and shot at everything. They said they were against the UP, but not everyone here was [with the UP]."[32] Marisel, a resident of Alfonso López who stayed in the community, said that "strange men drove around in cars and shot anywhere. They were crazy; they ran across rooftops. We hid under the beds, but I don't know why. They would come in and kill people anyways."[33]

The military also acknowledged that paramilitaries targeted the UP and particular communities. In a secret report prepared for the commander of the army dated October 1996, General Adolfo Clavijo notes,

> Without negating the responsibility that the forces of the left have in sustaining the conflict, as was noted previously, there is another actor that indiscriminately causes deaths in the zone: paramilitaries. . . . The paramilitaries shoot at auxiliaries and presumed collaborators of the FARC and the ELN, the political leaders of the UP and the PCC and the population that lives in regions of influence of these groups. They commit selective assassinations and massacres. They use as terrorist objectives, for their genocides, the banana plantations and the neighborhoods [*barrios de invasión*] of the FARC, the UP and the PCC. (Clavijo Ardila 1996, 11)

Years later, the formalization of property in Policarpa was extremely difficult to undertake, Mario Agudelo told me.[34] During his time as mayor of Apartadó, he tried to push for formalization but he was unable to because paramilitaries brought in people to take over the houses.

---

30. Interview with the author, Medellín, May 14, 2007.
31. Interview with the author, Medellín, May 23, 2008.
32. Interview with the author, Apartadó, June 9, 2008.
33. Interview with the author, Apartadó, June 9, 2008.
34. Interview with the author, Medellín, May 14, 2008.

Taken together, the interview and archival evidence indicate that paramilitaries collectively targeted Apartadó residents who were perceived to be disloyal, in order to politically cleanse the city. Displacement was not just an unintended byproduct of violence. In addition, if paramilitaries targeted people based on class, they should have targeted Comuna 2 as well. Comuna 2 was populated by people who had a lot in common with their neighbors in Comuna 1—they were mostly banana workers and union members—yet Comuna 2 seemed to have suffered little to no targeting by paramilitary groups. The difference is that Comuna 2 was populated by EPL supporters and demobilized members.[35]

But if paramilitaries successfully politically cleansed residents associated with the UP in the city of Apartadó, how did UP supporters in the rural community avoid a similar fate? I turn to this question in the next section.

Rural Resistance

The Peace Community   As indicated in the archival materials above, San José de Apartadó was also targeted by counterinsurgents. Given its ties to the UP, reflected in the election returns and well-known in the area, it is not surprising. A book recounting the presence of the PCC, FARC, and UP in the region states, "The case of San José is perhaps one of the most representative and successful in the work of the construction of the [Communist] Party in the region of Urabá" (Reiniciar 2006, 47). All twenty-three *veredas* of the area were organized by the party (49). What is surprising is how the communities responded to paramilitary violence.

Pastoral Social states, "The inhabitants of the hamlets in the Serrania de Abibe since 1993 have felt pressured by paramilitaries, obligating hundreds of campesinos to temporarily abandon their homes. It has been three years of the campesinos leaving their lands and returning later. However, in 1996, the pressure became unbearable and the displaced arrived to San José de Apartadó as faithful witnesses of 'orders to abandon' [their land]

---

35. Instead, the violence in that neighborhood was predominantly perpetrated by the FARC and its allies, including a 1992 massacre that left thirty-four people dead. This violence is consistent with my argument as well: during competition for territorial control, insurgents targeted rivals in an attempt to retain influence.

[*ordenes de desalojo*]" (Pastoral Social 2001b, 94).[36] In March 1997, hundreds of campesinos from the rural settlements surrounding San José de Apartadó arrived in the city of Apartadó (Pastoral Social 2001b, 94–95). Some settlements, such as La Resbalosa and Mulatos, are an eight-hour walk into the mountains from the town of San José de Apartadó. Residents claimed that paramilitaries threatened them and that the air force bombed the area. The commander of the area army brigade, General Rito Alejo del Rio, redeployed troops stationed from a few rural communities to the towns in 1996. As a result, one of his subordinates, Colonel Carlos Velásquez, denounced him for colluding with paramilitaries (Velásquez 1996). He alleged that the abandoned rural communities all shared a reputation for supporting the FARC. Velásquez told me, "Everyone knew there would be massacres in those communities [by the paramilitaries]." When I asked him which communities were perceived to be FARC loyalists, he listed four rural communities in Urabá; San José de Apartadó was on the top of the list.[37] Historian Carlos Ortiz notes, "Localities of complete or majority leftist presence, where, obviously, we cannot rule out that there were guerrillas among the population, were special objects of these actions: Belén and San José, two of the principal [targets]" (Ortiz Sarmiento 2007, 149). The families who left—an estimated eighty-seven, according to the archives, and ninety according to the Catholic Church (Pastoral Social 2001b, 95)—were housed in the municipal coliseum in Apartadó.

While the families were there, some families formed the idea of a "peace community." They were supported by the Catholic diocese of Apartadó and by a nongovernmental organization called Justice and Peace (Justicia y Paz). They eventually returned to their homes in the hamlets and town of San José de Apartadó. Eight days later, according to María, a cofounder of the community, the paramilitaries returned.[38] She says they threatened to decapitate people and gave them five days to leave. Residents had three

36. To refer to rural residents, I follow the terminology of Wood (2003): campesino does not quite translate as "peasant."

37. Interview with the author, Bogotá, March 29, 2008. Colonel Velásquez was forced to retire as a result. Though an investigation into the paramilitary ties of General Rito Alejo del Río was begun in 2001, he wasn't arrested until 2008. His trial began in 2010, after years of delays. In 2012, he was convicted of abetting the murder of a campesino in Urabá and sentenced to twenty-five years in prison. Colonel Velásquez and Gloria Cuartas testified against him, and several confessions of paramilitary leaders were used to convict him.

38. María is a pseudonym.

options: sell the land, leave, or die.[39] Still, they stayed. In March 1997, the peace community was officially created. It declared neutrality, meaning that the community would not interact with any armed actor, including the state.

The community continued to suffer violence over the years. By María's count, 180 community members were killed over the years, more than three-quarters of which she attributed to the paramilitaries and the army (Amnesty International reported 170 between 1997 and 2008 [Secretariat 2008, 60]). The most recent massacre occurred in February 2005 and included women and children; several members of the army have been arrested and charged. Despite its claims, the community has been dogged by allegations that it is not neutral, including by a former FARC political commander of the 5th Front who demobilized in April 2009 (Monroy Giraldo 2009). It is plausible that the FARC displaced civilians it considered disloyal as well in an attempt to retain control of San José de Apartadó. Anecdotally, residents of the town of San José de Apartadó or surrounding hamlets who were not members of the peace community were targeted by the FARC for displacement, in addition to occasional targeting of peace community members themselves.[40]

A combination of a strict internal hierarchy and external support explain the community's survival and individuals' decisions to stay in spite of the violence. The community makes decisions through a five-member elected council; members are supposed to serve six-month terms, though it seemed that several had de facto permanent posts. If families choose to leave the community, members are instructed to sever ties with them, a potentially effective disincentive for many.

In terms of external support, the community maintains close relationships with international NGOs, particularly the Fellowship for Reconciliation (FOR) and Peace Brigades International. These organizations provide volunteers who live in or make regular visits to the community and denounce violence against its members to a wide network of activists. The community officially broke relations first with the church, then with Justicia y Paz, though informally the ties were maintained through two trusted organizers. I think these factors increased the cost of collective

---

39. Interview with the author, San José de Apartadó, July 2, 2007.
40. Interview with Mario Agudelo, Medellín, July 4, 2007.

violence against the community for paramilitary groups and the state, but it has nevertheless persisted over the years. Masullo (2017) argues that the FARC and the military are more sensitive to international pressure than the paramilitaries. Colombian army generals I interviewed complained that any time the military attempted to enter the zone, international advocacy organizations lobbied the Colombian government to pressure the military to withdraw.[41] The peace community in San José de Apartadó demonstrates that perceived loyalty does influence armed groups' behavior, but at the same time also suggests that civilians can resist political cleansing under some circumstances.

The Indigenous Community of Las Playas   The indigenous reserve Las Playas consolidated around the same time as the peace community and also still exists in the area, but it engaged the armed actors differently. In 1997, during the same paramilitary and military incursion that led to the formation of the peace community, indigenous members of the Embera-Katío community were told by the FARC to leave and join other rural residents in the coliseum in Apartadó.[42] But at this time, the *resguardo* was still not officially recognized, and the leaders feared they would not be able to reclaim their land if they left. As a result, community members decided to cluster in the school and began to rebuild homes nearby (the community was dispersed in the area up to two hours away on foot). The leaders went to town to inform the Organización Indígena de Antioquia (OIA) and Pastoral Social, the social welfare organization of the Roman Catholic Church, what was happening. In 1999, the community was officially recognized as a *resguardo* and received a legal collective title to the land.[43] The costs of remaining were extremely high: for three years, Marisel, a teacher and community leader who lives in the city of Apartadó, provided food for the community, passing through military, paramilitary, and guerrilla checkpoints frequently. But the community remains in the area.

---

41. Interview with the author, Bogotá, June 8, 2007.
42. Interview with Marisel, Apartadó, June 9, 2008.
43. Colombian law allows for the collective titling of land for both indigenous and Afro-Colombian communities.

In 1994, the OIA convened a meeting of the *cabildos* (the elected ruling body of the *resguardos*) in the region, anticipating the "coming conflict," according to Carlos Salazar, an organizer.[44] In the meeting they agreed to forbid indigenous community members from attending meetings outside of the communities, and they restricted movements in town centers. On occasions when (usually young) community members have been found to be collaborating with one side or another, they are subject to punishment decided on by the *cabildos*; the sentence is usually community labor for up to one year. Joining an armed group is also punishable; each of the three indigenous communities I visited in Urabá had cases in which the OIA helped them intervene with the FARC to allow the recruits to return to their communities. In extreme cases of rule violations (which also cover intrafamily violence and crimes against private property), each community has a small jail. Finally, the communities also arranged places where they would go in case of emergency, "*sitios de encuentro*," to avoid violence, as well as longer-term destinations, mostly in other *resguardos*, in the case of sustained or severe threats.[45]

The indigenous communities and the peace community differ in terms of their rules governing interactions with armed groups in the war. While the peace community rejects any interaction whatsoever with any armed actor, including the state, the OIA has helped communities maintain their autonomy by engaging armed group leaders. Masullo (2017) calls the former approach "confrontational non-cooperation" and the latter "brokered non-cooperation." In 1997, the FARC agreed not to recruit among the indigenous and to respect the *resguardo* boundaries. They do not always abide by the agreement, but the point is there was a basis from which to negotiate as a bloc larger than independent communities. When any of the fifteen *resguardos* in the Urabá region are threatened, all the representatives mobilize through the OIA to contact an armed group's

---

44. Interview with the author, Apartadó, July 24, 2007.

45. Not all indigenous communities in Colombia are as well organized internally as those in Antioquia. The OIA is one of the strongest regional indigenous organizations in Colombia, but it does not work much beyond the departmental boundaries. Just across the gulf on the Chocó side, the indigenous community liaison for Pastoral Social, Padre Juvenal, lamented that the communities are unorganized because they are so remote (interview with the author, Apartadó, June 25, 2007). It can take two days by river to reach some areas.

leaders and seek a resolution.[46] Usually it ends in the armed group's withdrawing from the *resguardo*, but that can take a long time. In Mutatá, for example, a municipality in the south of Urabá, the members of the indigenous community were displaced to the town and in surrounding rural areas for two years before they could return.

While paramilitaries, the military, and the FARC all seem to be suspicious of the indigenous communities in general, there is little evidence that Las Playas has been targeted for displacement since the initial incursion. It has not avoided indiscriminate violence in the form of armed groups pursuing one another through the *resguardo*. Internal divisions exist as well, which have produced some selective killings, as when the FARC killed three community members of Las Playas for denouncing others as collaborators of the group, though this is a relatively small number of killings compared to those perpetrated against the wider community and the peace community. The OIA and Pastoral Social both try to resolve internal disputes before they involve one of the armed actors. Pastoral Social has also encouraged communities to formalize the rules governing their communities.[47]

I suspect that the internal organization of the rural communities also shaped how they were targeted by armed groups. The combination of internal community monitoring and external advocacy not only enabled the indigenous community to stay in its territory, but also to avoid ongoing collective violence (in contrast to the peace community). It is difficult to systematically assess if Las Playas has been more secure relative to the peace community as a result, but qualitative evidence suggests it has been. The experience of the indigenous community—developing a credible reputation as neutral—also indicates that armed groups' perceptions of loyalties can change and their strategies can shift as a result.

---

46. For example, in 1995, the first massive displacement of an indigenous community since 1986 occurred in northern Urabá, from the *resguardo* El Volao. A leader was killed by the dissident EPL group, and the ACCU was active in the region. The community left, seeking refuge in the town of Necoclí and a distant *resguardo* in a neighboring municipality. In the meantime, the OIA was able to facilitate a meeting between community leaders and the leader of the dissident group, Francisco Caraballo, imprisoned outside Medellín, as well as with paramilitary leader Carlos Castaño. Both agreed to respect the *resguardo* and the community was able to return (interviews in El Volao, Necoclí, June 27, 2017).

47. Interview with Padre Juvenal, Apartadó, June 25, 2007.

In this chapter, by integrating individual-level data from nine communities with archival materials and interviews, I show that paramilitaries sought to displace civilians based on their perceived political loyalties. The data taken together strongly suggest that displacement was a goal of the armed groups in Apartadó based on the political identities of neighborhoods and communities. These data support the assessment that the city was politically cleansed.

At the same time, however, one area of Apartadó was unexpectedly able to avoid political cleansing. This suggests a counterintuitive result: areas that are the most desirable for counterinsurgents to politically cleanse may be the least likely to be cleansed. Of the two strongholds, one was cleansed by the paramilitaries but the other was able to resist. To the extent that the resistance could be replicated elsewhere and is systematically more likely where there are high numbers of a particular group, political cleansing is not a foregone conclusion. I offer an explanation for the communities' ability to resist that is based on their internal organization and their ties to external advocates who can reinforce resolve and increase the costs of collective targeting for armed groups.[48]

Focusing on the micro-dynamics of the communities and neighborhoods within Apartadó establishes persuasive evidence for the argument. Political cleansing is likely in the context of territorial conquest against those considered to be disloyal. What happened in Apartadó suggests that elections revealed these loyalties to outside counterinsurgent groups and provided an opportunity for local rivals to ally with them. The next chapter evaluates the extent to which similar dynamics took place in other municipalities within Colombia.

---

48. This explanation resonates with Masullo (2017), but he specifies that the external advocates are necessary for forming noncooperation, and internal mechanisms are necessary for sustaining it.

THE POLITICS OF DISPLACEMENT ACROSS COLOMBIA

Between 1993 and 1996, as we have seen, counterinsurgents expelled residents who appeared to favor a rival political agenda from the northwest municipality of Apartadó. These residents were perceived to support the insurgency, so targeting them collectively was justified by counterinsurgents. Expelling them was also expedient; cleansing the politically disloyal enabled the paramilitaries to wrest dominance of the area from the insurgents. But did these dynamics occur in other regions of Colombia, or was it restricted to Apartadó? This chapter evaluates this question by testing whether or not municipalities that supported the UP—the political party associated with the insurgents—were also the places with high levels of displacement recorded by the government.

Existing work on displacement both cross-nationally and within Colombia has focused on the relationship between violence and displacement, and the general formulation is that more violence leads to more displacement. My argument shows that the relationship is often inverted: violence increases because displacement is the goal. In other words, though violence provokes displacement, displacement is not just an un-intended byproduct of violence. Further, the argument specifies which civilians are likely to be targeted for displacement and why, which exist-ing theories do not. In this chapter, I provide evidence that municipali-ties in Colombia where the UP won votes in local elections were more likely to experience higher levels of displacement, and that once the po-litical dimension is accounted for, the relative impact of violence is less important.

Displacement and Democratic Reforms across Colombia

Armed groups are likely to attempt political cleansing during periods of conquest by targeting members of the population suspected of being dis-loyal. When loyalties can be inferred, armed groups can gain control of a territory more effectively by expelling the disloyal than by attempting to "convert" potentially hostile civilians. If my argument is correct, then areas where a rival's supporters have been identified should be more likely to be targeted for political cleansing. Specifically, municipalities where the insurgent-affiliated Unión Patriótica (UP) political party had an electoral presence should be more likely to experience higher levels of displace-ment, all else being equal. Counterinsurgent armed groups are more likely to collectively target civilians in these communities for political cleans-ing, either because they can identify them or because they are invited in by local elites seeking to defeat them in future elections. To test the argu-ment, I use a cross-sectional dataset at the municipal level that includes local-level electoral results, aggregate displacement, and a host of covari-ates that indicate violence, population, terrain, and socioeconomic factors that could also influence displacement.

Elections were held across Colombia, so I can compare displacement from municipalities where the UP was electorally successful to similar mu-nicipalities where the UP did not have a presence. To test my argument, I compare local electoral results for the UP during the 1990s across mu-nicipalities with displacement in those municipalities in subsequent years. This approach aids interpretation; by separating the time periods, we will not mistake displacement as the cause of UP political support (or the lack of it), rather than displacement as the consequence of UP political support.

This strategy also reflects the theory: I argue that political cleansing is only likely once such elections have taken place and have potentially revealed civilians' loyalties. Importantly, the identification of a rival's supporters at the collective level will not necessarily *cause* political cleansing. Rather, it provides an opportunity for an armed group to engage in collective targeting, given the intent to challenge for control of a territory. All things being equal, I would expect armed groups to take advantage of this opportunity at some point, but the precise timing would depend on a variety of factors. In addition, most theoretically relevant variables of interest do not vary over time in the dataset. As a result, the analysis here will be cross-sectional.

I also test my argument against alternatives with data available at the municipal level on a variety of indicators. Ideally, this analysis would take place at the community level, given the logic of the theory, as well as the local-level dynamics and variation identified within the municipality of Apartadó in the previous chapter. Systematic data at the submunicipal level, however, are not available for the entire country.

Data

In order to test my argument across communities in Colombia, I created a subnational dataset drawing from several sources.

Dependent Variable   As I explained in the theory chapter, collective targeting and political cleansing—the dependent variables of this book—are difficult phenomena to observe and measure because they are observationally equivalent to other forms of displacement. As a result, I rely on aggregate displacement data to measure the outcome of interest. Wherever political cleansing exists, I would expect the overall level of displacement to be higher because it would imply that entire groups are targeted and likely to leave a municipality. On the other hand, selective targeting is likely to lead to individual-level displacement and so would affect fewer people overall at any given time compared to collective targeting. Indiscriminate targeting, though it has the potential to affect large groups of people, is less likely to result in permanent displacement and therefore less likely to be reflected in the data. In any case, even where displacement due to selective and indiscriminate targeting exists, political cleansing is likely to *add* an additional set of victims, all other things being equal. In other words, while I expect different forms of displacement to be more likely at different time periods of armed group control, when considering an over-all time period, I do not expect forms of displacement to be substitutes, but rather to covary.

The data on displacement come from the Colombian government's registry of the displaced. Law 387 of 1997 mandated that the state register the displaced; it contains 2,169,874 registrations through June 2007.[1] The executive branch agency the Department of Social Prosperity (Departamento de Prosperidad Social, or DPS) manages the registration of households and individuals who are displaced. To register, displaced individuals and households must approach a government agency and respond to a questionnaire.[2] Government officials in regional offices then review the questionnaire to assess whether or not the claim of displacement is credible. If the application is found to be plausible, then the household enters into the Unique Victim Registry (Registro Único de Víctimas, or RUV)[3] and becomes eligible for humanitarian assistance from the government.[4] In an August 2006 Constitutional Court decision (T-025), the government was found to be delinquent in attending to the entire IDP population, and the government acknowledged that its database could not be considered an estimate of the total number of displaced. At the same time, Ibáñez and

---

1. The database was provided to the Center for the Study of Development Economics (CEDE) at the Universidad de los Andes in Bogotá, where I was an affiliated researcher during 2008.

2. The only exception is with massive displacements. If a displacement appears to be on a massive scale, government enumerators go to the arrival point of the majority of the displaced (based on reports from regional government offices and nongovernmental organizations such as the International Committee of the Red Cross), collect the testimony of a community leader, and register all households in the area. The RUV dataset on mass displacement includes events of at least fifty individuals or ten households leaving a community (over some undefined but presumably short time span).

3. Previously, the registry was known as the Unique Registration System (Sistema Único de Registro, or SUR) and was maintained by the executive-branch agency Social Action (Acción Social), which was folded into the Department of Social Prosperity under the Santos administration. The administration also created a Special Unit for Victims, which oversees the implementation of the Victims Law of 2011.

4. Once registered as an IDP, the household is entitled to three months of rent and groceries. There is generally a long delay between the time of entrance into the RUV and receipt of assistance.

Velásquez (2006) find no evidence of a systematic attempt by the government to refuse certain types of registrants, but they do estimate that up to 30 percent of the IDP population is not registered with the RUV; lack of information about how to register seems to be the main reason.[5]

The data on the displaced in Colombia are among the best on displacement in the world. Azerbaijan is the only other country that records individual-level characteristics of the displaced (Jennings et al. 2008). Nonetheless, one concern with using observational data is measurement error.[6] For example, if the data are less likely to include certain types of displaced people, such as those from particular classes or regions or political or ethnic backgrounds, then we might make the wrong inferences about which factors on average influence displacement levels. If there are very few people who registered with the RUV who were displaced by government forces, for example—which is a reasonable concern given that the government manages the RUV and such victims might fear retribution of some kind—then we might wrongly conclude that the government did not provoke any displacement. My stronger suspicion is that IDPs targeted early on were the least likely to register at any point, partly because the registration system was not implemented until 1997 and partly because these IDPs were targeted by paramilitary forces associated with the government and feared identification as guerrilla sympathizers. Such an underrepresentation of precisely whom I would expect to be most likely to be affected by political cleansing means that the estimates of the relationship I make in the next section are likely to be biased downward, that is, lower than the true value. Despite this possibility, the data are still useful aggregated

---

5. CODHES is another source of data on the displaced, but it estimates numbers of people arriving to a municipality. Additionally, the RUV does not register households more than once, whereas CODHES counts number of displacements, not households. CODHES also includes those displaced by aerial fumigation of coca plantations, while the SUR does not. While the CODHES estimates are useful for offering an additional impression of variation in displacement over time, they cannot be used to analyze causes of displacement because the aggregate estimates are of IDPs arriving *to* municipalities. The data do not include information on where individuals were displaced *from*.

6. Methods to address potential errors in the data, such as multiple systems estimation, are not possible as of yet because there are not enough independent, precise data sources on displacement for the entire country. While the Catholic Church has collected its own registry of the displaced, it is no longer independent of the state's RUV database. Priests at local parishes are now instructed to direct IDPs to state authorities to register before returning and receiving aid from the church's social assistance organization, Pastoral Social. Further, the CODHES data are estimates, not registrations.

over 1998 and 2006 because the measurement error over that time span is nonsystematic. It is likely, for example, that IDPs from some areas of the country at certain periods of the war were less likely to register than counterparts from other regions. Aggregation over time, however, helps to mitigate these biases. In addition, access to registration improved after 2000 across the country (Ibáñez and Velásquez 2006), and the offer of humanitarian assistance was a likely strong incentive for IDPs to register regardless of the actor responsible. Finally, because the data measure the dependent variable, the primary concern is attenuation bias in the estimates.

I aggregate the individual-level RUV displacement registrations by municipality between 1998 and 2006, the final full year for which I have data. This constraint is consistent with the theoretical framework of this project. As discussed in chapter 1, my theory provides a general implication for the timing of political cleansing: it should occur after a group-based identity is linked to a perception of loyalty to insurgents and in the context of a counterinsurgent campaign. The argument, however, does not account for precise timing, which also depends on factors such as the resources of the armed group, the emergence of local allies, and the location of the municipalities. The fact that this statewide analysis is limited to the time period following the creation of the umbrella paramilitary force in 1997, the AUC, is therefore consistent with the theory. Before this year, displacement was limited to a few regions of the country (which, consistent with the theory, were areas of strong UP support, as described in chapter 4). In addition, structuring the analysis as one of aggregate municipal displacement between 1998 and 2006, the period following the electoral data for the UP, allows me to exclude the possibility that displacement leads to increased support for the UP rather than vice versa.

Again, by using the aggregate estimate of displacement, I assume that political cleansing increases the total number of IDPs from a municipality. In the absence of a direct indicator of collective targeting, this is the best we can do empirically. In addition, it is reasonable to assume that over the period of time in question (1998–2006), the various forms of displacement are roughly likely to covary, and the cumulative measure of displacement is likely to capture the span of all types. If my argument is correct, different forms of displacement are likely during different time periods.[7]

---

7. For example, instances of individual escape in response to selective targeting are likelier during periods when one armed group exercises dominant but not complete control of a

Independent Variables   The argument incorporates two mechanisms that account for armed groups' targeting of civilians for expulsion: perceived civilian loyalties and alliances with locals who would stand to benefit from expelling political rivals. The indicator I use for both is the local-level electoral share for the Unión Patriótica political party. In the previous two chapters, I described the formal and informal connections between the UP and the FARC and the perception among counterinsurgent groups that UP supporters were therefore linked to the armed group as well. Further, wherever the UP was successful, it challenged existing political elites' hold on local power. I compile the average vote share for local council elections at the municipal level between 1990 and 1997.[8] *Concejos*, or councils, manage the affairs of municipalities as the local legislative body; the *alcalde* is the executive, equivalent to a mayor, though with jurisdiction over all communities within a municipality. Residents elect *concejales*, or councilors, to represent them. The UP contested council and mayoral elections across the country, and the electoral results reflect the local political cleavage at that time. As a result, the local electoral outcomes are reasonable indicators of my primary independent variable, and they have the added advantage of being systematically collected across the country.

To indicate the presence of UP supporters before the counterinsurgency campaign by paramilitary groups, I take the average UP vote share from the 1990, 1992, 1994, and 1997 elections, by municipality. As noted in chapter 4, the UP experienced declining support throughout the 1990s and did not recover after the FARC prohibited electoral participation in 1997. The party lost its legal standing in 2002 for lack of sufficient support. I also create an alternative indicator, a dummy variable equal to 1 if the UP won votes in any of these elections. The UP won some percentage of the council vote in 205 municipalities and won at least one seat in 141. In other words, the party established some kind of

---

community. Evasion is likelier when armed groups do not have a presence in a territory but are aiming to disrupt a rival's operations with indiscriminate violence.

8. Data on electoral outcomes come from the Registraduría Nacional in Bogotá, the institution responsible for administering and monitoring elections in Colombia. I thank Fabio Sánchez for sharing the data. Elections for council were closed-list, proportional representation.

presence in roughly 20 percent of the municipalities of the country, but had actual political representation at the local level in about 15 percent of the country.[9] The average UP vote share across all municipalities was only 2 percent.[10]

Control Variables   According to the predominant alternative argument in the literature, the variation in UP support across municipalities should not have a relationship with displacement *independent* of levels of violence. To test for this possibility, I include data on violence from the Colombian National Police.[11] The police data track violent events by type, municipality, and date based on reporting in municipalities. It is notoriously difficult to collect accurate data on violent events and homicides during civil wars (Seybolt, Aronson, and Fischhoff 2013; Price and Gohdes 2014). Nevertheless, these data represent the best available. They include the details of the location, type, and date of each event. I include any violent action attributed to paramilitaries and to the FARC during both the early period (1990–1997) and the later period (1998–2006), as well as any clashes between the two groups. Though these actors are not the only ones perpetrating violence, they are the most prominent and most likely to be involved in displacement as expected by the framework. Further, events are relatively easier to document and count compared to the number of victims—many of which go unreported or are attributed to the wrong perpetrator—which reduces the likelihood of measurement error.

---

9. Thirteen municipalities stand out for their unusually high support for the UP—over 38 percent, on average. In the analyses below I include them, and in appendix Table A.4, I drop them. The results become even stronger without these municipalities, and as I describe in the table, I believe the reason is that displacement occurred earlier in these municipalities (as in Apartadó) and was therefore not recorded in the dataset I use.

10. The units of analysis are important: municipalities comprise many communities. For example, the average electoral return for the UP in Apartadó was 40 percent. This belies the distribution of those votes, however. In the rural communities, one community backed the party with 90 percent of the vote, while another supported its UP candidate with only 20 percent of the vote. In the city, neighborhoods similarly varied in their support.

11. I also use violence data from another source—the Center for the Study of Economic Development (Centro de Estudios de Desarrollo Económico, or CEDE) at the Universidad de los Andes in Bogotá—as a robustness check. This dataset combines police reports with local press reports. The results are included in the appendix and are consistent with the analyses using the police data alone.

As robustness checks, I also use the total number of civilian victims recorded as well as the number of massacres recorded. The results remain robust. I also include a measure of the number of homicides for each municipality. I use the violence indicators to assess whether or not violence fully accounts for the displacement, as the alternative account would hold.

In addition to the violence variables, I also include a series of controls that may have an impact on the levels of displacement across Colombia based on insights from the civil war and existing displacement literature. Data on elevation, the size of the municipality, the presence of roads in 1995 (in km), and the linear distance of the municipality from the department capital were provided by the Center for the Study of Economic Development (Centro de Estudios de Desarrollo Económico, or CEDE).[12] Each variable indicates how easily civilians could feasibly opt to leave the municipality. Those municipalities that are large, that have "rough" terrain and few roads, and are distant from the nearest large city should be more difficult for people to exit, even when faced with substantial threats. In Nepal, for instance, Adhikari (2012) finds that the presence of roads were important indicators of the probability that a resident would leave. I also include the natural log of the municipal population in 1993, based on the census. These data were obtained from the Department of National Statistics (Departamento Administrativo Nacional de Estadística, or DANE). Larger populations might be more attractive targets for armed groups and may make the sort of resistance to cleansing described in the previous chapter more difficult to mount.

Controls related to poverty and municipal resources are also included. Municipalities that are poorer may be more likely to produce displacement because there are fewer incentives for civilians to risk violence and stay.[13] Ibáñez (2008) finds that municipalities with high levels of poverty have higher levels of displacement after 1998. It could be that poorer peasants are more likely to be targeted or displaced because they do not

---

12. The CEDE recently made all of its data available for public use at https://datoscede.uniandes.edu.co.

13. Some observers also claim that displacement is a product of economic motivations. While it is true that Colombia, as with many developing states, has high levels of internal rural-urban migration, the data used here are explicitly violence- or conflict-related migration data. As described in the previous section, government officials only include those civilians whose claims of displacement are plausible.

have title to their land, so it is more easily usurped (Reyes Posada 2009). To capture measures of poverty, I include the "basic needs unsatisfied" index (NBI), which measures the proportion of a municipal population living in extreme poverty, calculated from the 2005 census. The average municipal GDP over the 1998–2006 period is also included, based on the calculations by the CEDE.

Finally, I also include data on the median transfers and royalties received by municipalities over the 1998–2006 period. Some scholars have suggested that these resources, which municipalities began to receive in the 1990s, made some attractive targets for armed groups (Sánchez and Mar Palau 2006; Sánchez and Chacón 2005; Eaton 2006). The transfers variable is included to account for the possibility that these factors, rather than the political profile of municipal residents, led to an increase in the dispute for territorial control between armed groups (which could lead to displacement as the result of indiscriminate violence rather than collective targeting). The royalties variable also indicates the possibility that displacement overlapped with areas of rich natural resources, for armed groups' economic gain.

Table 6.1 presents the descriptive statistics for the variables used in the analysis.

TABLE 6.1. Descriptive statistics

	Obs.	Mean	Std. dev.	Min.	Max.
IDPs, total (1998–2006)	1,103	2,002.04	4,421.29	1	56,926
IDPs (natural log) ('98–'06)	1,103	6.05	1.95	0	10.95
=1 if any UP votes, ('90–'97)	1,122	0.18	0.39	0	1
UP vote share avg. ('90–'97)	1,122	0.02	0.08	0	0.726
FARC actions ('88–'97)	1,117	41.34	145.15	0	1,830
FARC actions ('98–'06)	1,117	163.39	478.36	0	5,996
Paramilitary actions ('98–'06)	1,117	23.08	104.64	0	2,298
Paramilitary actions ('88–'97)	1,117	0.01	0.10	0	2
FARC-paramilitary clashes ('98–'06)	1,117	0.37	1.23	0	12

(*Continued*)

TABLE 6.1. Continued

	Obs.	Mean	Std. dev.	Min.	Max.
Homicides, total ('98–'06)	1,117	15.83	58.49	0	1,154.0
Homicides, total ('88–'97)	1,117	8.58	37.37	0	1,010.0
Population 1993, natural log	1,044	9.54	1.07	4.594	15.50
Distance from dept. capital, linear	1,118	81.31	60.32	0	493.1
Elevation, meters	1,058	1,183.33	1,162.54	2	25,221.0
Area (km²)	1,122	1,017.60	3,201.21	15	65,674.0
Constructed roads in 1995 (km)	1,061	66,498.17	87,486.74	0	962,602.5
NBI, 2005	1,117	45.09	21.11	5.360	100.0
Municipal GDP per capita, average ('98–'06)	1,122	0.85	2.94	0	59.51
Royalties, median ('98–'06)	1,098	224.62	1,418.84	0	19,923.0
Transfers per capita, median ('98–'06)	1,028	0.03	0.02	0	0.255
N	1,122				

Bivariate Comparison

If we first compare the variation in UP electoral success with the levels of displacement in simple bivariate analyses, we see a strong relationship. Figure 6.1 shows the average proportion of the population displaced from municipalities with UP presence and without UP presence.

Municipalities that supported the UP experienced higher levels of displacement than non-UP municipalities.[14] On average, UP municipalities are associated with about three thousand more cumulative IDPs than non-UP municipalities.

Figure 6.2 shows the scatter plot of IDP population by UP vote share.

The scatter plot also indicates a relationship between UP electoral success and displacement: as the vote share for the UP increases in a municipality, so does the average number of IDPs. A bivariate regression indicates that

---

14. Nonetheless, non-UP municipalities also suffered substantial displacement. I should note that I still expect the mechanisms of my argument to apply in municipalities without a UP presence; that is, where group loyalties can be inferred by armed groups, the disloyal should be collectively targeted for expulsion during conquest. Without an indicator of loyalties across municipalities, however, it is difficult to observe or test the argument.

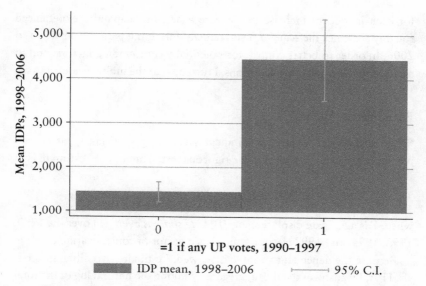

Figure 6.1. Mean municipal IDPs 1998–2006 by UP presence 1990–1997.
Data from RUV and Registraduría Nacional.

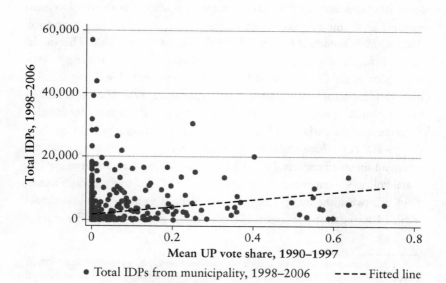

Figure 6.2. IDPs 1998–2006 and UP vote share 1990–1997.
Data from RUV and Registraduría Nacional.

for each increment increase in UP vote share, municipalities experienced roughly six times the scale of displacement during the period from 1998 to 2006. In order to better control for potentially confounding factors, and to account for alternative explanations, I turn now to the multivariate analysis.

Econometric Analysis

While the bivariate comparison indicates a striking relationship, an econometric analysis allows for a more rigorous test. The model I estimate is

$$Y = \alpha + \beta * \text{UP Vote Share} + \delta * X$$

where *Y* is aggregate displacement, *UP vote share* is averaged over the 1990, 1992, 1994, and 1997 elections, and *X* is a vector of control variables.

Because the dependent variable is skewed, I estimate two different models. First, I transform the IDP aggregate by taking the natural log of the total to adjust for its nonnormal distribution.[15] Then I estimate a linear ordinary least squares (OLS) model to reflect the theoretical relationship posited: higher levels of UP support in a municipality should correspond to higher levels of displacement from that municipality. I also leave the displacement variable as a count variable and estimate a negative binomial regression that explicitly models the dispersion of the dependent variable. This model accounts for the dispersion of the dependent variable and provides a robustness check of the OLS analysis. The results are presented in Table 6.2. Robust standard errors are clustered at the department level. The linear models have a high R-squared, indicating that the full model accounts for roughly 55 percent of the variation observed in displacement across Colombia.[16]

The *UP vote share* variable is substantively and statistically significant across all six specifications. Model 1 includes the violence data from the National Police. Violent events attributed to the FARC and to the paramilitaries, divided between the two periods, are included, as well as overall homicides recorded during the two periods. *UP vote share* is statistically significant at the

---

15. All municipalities register at least one displaced person between 1998 and 2006, alleviating concerns that such a transformation would lead to dropping observations since the log of zero is undefined.

16. I also ran the models with alternative measures of the dependent variable, such as the proportion of a municipal population displaced; all were significant at the 99 percent level, and all had similar substantive effects. These tables are available in the appendix.

TABLE 6.2. Average UP vote share, 1988–1997, and municipal displacement, 1998–2006

	OLS – DV: IDPs (natural log)			Negative binomial – DV: IDPs		
	(1)	(2)	(3)	(4)	(5)	(6)
UP vote share	2.57***	2.12***	1.66**	2.25***	2.44***	1.60**
	(0.70)	(0.67)	(0.64)	(0.83)	(0.80)	(0.63)
FARC actions ('98–'06)	0.00**	0.00**	0.00**	0.00***	0.00***	0.00***
	(0.00)	(0.00)	(0.00)	(0.00)	(0.00)	(0.00)
FARC actions ('88–'97)	0.00**	0.00	0.00	0.00	−0.00	0.00
	(0.00)	(0.00)	(0.00)	(0.00)	(0.00)	(0.00)
Paramilitary actions ('98–'06)	0.00	0.00*	0.00*	0.00	0.00	0.00*
	(0.00)	(0.00)	(0.00)	(0.00)	(0.00)	(0.00)
Paramilitary actions ('88–'97)	1.03***	0.36	0.52**	0.41**	0.28*	0.49***
	(0.21)	(0.26)	(0.24)	(0.16)	(0.16)	(0.18)
FARC-paramilitary clashes ('98–'06)	0.37***	0.29***	0.26***	0.31***	0.28***	0.23***
	(0.07)	(0.05)	(0.05)	(0.08)	(0.07)	(0.07)
Homicides, total ('98–'06)	0.00***	−0.00	−0.00	0.00	−0.00	−0.00
	(0.00)	(0.00)	(0.00)	(0.00)	(0.00)	(0.00)
Homicides, total ('88–'97)	−0.00	−0.01***	−0.01***	0.00	−0.01***	−0.01***
	(0.00)	(0.00)	(0.00)	(0.01)	(0.00)	(0.00)
1993 population, natural log		0.85***	0.94***		0.82***	0.83***
		(0.11)	(0.13)		(0.11)	(0.12)
Area (km²)		0.00	0.00		0.00	0.00
		(0.00)	(0.00)		(0.00)	(0.00)
Elevation, meters		−0.00	−0.00		−0.00***	−0.00***
		(0.00)	(0.00)		(0.00)	(0.00)
Distance from dept. capital, linear		0.00**	0.00		0.00**	0.00
		(0.00)	(0.00)		(0.00)	(0.00)
Constructed roads in 1995 (km)		0.00	−0.00		0.00	0.00
		(0.00)	(0.00)		(0.00)	(0.00)
Municipal GDP per capita, average			−0.04			−0.04
			(0.03)			(0.03)

(Continued)

TABLE 6.2. Continued

	OLS – DV: IDPs (natural log)			Negative binomial – DV: IDPs		
	(1)	(2)	(3)	(4)	(5)	(6)
Royalties, median, '98–'06			0.00 (0.00)			0.00 (0.00)
Transfers per capita, median '98–'06			2.84 (3.58)			1.33 (3.65)
NBI, 2005			0.02*** (0.01)			0.02*** (0.00)
Constant	5.60*** (0.31)	–2.21* (1.22)	–3.92*** (1.41)	6.61*** (0.26)	–1.39 (1.10)	–2.42* (1.26)
lnalpha constant				0.54*** (0.10)	0.28*** (0.09)	0.18* (0.10)
Observations	1,102	1,012	1,001	1,102	1,012	1,001
R^2	0.274	0.506	0.547			

* $p < 0.10$, ** $p < 0.05$, *** $p < 0.01$

Note: Standard errors in parentheses clustered at the department level.

99 percent level and, importantly, has a much larger substantive effect than the violence indicators. As I explained in the description of the data, the likely bias on these effects is downward, given the disincentives for IDPs displaced by paramilitaries to register, especially in the early periods of registration.

Model 2 includes the geographic and population controls, including the *1993 population natural log, Area, Elevation, Distance from the department capital,* and *Constructed roads in 1995.* The substantive effect of *UP vote share* dampens slightly, but remains statistically significant.

Model 3 includes indicators of poverty and municipal resources. Again, the *UP vote share* variable is substantively and statistically significant, this time at the 95 percent level. Models 4 through 6 replicate Models 1 through 3, but estimate a negative binomial model with the count IDP variable. As indicated in the table, the results are strongly consistent with the OLS estimations.

These models are replicated with alternative indicators of violence—the reported number of victims rather than events—in Table 6.3.

One potential concern with the data is spatial dependence. If displacement from one municipality is more likely because of displacement from a nearby municipality, then the values of the dependent variable would not be independent of one another. Such dependence would bias the results. I check for spatial autocorrelation in the displacement data, and the I-Moran's statistic (0.201, significant at the 99 percent level) indicates that the data are spatially correlated. As a result, I rerun the models,

TABLE 6.3. Main models with alternative indicators of violence from police data

	OLS			Negative binomial		
	(1)	(2)	(3)	(4)	(5)	(6)
UP vote share	4.44***	3.30***	2.77***	3.07***	2.98***	2.60***
	(0.71)	(0.54)	(0.54)	(0.62)	(0.51)	(0.51)
Total victims, '88–'97	0.01**	0.01*	0.01	0.01***	0.01**	0.01*
	(0.00)	(0.00)	(0.00)	(0.00)	(0.00)	(0.00)
Total victims, '98–'06	0.00***	0.00***	0.00***	0.01***	0.00***	0.00***
	(0.00)	(0.00)	(0.00)	(0.00)	(0.00)	(0.00)
Total massacres, '98–'06	0.08	0.08	0.08*	0.12***	0.10***	0.11***
	(0.06)	(0.05)	(0.05)	(0.03)	(0.04)	(0.04)
Total massacres, '88–'97	−0.19***	−0.09	−0.09*	−0.11**	−0.06	−0.08**
	(0.06)	(0.05)	(0.05)	(0.05)	(0.04)	(0.03)
Total homicides, '98–'06	−0.01*	−0.01**	−0.01**	−0.01	−0.01***	−0.01***
	(0.00)	(0.00)	(0.00)	(0.00)	(0.00)	(0.00)
Total homicides, '88–'97	−0.02	−0.02**	−0.02	−0.03***	−0.03***	−0.02
	(0.01)	(0.01)	(0.01)	(0.01)	(0.01)	(0.01)
1993 population, ln		0.82***	0.86***		0.78***	0.75***
		(0.12)	(0.14)		(0.12)	(0.13)
Area (km²)		0.00**	0.00*		0.00	0.00
		(0.00)	(0.00)		(0.00)	(0.00)
Elevation, meters		−0.00	−0.00		−0.00***	−0.00***
		(0.00)	(0.00)		(0.00)	(0.00)

(*Continued*)

TABLE 6.3. Continued

	OLS			Negative binomial		
	(1)	(2)	(3)	(4)	(5)	(6)
Distance from dept. capital, linear		0.00** (0.00)	0.00 (0.00)		0.00** (0.00)	0.00 (0.00)
Constructed roads in 1995 (km)		0.00 (0.00)	−0.00 (0.00)		0.00 (0.00)	0.00 (0.00)
Municipal GDP per capita, average			−0.02 (0.03)			−0.03 (0.02)
Royalties, median '98–'06			0.00* (0.00)			0.00 (0.00)
Transfers per capita, median '98–'06			0.78 (3.57)			−0.38 (2.94)
NBI, 2005			0.02*** (0.01)			0.02*** (0.00)
Constant	5.59*** (0.31)	−1.95 (1.30)	−3.22** (1.52)	6.50*** (0.26)	−1.06 (1.20)	−1.59 (1.33)
lnalpha constant				0.52*** (0.10)	0.30*** (0.09)	0.21** (0.10)
Observations	1,102	1,012	1,001	1,102	1,012	1,001
R^2	0.256	0.490	0.534			

* $p < 0.10$, ** $p < 0.05$, *** $p < 0.01$

Note: Standard errors in parentheses clustered at the department level.

incorporating a spatial lag in Models 1 through 3 of Table 6.4, and then a spatial error term in Models 4 through 6.[17]

---

17. The spatial lag models incorporate neighboring municipalities' values of the dependent variable, and spatial error models take into account spatial correlation in the error term. The results here are based on analyses with a distance-based (inverse distance) weights matrix (distance band: $0.0 < d \leq 4.0$), which is row-standardized.

TABLE 6.4. Spatial dependence models

DV: IDPs, 1998–2006 (ln)	Spatial lag models			Spatial error models		
	(1)	(2)	(3)	(4)	(5)	(6)
UP vote share	2.15*** (0.54)	1.76*** (0.53)	1.64*** (0.54)	2.18*** (0.54)	1.67*** (0.53)	1.39** (0.54)
FARC actions ('98–'06)	0.00*** (0.00)	0.00*** (0.00)	0.00*** (0.00)	0.00*** (0.00)	0.00*** (0.00)	0.00*** (0.00)
FARC actions ('88–'97)	0.00*** (0.00)	0.00** (0.00)	0.00 (0.00)	0.00*** (0.00)	0.00** (0.00)	0.00* (0.00)
Paramilitary actions ('98–'06)	0.00** (0.00)	0.00** (0.00)	0.00* (0.00)	0.00** (0.00)	0.00** (0.00)	0.00 (0.00)
Paramilitary actions ('88–'97)	0.82*** (0.24)	0.49** (0.23)	0.50** (0.21)	0.81*** (0.22)	0.48** (0.22)	0.53*** (0.19)
FARC-paramilitary clashes ('98–'06)	0.33*** (0.04)	0.28*** (0.04)	0.27*** (0.04)	0.31*** (0.04)	0.25*** (0.04)	0.23*** (0.04)
Homicides, total ('98–'06)	0.00*** (0.00)	0.00*** (0.00)	0.00* (0.00)	0.00*** (0.00)	0.00*** (0.00)	0.00** (0.00)
Homicides, total ('88–'97)	−0.00 (0.00)	−0.00 (0.00)		−0.00 (0.00)	−0.00 (0.00)	
1993 population, natural log		0.16*** (0.02)	0.19*** (0.02)		0.16*** (0.02)	0.19*** (0.02)
Area (km²)		0.00*** (0.00)	0.00 (0.00)		0.00*** (0.00)	0.00*** (0.00)
Elevation, meters		−0.00** (0.00)	−0.00** (0.00)		−0.00* (0.00)	−0.00** (0.00)
Distance from dept. capital, linear		0.00*** (0.00)	0.00** (0.00)		0.00*** (0.00)	0.00** (0.00)
Constructed roads in 1995 (km)		0.00* (0.00)	0.00 (0.00)		0.00* (0.00)	0.00 (0.00)
Municipal GDP per capita, average			−0.02 (0.02)			−0.01 (0.02)

(*Continued*)

TABLE 6.4. Continued

DV: IDPs, 1998–2006 (ln)	Spatial lag models			Spatial error models		
	(1)	(2)	(3)	(4)	(5)	(6)
Royalties, median '98–'06			0.00 (0.00)			0.00 (0.00)
Transfers per capita, median '98–'06			−10.06*** (2.26)			−11.54*** (2.53)
NBI, 2005			0.01*** (0.00)			0.02*** (0.00)
Constant	−0.14* (0.08)	−1.57*** (0.25)	−2.01*** (0.29)	14.43** (7.01)	10.54* (5.48)	7.92* (4.13)
rho constant	0.99*** (0.01)	0.99*** (0.01)	0.98*** (0.01)			
sigma constant	1.47*** (0.04)	1.37*** (0.04)	1.33*** (0.04)	1.50*** (0.04)	1.39*** (0.03)	1.35*** (0.04)
lambda constant				0.99*** (0.01)	0.99*** (0.01)	0.98*** (0.01)
Observations	1,121	1,121	1,121	1,121	1,121	1,121

* $p < 0.10$, ** $p < 0.05$, *** $p < 0.01$

Note: Robust standard errors in parentheses.

These results indicate that the influence of *UP vote share* is robust to models that account for spatial dependence in the data, and that the substantive effects of the variables remain similar to those in the OLS and negative binomial models.

Interpretation   The full model (i.e., Models 3 and 6 of Table 6.2; Models 3 and 6 of Table 6.3) indicates that a one-unit increase in the UP vote share average between 1990 and 1997 is associated with a 160 percent increase in the level of displacement from a municipality between 1998 and 2006. To interpret this association with meaningful values of UP electoral success, I use the Clarify package for Stata (King, Tomz, and Wittenberg 2000). If we simulate the full model (using OLS) one thousand times, we can estimate the change in the level of displacement based on shifting the (hypothetical) UP vote share from one standard deviation below to one standard deviation above the mean (0 to 10 percent of the vote), while holding all other covariates at their means. Such a shift would lead to an estimated 17 percent increase in the level of displacement in a municipality. Moving the vote share for the UP to two standard deviations above the mean (from 0 to 18 percent of the vote) is associated with an estimated 30 percent increase in the scale of displacement. Finally, moving from no UP support to the maximum support the party received (73 percent in La Uribe, Macarena, a historical stronghold of the FARC), the estimated level of displacement increases by 119 percent. These estimates affirm that the relationship between UP vote share and displacement is a substantively important one that accounts for a larger share of displacement than other covariates. In other words, once an indicator of residents' political loyalties (or more broadly, of municipal politics) is incorporated into the analyses, it reveals the importance of not just violence but also the politics of displacement.

The control variables reveal some interesting findings. These models indicate that violence—as measured by actions perpetrated by the two main armed groups—contributes to displacement, but, surprisingly, not in a substantive way. The factor of paramilitary events through 1997 has the largest impact on displacement between 1998 and 2006, but it is substantively small and sensitive to model specifications. Clashes between the FARC and paramilitaries from 1998 through 2006 are more stable across models and account for increases of about 26 percent in the level of displacement over the same time period. Such clashes are more likely to take place in municipalities that the armed groups actively dispute, which is consistent with the second component of the theoretical framework: displacement is more likely during attempts at conquest (by paramilitaries) or to repel conquest (the insurgents).

The geographical variables are not substantively important in these models. The log of municipal population is significant across models, indicating that more populous municipalities were more likely to suffer displacement.

The level of poverty is positively associated with levels of displacement, which is consistent with findings that those without a formal land title are more likely to be displaced (Ibáñez 2008). It is inconsistent, however, with the idea that poorer individuals are trapped by a lack of resources. The quantity of transfers and royalties that a municipality received is not associated with displacement, which indicates that targeting civilians does not depend on how many resources the municipality receives or how much of its economy depends on the exploitation of natural resources.

Overall, the results are consistent with my argument. Municipalities that had a previous UP presence were more likely to experience higher levels of displacement, all other things being equal. The robust and substantively important results of the multivariate analyses are consistent with my expectations based on the theory. If UP presence were irrelevant to displacement, we would expect no systematic difference among municipalities with different levels of UP vote share. At the same time, alternative arguments for which indicators are available do not find support.[18]

While the results are consistent with my expectations, it may be that forms of displacement other than political cleansing account for the higher level of displacement from municipalities with UP voters. To rule out such an alternative explanation, ideally we would have more precise information on *who* left the municipalities. But this kind of information is unavailable on a large scale, even aggregated to the municipal level, for practical and ethical reasons. One advantage of this type of analysis is that it does not rely on self-reported motivations and behavior, which, if my argument is correct, individuals would have strong incentives to conceal. Paired with the findings of the previous chapter, these results likely reflect the mechanisms underpinning the theory. Additionally, survey work by Ibáñez (2008) and colleagues suggests that the majority of displaced individuals cite direct threats as the most relevant precipitator in their decision to leave their community. I also find that residents of UP strongholds were the most likely to leave the municipality, which I describe in the previous chapter.

Local political loyalties shape the strategies that armed groups use and civilians' responses to those strategies. While such political cleavages are difficult to observe in a systematic and widespread manner, in this chapter I use local electoral results from municipalities in Colombia as a proxy for

---

18. Additional models with alternative indicators are included in the appendix.

one type of these local loyalties. I find that those municipalities where the UP—the political party associated with the FARC—won at least a portion of the vote share in local elections between 1990 and 1997 experienced higher levels of displacement between 1998 and 2006, even controlling for the presence of armed groups and levels of violence.

While ecological correlations such as these are inherently limited in light of the challenges of collecting large-scale, systematic data on disaggregated forms of displacement, the empirical strategy of this chapter is appropriate. The findings of the previous chapter, moreover, lend confidence to the inferences here. Additionally, this approach constitutes a contribution to an emerging literature that studies subnational patterns of civil war displacement (Ibáñez 2008; Adhikari 2012; Zhukov 2014; Balcells and Steele 2016).

The dominant goal of political cleansing was not to gerrymander and win elections. Rather, counterinsurgents used electoral outcomes as signals of loyalties and then targeted civilians in such a way as to maximize the likelihood of gaining control of the territory. Sometimes, as I argued previously, local elites threatened by the UP's electoral inroads invited paramilitaries into their communities. Later, as work by López Hernández (2005) and Acemoglu, Robinson, and Santos (2013) shows, paramilitary groups did participate in electoral fraud and coercion in order to win local and regional offices and influence national policies. In this effort, displacement may have played a role. It is more likely, however, that the paramilitaries successfully co-opted, corrupted, and coerced both political candidates and voters. This line of reasoning helps us make sense of the apparent overall decrease in displacement beginning around the time the UP reached its ultimate decline; by that time—2002—the counterinsurgent push had reached far beyond the initial regions where the strategy was begun (described in the previous chapter). Additionally, paramilitaries were in talks with the government to demobilize.

Civil war in the context of democratic institutions—especially competitive elections—can take on dangerous characteristics. Politics in such an unstable context are especially dangerous for civilians. These institutions are one way to form links between the "macro cleavage" and local politics (Kalyvas 2003). The finding of this chapter is that such a mapping is particularly dangerous to civilians. When their position relative to the macro cleavage can be inferred by outside armed actors, they are more vulnerable to collective targeting. The sad irony is that as elections enhance participation and representation, they are more likely to endanger civilians. Rational civilians will eventually abstain or misrepresent their true preferences in order to protect themselves, which undermines the goals that elections are meant to serve.

CONCLUSION

Democracy, Displacement, and the State

This book began with Arturo's story. After violence engulfed his neighborhood and it became too much for him to bear, he left his home, his job, and his community for the relative safety of a settlement at the edge of Medellín. Millions of people each year face similar, wrenching decisions.

But the increasing violence was only one part of the story. Who perpetrated the violence, how they did so, and why turn out to be crucial for understanding Arturo's predicament in particular and civilian displacement during war in general. A counterinsurgent armed group considered Arturo and his neighbors disloyal and untrustworthy and targeted them with violence to expel them from the community. Expelling them from the community enabled the counterinsurgents to wrest control from the insurgent group that had established a presence there over two decades. But Arturo was not a member of a sect or an ethnic group. He was a resident of a neighborhood that overwhelmingly supported a political party associated with insurgents. The history of Arturo's neighborhood shows that civilian displacement during civil wars is not only a byproduct of violence;

it is also an end in itself. What's more, armed groups cleanse communities to gain control of them, even when they do not target based on ethnicity.

The conceptual framework that anchors the book helps to make sense of civilian displacement in Colombia and across contemporary civil wars. Civilians' decisions to stay in or leave a community depend not on the level of violence they face, but rather on the way armed groups target them. Each form of targeting is associated with a distinct type of displacement: individuals escape from selective targeting, they evade indiscriminate violence, and they experience political cleansing after facing collective targeting. In addition to providing a new characterization of displacement during wars that effectively captures the range of displacement forms, the conceptual framework shows that each type requires its own causal explanation.

The explanatory focus of the book is on political cleansing because it is the form of displacement that armed groups purposefully try to provoke. Political cleansing is not, in other words, an unintended consequence of other forms of violence, such as bombings or a thwarted assassination attempt. Unlike the other forms of targeting, which have ends other than displacement, armed groups use collective targeting to generate an exodus of a particular group of civilians. Collective targeting is effective because when civilians are targeted because of a shared trait, their safety is tied to others' decisions. If everyone stays, it reduces any one household's risk of suffering direct violence. Given sustained violence directed at their group, however, it is likely that households will decide to leave, triggering others to follow suit. Based on this logic, I develop a theory for when and where armed groups are likely to employ collective targeting to cleanse communities and thereby gain an advantage over a rival.

When armed groups compete for control over a community, they seek to displace disloyal civilians because such displacement undermines the rival armed group's presence and is more effective than killing or attempting to convert those who are disloyal. To eliminate nonsupporters, armed groups need to be able to tell who is loyal and who is not. Although information about civilian preferences is difficult to obtain in the context of civil wars, elections conducted before or during a violent conflict are one way armed groups can identify those who are disloyal. Elections also change the incentives of local elites, who are enticed to ally with outside armed groups to protect or regain their political power.

The book reveals that in spite of how displacement is commonly perceived in Colombia and other nonethnic civil wars as haphazard, armed groups also purposefully targeted groups of civilians for expulsion. Counterinsurgents provoked political cleansing as they pursued the conquest of new territories. Political cleansing became possible following the introduction of local elections in Colombia, which revealed where supporters of the opposition political party resided and fostered new alliances between local elites and armed groups. Drawing on archival materials, interviews, and quantitative data, the book shows that this pattern of targeting and expulsion existed across communities in Colombia.

The book also uncovered rare instances of community resistance to political cleansing in spite of the collective targeting and violence the community faced. The experiences of the San José de Apartadó peace community and the Las Playas indigenous reserve in Apartadó suggest a combination of strong internal rules and external assistance helped them maintain a core of residents who withstood the violence together. The internal rules create incentives and punishment for community members who consider leaving, and the external assistance can provide key support for these internal mechanisms as well as, in some cases, indirect protection against further violence by raising the costs of the violence for perpetrators. Although this speculation is left untested in the book, it is consistent with the logic of collective targeting; to the extent that the targeted group is large enough, any particular household could be safer remaining with the group than relocating. At the same time, retaining enough residents to be relatively safe is a difficult collective-action problem for communities to solve, so internal and external institutions are key. This finding contributes to emerging scholarly work on the agency of civilians in civil wars (e.g., Kaplan 2013; Masullo 2017).

Displacement and Political Cleansing beyond Colombia

Though the empirical work of this book is drawn from Colombia, IDPs and refugees from other civil wars have described their decisions to leave their homes in ways that echo the conceptual framework of the book. People report leaving in response to direct threats to their safety (selective targeting), fear of generalized violence (indiscriminate targeting), and threats against their ethnic group, sect, or neighborhood (collective targeting). Across civil wars, individuals escape violence, communities move out of the way of violence, and still others whose loyalties are suspect are "cleansed" from their communities.

In addition, my argument for when and where political cleansing is most likely is consistent with emerging evidence from within other non-ethnic wars as well. Balcells and Steele (2016) find that displacement patterns in Catalonia during the Spanish Civil War are consistent with targeting based on the 1936 elections prior to the outbreak of the war. Districts where nationalists were successful experienced higher levels of displacement by Republicans than other districts. During the Soviet counterinsurgency campaign in postwar Ukraine, Zhukov (2014) finds that the Soviets targeted communities for resettlement that had been under partisan control in 1942. Communities' prior association with nationalists made them targets for cleansing. Finally, even in a conventional ethnic civil war such as the Bosnian war, Bulutgil (2009) finds that the timing of cleansing was linked to which political parties communities supported.

The theory also implies when and where cleansing should be likely across wars. One key factor is the revelation or creation of new cleavages that allow armed groups to detect civilians' loyalties or "side" in a war. A shift in a war's cleavage toward one based on collective identities should lead to an increase in collective targeting and political cleansing because they allow armed groups to attribute loyalties to groups of civilians. Mann (2005) and Bulutgil (2016) have written about how processes shaping the onset of war—democratization and territorial expansion—can activate fault lines in a country and shape how ethnic groups mobilize and how this can increase the likelihood of an ethnic cleavage. Such wars are likely to feature high levels of collective targeting and cleansing.

In other instances, the cleavage can shift due to the dynamics of the war itself. As Kalyvas (2008) points out, this is often a strategy by an armed group to broaden its base. Where armed groups succeed in associating ethnic identities with their cause, members of the ethnic group also have a strong incentive to align with them for protection (Kalyvas 2008; Kalyvas and Kocher 2007), or they may do so out of moral outrage following victimization (Wood 2003; Cederman, Gleditsch, and Buhaug 2013). In turn, members of the ethnic group are likely to be perceived as loyal to one armed group or another and thus as legitimate targets.

The insurgency in Iraq dramatically changed in such a way. For the first two and a half years of the war following the US invasion, there were thousands of refugees and internally displaced persons, but the scale was smaller than expected. Humanitarian organizations anticipated hundreds of thousands of refugees and constructed camps along the Syrian border to attend to their needs (Margesson, Bruno, and Sharp 2009, 7), but hardly anyone came. Then the shrine in Samarra was bombed in February 2006, and displacement tripled within months. Amnesty International reported, "Thousands of civilians were driven from their homes in mixed neighborhoods in Baghdad. Both Sunni and Shi'a armed groups were responsible for the 'cleansing' drive" (Amnesty International 2007). By the end of 2008, the IDMC (2008) estimated that 1.6 million people had left their homes and resettled in new communities within Iraq since February 2006, and another two million had left the country. In contrast, roughly 190,000 had been displaced between 2003 and early 2006.

Cleavages are important because they influence armed groups' and civilians' strategies. Political cleansing becomes an option available to armed groups when collective identities are linked to one side of the war or another. As a result, policymakers and the international community should avoid triggering such shifts to the extent possible. This responsibility is often overlooked, especially in nonethnic civil wars, because collective targeting is viewed as an "ethnic issue." The introduction of competitive elections in particular is an important possible source of cleavage revelation and even creation during war, which suggests that one area to exercise caution is the implementation and design of elections during civil wars. Democratization in the context of ongoing civil wars is a popular policy prescription (Autesserre 2010), and elections have already been held during many civil wars. According to Hyde and Marinov (2012), sixty-five civil wars between the end of World War II and 2004 featured competitive legislative elections, roughly half of all civil wars during this period (Steele and Schubiger 2015). The Colombian case is in many ways a warning about the dangers of democratization during civil war, but it also points to how electoral institutions could be designed to protect against an increase in violence against civilians.

First, local-level elections for representatives of neighborhoods or small communities should be avoided in civil war settings because they allow armed groups to make a connection between where people live and how they vote. Since individuals' votes are generally unknown, armed groups have to make an inference between the elected official's party affiliation and the preferences and loyalties of her supporters. Fortunately, relatively few irregular civil wars have featured local-level elections similar to those held in Colombia. According to Keefer (2010), Algeria, Bangladesh, India, and Peru, for instance, all held elections in regions where an ongoing insurgency was active. (Several others held local elections in regions where the government had full control during this period. Information on the type of civil war comes from Kalyvas and Balcells [2010]).

A shared trait among the eight conflicts in these four countries (India held elections in areas of four separate insurgencies) suggests a second aspect of dangerous elections: the participation of political parties linked to an active armed group. In Algeria, Peru, Bangladesh, and India, the political parties contesting the local elections were disconnected from active insurgencies, either because they were barred from running, as in the case of the GIA in Algeria, or because the insurgencies themselves opted not to engage directly in electoral politics, as in the cases of Peru, Bangladesh, and India. If the competitive political parties all denounce insurgents, then electing members of different parties will not reveal much information about possible sympathizers and their links to competing armed groups. One possible exception is abstention. If abstention is associated with one side or another in the conflict, then it might be a basis for targeting. In Colombia, abstention was not informative. Voter turnout was not especially high anywhere, so it was not possible to infer what areas of abstention were linked to FARC influence.

In related work with Livia Schubiger, we argue that in addition to the existence of a political party affiliated with an armed group and territorial-based local elections, two other factors in Colombia were important: politicians were unused to electoral competition and so were more willing to take measures to undermine fair elections to maintain their positions; and the state was unable (and some of it was unwilling) to restrain decentralized counterinsurgents (Steele and Schubiger 2015). These factors interacted to create an especially dangerous environment for democratization, and though they do not all come together in other civil war settings, they could in theory. As a result, it is important for policymakers to be aware of them when considering the introduction of elections.

When the state refuses to hold elections in regions not under its control, it can help to protect civilians living in contested regions. Afghanistan and Cambodia each held local elections during their civil wars in the 1980s, but both states restricted competition and held elections only in territories under the full control of the government. This, though, is still potentially risky. In Colombia, holding elections within controlled territory might have provided armed groups with enough information or new allies, or both, to expand their presence into those areas. Further, excluding the very citizens living in the context of an ongoing civil war from participation in elections seemingly undermines any normative impetus for holding elections in the first place.

A final risk of holding elections in a civil war setting is that they can prompt new cleavages, not just reveal existing ones. Political mobilization can lead to polarization even in established democracies; such polarization can be deadly in civil war settings. Returning to Iraq, prior to the shift to a sectarian cleavage in 2006, international actors introduced elections. The International Crisis Group (2006) reported that mobilization into political parties precipitated the sectarian cleavage shift. The year 2005, it said,

> will be remembered as the year Iraq's latent sectarianism took wings, perme-
> ating the political discourse and precipitating incidents of appalling violence
> and sectarian "cleansing." The elections that bracketed the year, in Janu-
> ary and December, underscored the newly acquired prominence of religion,
> perhaps the most significant development since the regime's ouster. With
> mosques turned into party headquarters and clerics outfitting themselves as
> politicians, Iraqis searching for leadership and stability in profoundly uncer-
> tain times essentially turned the elections into confessional exercises.

This account suggests that without elections and the accompanying political mobilization, the sectarian cleavage may not have emerged in Iraq. If the sectarian cleavage had not emerged, political cleansing would have been less likely or at least less prevalent. Policymakers that favor democratization during an ongoing war face a stark choice: implement restrictive elections or risk triggering new forms and levels of violence against civilians. Given that the risk of such violence increases as elections approach the normative goals of representation and participation, it raises the question whether or not holding elections during ongoing civil wars is worth it at all.

Theoretical Contributions and Extensions

Cleavage formation and shifts are important because they are connected to armed groups' ability to use collective targeting as a wartime tactic. Without the concept of collective targeting, we miss a key aspect of violence during civil wars—political cleansing—and therefore cannot explain it or understand its effects. A related core finding is that political cleansing is not an ancillary outcome of other forms of violence but requires an explanation in its own right. These advances contribute to a growing body of scholarship that studies patterns of violence during civil wars and expands efforts to explain aspects of civil wars beyond lethal violence, such as sexual violence (Wood 2006) and armed group governance (Arjona 2016; Mampilly 2011). The description and explanation of displacement also provides insights into overlooked dimensions of civil wars, and by extension contemporary state building.

The book revives the idea that political identities and institutions are integral to civilian displacement during war. The typical focus of collective targeting is ethnic (e.g., Fjelde and Hultman 2014) or sectarian, perhaps because these forms are the most apparent. While sometimes hatred or animosity is the genesis of such targeting (Petersen 2002, Bulutgil 2015), which makes it seem distinct from political targeting, many times the motivation for targeting based on ethnicity or sect is strategic, after the identities have been politicized. Historically, the bases of collective targeting are linked to politics because refugees and the internally displaced are often part of a political project. Arendt (1948) pointed out that the refugee crisis facing Europe following World War II was not a new phenomenon at the time: "In the long memory of history, forced migrations of individuals or whole groups of people for political or economic reasons look like everyday occurrences" (293). In the mid-twentieth century, states determined who could be citizens. As Tilly (1992, 203) put it, "Because those who control states define whole populations as their enemies, wars generate refugees at a huge rate." Such "enemies," noted Arendt (1948), were defined by birthright or loyalty.

Birthright and loyalty still factor into displacement during contemporary wars, especially during insurgencies, because wars directly involve civilians in the competition for power (Kalyvas 2006). Moreover, civilians' behavior *is* political during wars (Trinquier 1964), and armed groups can and do behave in strategic ways toward them, including in terms of displacement. As loyalty figures into the formation of the nation-state, it also matters in the formation of the "counterinsurgent state" (Rich and Stubbs 1997) through collective targeting and political cleansing.

A key development in contemporary civil wars in comparison with Arendt's postwar period is the emphasis on democratization. As we have seen, the process can endanger civilians by revealing loyalties and fostering new alliances, both of which can lead to collective targeting and cleansing. The "calamity" that results has not only humanitarian implications but also political consequences (Arendt 1948).

Political cleansing and displacement shape contemporary state building in important ways when it is conducted by the state or by its allies or insurgent groups. From the state's perspective, those judged to be loyal— based on ethnicity, sect, or political affiliation—are permitted to live in areas under contested control, while those who are unreliable are forced to leave during counterinsurgent conquest. This method of targeting during contestation indicates that political loyalties are essential to contestation and to nonlethal forms of violence. Once the political misfits are expelled from a community, the remaining civilians denounce one another based on their private motives (Kalyvas 2006). As long as civilians are loyal to the state, they are permitted to stay on the periphery, and to do so they form a tacit contract with the counterinsurgents to comply. In this way, the state extends its presence.

The disloyal, in contrast, have to relocate. Once they have been targeted and leave their communities, where the displaced resettle can alter the political development of a state. The location of resettlement depends on where the displaced anticipate relative security and on humanitarian assistance. The perpetrators of the original violence influence where the displaced will be safe, and the providers of assistance either disburse aid within the state or across international borders. Following the logic of targeting and displacement, I identify three resettlement patterns: expulsion, segregation, and integration.

When targeted by state forces or its allies, the displaced are likely to move to an area beyond the control of the state for safety, either within or across its borders. Sometimes international assistance is available, which can increase the likelihood that the displaced will cross the border. This creates an overall pattern of expulsion of the disloyal. To the extent that assistance is instead provided by insurgents, the displaced are more likely to stay within the state. When the targeted group remains within the state, segregation of loyal and disloyal groups emerges as the pattern.

If the displacement was provoked by insurgents, then the likely destination is an area controlled by the state, especially if assistance is available in some form. In this case, the resettlement pattern resembles integration, even if the state does not actively incorporate the displaced.

While expectations about these resettlement patterns requires empirical investigation and testing, the extension demonstrates that the forms of displacement outlined in the book not only enhance our understanding of this important form of civil war violence, but also have the potential to shed light on resettlement patterns. *Forms* of resettlement are equally likely to affect the political development of a country and its neighbors as the *scale* of displacement and resettlement.

Expulsion, when the displaced leave the country and become refugees, can lead to the spread of violence and war across borders (Salehyan and Gleditsch 2006; Lischer 2005). A devastating example stems from Rwandan refugees in the Democratic Republic of Congo. International expulsion can also create a lasting source of tension between countries and a motivation for irredentist activity, particularly if ethnic groups span an international border as a result of refugee movements. Finally, when a substantial proportion of a state's population leaves, it can dramatically alter the demographic balance of the country, which in turn can influence the formation of new, politically relevant cleavages.

When the displaced remain within a state's borders but are segregated into particular regions, this can also fundamentally shape the political trajectory of a country. Newly settled and segregated regions can lead to alternative, autonomous forms of governance. In Iraq, prominent US policymakers called for the creation of autonomous regions for Sunnis, Shi'ites, and Kurds (Biden and Gelb 2006). In turn, segregation can create lasting regional divisions, can form the basis for geographically or ethnically restrictive political parties, or can even foster demands for secession.

The third pattern of resettlement—integration—is likely to contribute to the growth of cities and the urbanization of a country. Though insurgents might maintain urban networks, states have an advantage in controlling and governing cities (Kocher 2004). The internally displaced, having abandoned their assets and commonly without capital, are likely to form part of the urban poor. Integration of the displaced from the periphery into cities generally favors states, which can thereby more easily monitor those who were perceived to be disloyal; and it can avoid the international conflicts that expulsion could incite or the long-term challenges that segregation could.

Colombia's history reflects a shift in resettlement from a mix of expulsion and segregation to predominant integration. During and following La Violencia, the state managed to absorb the displaced who arrived in the outskirts of cities, albeit modestly. Another substantial portion of the displaced, though, fled to unsettled territories that remained abandoned by the state. By and large, these displaced were radical Liberals or communists, targeted by armed groups associated with members of local governments or the central government. Rather than relocate to another state, though, the "refugees" settled on the periphery of the Colombian state, beyond the reach of its bureaucracy and the rule of law. The armed groups that emerged from La Violencia also found refuge in these territories and over the years developed strong ties to communities, some of which they helped create. When the state and its allies attempted to extend sovereignty throughout its territory decades later, they encountered powerful insurgents that mounted long-term rebellions. The civilians who associated with them—the so-called disloyal—were not trusted by the state or its allies to continue unmonitored and unassimilated on the periphery. But in contrast to the expulsions of the mid-twentieth century, these disloyal did not leave the country or relocate to unsettled territory half a century later. Rather, they have gone in the opposite direction: from the edges of the state back into the core, arriving in cities for safety and support.

Colombia is now undergoing a major attempt to build the state in the context of the peace agreement with the FARC and peace talks with the ELN. History shows, though, that not only do the powerful armed actors have to be incorporated into the new state, but that the most vulnerable segment of society—the displaced—have to be at the center of this project. More than six million people have been uprooted over the last twenty-five years in Colombia, more than 12 percent of the population. How the government integrates the displaced, through recognition, reparation, and restitution, will once again be a cornerstone of Colombia's future stability, development, and democracy.

APPENDIX

TABLE A.1. Main models with CEDE violence data

	(1)	(2)	(3)	(4)	(5)	(6)
	OLS			Negative binomial		
UP vote share	5.57*** (0.68)	4.13*** (0.60)	3.39*** (0.59)	3.79*** (0.72)	3.33*** (0.79)	2.36*** (0.69)
Total massacres, '93–'06	0.16*** (0.04)	0.03 (0.02)	0.03* (0.02)	0.21*** (0.05)	0.12*** (0.03)	0.14*** (0.03)
Total homicides, '98–'06	0.01* (0.00)	0.00 (0.00)	0.00 (0.00)	0.01* (0.00)	–0.00 (0.00)	–0.00 (0.00)
Total homicides, '88–'97	–0.01* (0.01)			–0.01 (0.01)		
1993 population, ln		0.86*** (0.12)	0.91*** (0.14)		0.83*** (0.13)	0.77*** (0.14)

(Continued)

TABLE A.1. Continued

	(1)	(2)	(3)	(4)	(5)	(6)
		OLS			Negative binomial	
Area (km²)		0.00**	0.00*		0.00*	0.00*
		(0.00)	(0.00)		(0.00)	(0.00)
Elevation, meters		−0.00	−0.00		−0.00***	−0.00***
		(0.00)	(0.00)		(0.00)	(0.00)
Distance from dept. capital, linear		0.00**	0.00		0.00**	0.00
		(0.00)	(0.00)		(0.00)	(0.00)
Constructed roads in 1995 (km)		0.00	0.00		0.00	−0.00
		(0.00)	(0.00)		(0.00)	(0.00)
Municipal GDP per capita, average			−0.02			−0.01
			(0.03)			(0.02)
Royalties, median '98–'06			0.00			0.00
			(0.00)			(0.00)
Transfers per capita, median '98–'06			0.92			−1.56
			(3.90)			(2.88)
NBI, 2005			0.02***			0.02***
			(0.01)			(0.00)
Constant	5.73***	−2.25*	−3.69**	6.85***	−1.29	−1.71
	(0.31)	(1.27)	(1.52)	(0.25)	(1.31)	(1.46)
lnalpha constant				0.66***	0.44***	0.35***
				(0.10)	(0.08)	(0.10)
Observations	1,102	1,012	1,001	1,102	1,012	1,001
R^2	0.168	0.425	0.480			

* $p < 0.10$, ** $p < 0.05$, *** $p < 0.01$

Note: Standard errors in parentheses clustetred at the department level.

TABLE A.2. Main OLS models with IDPs as proportion of 1993 population

DV: IDPs, 1998–2006 (ln)	(1)	(2)	(3)
		OLS	
UP vote share	0.40***	0.35**	0.31**
	(0.13)	(0.13)	(0.13)
FARC actions ('98–'06)	0.00*	0.00*	0.00*
	(0.00)	(0.00)	(0.00)
FARC actions ('88–'97)	−0.00	−0.00	−0.00
	(0.00)	(0.00)	(0.00)
Paramilitary actions ('98–'06)	0.00	0.00	0.00
	(0.00)	(0.00)	(0.00)
Paramilitary actions ('88–'97)	−0.01	−0.03	−0.02
	(0.02)	(0.02)	(0.02)
FARC-paramilitary clashes ('98–'06)	0.04***	0.04***	0.04***
	(0.01)	(0.01)	(0.01)
Homicides, total ('98–'06)	−0.00*	−0.00	−0.00
	(0.00)	(0.00)	(0.00)
Homicides, total ('88–'97)	−0.00***	−0.00**	−0.00
	(0.00)	(0.00)	(0.00)
1993 population, natural log		−0.01	−0.00
		(0.01)	(0.01)
Area (km²)		0.00	0.00
		(0.00)	(0.00)
Elevation, meters		−0.00*	−0.00**
		(0.00)	(0.00)
Distance from dept. capital, linear		0.00*	0.00
		(0.00)	(0.00)
Constructed roads in 1995 (km)		−0.00	−0.00*
		(0.00)	(0.00)
Municipal GDP per capita, average			−0.00
			(0.00)
Royalties, median '98–'06			−0.00
			(0.00)
Transfers per capita, median '98–'06			0.14
			(0.38)
NBI, 2005			0.00***
			(0.00)
Constant	0.07***	0.13*	0.02
	(0.01)	(0.07)	(0.10)
Observations	1,029	1,012	1,001
R^2	0.289	0.336	0.367

* $p < 0.10$, ** $p < 0.05$, *** $p < 0.01$

Note: Standard errors in parentheses clustered at the department level.

TABLE A.3. Main OLS models with UP presence dummy and UP seats won

DV: IDPs, 1998–2006 (ln)	(1)	(2)	(3)	(4)	(5)	(6)
=1 if any UP votes ('90–'97)	0.62** (0.23)	0.15 (0.17)	0.28* (0.14)			
UP council seats, avg. ('90–'97)				0.07** (0.03)	0.06** (0.03)	0.04* (0.02)
FARC actions ('98–'06)	0.00** (0.00)	0.00** (0.00)	0.00** (0.00)	0.00** (0.00)	0.00** (0.00)	0.00** (0.00)
FARC actions ('88–'97)	0.00** (0.00)	0.00 (0.00)	0.00 (0.00)	0.00* (0.00)	0.00 (0.00)	0.00 (0.00)
Paramilitary actions ('98–'06)	0.00 (0.00)	0.00 (0.00)	0.00* (0.00)	0.00 (0.00)	0.00* (0.00)	0.00* (0.00)
Paramilitary actions ('88–'97)	1.14*** (0.22)	0.46 (0.28)	0.60** (0.25)	0.96*** (0.20)	0.30 (0.26)	0.48* (0.23)
FARC-paramilitary clashes ('98–'06)	0.38*** (0.07)	0.31*** (0.05)	0.26*** (0.05)	0.38*** (0.07)	0.30*** (0.05)	0.26*** (0.05)
Homicides, total ('98–'06)	0.00** (0.00)	–0.00 (0.00)	–0.00 (0.00)	0.00*** (0.00)	–0.00 (0.00)	–0.00 (0.00)
Homicides, total ('88–'97)	–0.00 (0.00)	–0.01*** (0.00)	–0.01*** (0.00)	–0.00 (0.00)	–0.01*** (0.00)	–0.01*** (0.00)
1993 population, natural log		0.82*** (0.11)	0.90*** (0.13)		0.85*** (0.11)	0.93*** (0.13)
Area (km^2)		0.00 (0.00)	0.00 (0.00)		0.00 (0.00)	0.00 (0.00)
Elevation, meters		–0.00 (0.00)	–0.00 (0.00)		–0.00 (0.00)	–0.00 (0.00)
Distance from dept. capital, linear		0.00** (0.00)	0.00 (0.00)		0.00** (0.00)	0.00 (0.00)
Constructed roads in 1995 (km)		–0.00 (0.00)	–0.00 (0.00)		0.00 (0.00)	–0.00 (0.00)
Municipal GDP per capita, average			–0.05 (0.03)			–0.04 (0.03)

DV: IDPs, 1998–2006 (ln)	(1)	(2)	(3)	(4)	(5)	(6)
Royalties, median '98–'06			0.00 (0.00)			0.00 (0.00)
Transfers per capita, median 9806			2.55 (3.62)			2.69 (3.59)
NBI, 2005			0.02*** (0.01)			0.02*** (0.01)
Constant	5.55*** (0.32)	−2.01 (1.26)	−3.62** (1.42)	5.61*** (0.31)	−2.20* (1.24)	−3.87** (1.42)
Observations R^2	1,102 0.278	1,012 0.500	1,001 0.546	1,102 0.270	1,012 0.504	1,001 0.546

* $p < 0.10$, ** $p < 0.05$, *** $p < 0.01$

Note: Standard errors in parentheses clustered at the department level.

TABLE A.4. Main models, excluding outliers of UP vote share

	(1)	(2)	(3)	(4)	(5)	(6)
	OLS			Negative binomial		
UP vote share	4.98*** (1.08)	4.08*** (1.20)	3.54*** (0.96)	3.78*** (0.92)	4.28*** (1.09)	3.20*** (0.76)
FARC actions ('98–'06)	0.00** (0.00)	0.00** (0.00)	0.00** (0.00)	0.00*** (0.00)	0.00*** (0.00)	0.00*** (0.00)
FARC actions ('88–'97)	0.00** (0.00)	0.00 (0.00)	0.00 (0.00)	0.00 (0.00)	−0.00 (0.00)	−0.00 (0.00)
Paramilitary actions ('98–'06)	0.00 (0.00)	0.00 (0.00)	0.00* (0.00)	0.00 (0.00)	0.00 (0.00)	0.00* (0.00)
Paramilitary actions ('88–'97)	0.82*** (0.22)	0.22 (0.26)	0.38 (0.23)	0.35** (0.15)	0.17 (0.16)	0.36** (0.17)
FARC-paramilitary clashes ('98–'06)	0.38*** (0.08)	0.30*** (0.06)	0.27*** (0.06)	0.32*** (0.08)	0.28*** (0.08)	0.24*** (0.07)
Homicides, total ('98–'06)	0.00*** (0.00)	−0.00 (0.00)	−0.00 (0.00)	0.00 (0.00)	−0.00 (0.00)	−0.00 (0.00)

(Continued)

TABLE A.4. Continued

	(1)	(2)	(3)	(4)	(5)	(6)
		OLS			Negative binomial	
Homicides, total ('88–'97)	−0.00 (0.00)	−0.00*** (0.00)	−0.01*** (0.00)	0.00 (0.01)	−0.01*** (0.00)	−0.01*** (0.00)
1993 population		0.85*** (0.11)	0.95*** (0.13)		0.81*** (0.11)	0.83*** (0.11)
Area (km²)		0.00 (0.00)	0.00 (0.00)		0.00 (0.00)	0.00 (0.00)
Elevation, meters		−0.00 (0.00)	−0.00 (0.00)		−0.00*** (0.00)	−0.00*** (0.00)
Distance from dept. capital, linear		0.00** (0.00)	0.00 (0.00)		0.00** (0.00)	0.00 (0.00)
Constructed roads in 1995 (km)		0.00 (0.00)	−0.00 (0.00)		0.00 (0.00)	0.00 (0.00)
Municipal GDP per capita, average			−0.04 (0.03)			−0.04 (0.03)
Royalties, median '98–'06			0.00 (0.00)			0.00 (0.00)
Transfers per capita, median '98–'06			3.07 (3.44)			1.60 (3.56)
NBI, 2005			0.02*** (0.01)			0.02*** (0.00)
Constant	5.57*** (0.31)	−2.24* (1.22)	−4.05*** (1.38)	6.58*** (0.26)	−1.38 (1.09)	−2.46** (1.24)
lnalpha constant				0.54*** (0.11)	0.28*** (0.08)	0.17* (0.10)
Observations	1,089	999	988	1,089	999	988
R^2	0.270	0.504	0.548			

* $p < 0.10$, ** $p < 0.05$, *** $p < 0.01$

Notes: Standard errors in parentheses clustered at the department level. Outliers are thirteen municipalities that received an average UP vote share of 38%, a much higher proportion of the vote than the mean (2%). The results indicate a more robust relationship without these municipalities because they experienced higher levels of displacement prior to 1998, when this dataset begins. This timing is consistent with the evidence in chapter 4.

REFERENCES

Acemoglu, Daron, James A. Robinson, and Rafael J. Santos. 2013. "The Monopoly of Violence: Evidence from Colombia." *Journal of the European Economic Association* 11 (1): 5–44.

Actas. 1995. Comité de Vigilancia Epidemiológica en Violencia. Vols. 1–5. Apartadó: Municipal Archives.

———. 1996. Comité de Vigilancia Epidemiológica en Violencia. Vols. 6–15. Apartadó: Municipal Archives.

———. 1997. Comité de Vigilancia Epidemiológica en Violencia. Vols. 16–27. Apartadó: Municipal Archives.

Adhikari, Prakash. 2012. "The Plight of the Forgotten Ones: Civil War and Forced Migration." *International Studies Quarterly* 56 (3): 590–606.

Albertus, Michael, and Oliver Kaplan. 2013. "Land Reform as a Counterinsurgency Policy Evidence from Colombia." *Journal of Conflict Resolution* 57 (2): 198–231.

Amnesty International. 1997. *¿Qué debemos hacer para seguir viviendo? Los desplazados internos de Colombia desposeídos y exiliados en su propia tierra*. London: Amnesty International.

———. 2007. *Amnesty International Report 2007—Iraq*. http://www.refworld.org/docid/46558ecf5.html.

Arendt, Hannah. 1948. *The Origins of Totalitarianism*. London: André Deutsch.

Arjona, Ana. 2014. "Wartime Institutions: A Research Agenda." *Journal of Conflict Resolution* 58 (8): 1360–89.

———. 2016. *Rebelocracy: Social Order in the Colombian Civil War*. New York: Cambridge University Press.

Autesserre, Séverine. 2010. *The Trouble with the Congo: Local Violence and the Failure of International Peacebuilding*. New York: Cambridge University Press.

Bagley, Bruce M. 1988. "Colombia and the War on Drugs." *Foreign Affairs* 67 (1): 70–92.

Balcells, Laia. 2017. *Rivalry and Revenge: The Politics of Violence in Civil Wars*. New York: Cambridge University Press.

Balcells, Laia, and Abbey Steele. 2016. "Warfare, Political Identities, and Displacement in Spain and Colombia." *Political Geography* 51 (March): 15–29.

Bejarano, Ana María. 2001. "The Constitution of 1991: An Institutional Evaluation Seven Years Later." In *Violence in Colombia, 1990–2000: Waging War and Negotiating Peace*, edited by Charles Bergquist, Ricardo Peñaranda, and Gonzalo Sánchez, 53–74. Wilmington, DE: Scholarly Resources.

Bergquist, Charles. 1992. "The Labor Movement (1930–1946) and the Origins of the Violence." In *Violence in Colombia: The Contemporary Crisis in Historical Perspective*, edited by Charles Bergquist, Ricardo Peñaranda, and Gonzalo Sánchez, 51–72. Wilmington, DE: Scholarly Resources.

Biden, Joseph R., and Leslie H. Gelb. 2006. "Unity through Autonomy in Iraq." *New York Times*, May 1. http://www.nytimes.com/2006/05/01/opinion/01biden.html.

Branch, Adam. 2008. "Against Humanitarian Impunity: Rethinking Responsibility for Displacement and Disaster in Northern Uganda." *Journal of Intervention and Statebuilding* 2 (2): 151–73.

Bringa, Tone, and Debbie Christie. 1993. *We Are All Neighbors*. TV Film Production, ITV.

Brubaker, Rogers, and David D. Laitin. 1998. "Ethnic and Nationalist Violence." *Annual Review of Sociology* 24 (4): 423–52.

Bulutgil, H. Zeynep. 2009. "Territorial Conflict and Ethnic Cleansing." PhD diss., University of Chicago.

———. 2015. "Social Cleavages, Wartime Experiences, and Ethnic Cleansing in Europe." *Journal of Peace Research* 52 (5): 577–90.

———. 2016. *The Roots of Ethnic Cleansing in Europe*. New York: Cambridge University Press.

Bushnell, David. 1993. *The Making of Modern Colombia: A Nation in Spite of Itself*. Berkeley: University of California Press.

Cardona, Christopher Michael. 2008. "Politicians, Soldiers, and Cops: Colombia's La Violencia in Comparative Perspective." PhD diss., University of California, Berkeley.

Caris, Charles C., and Samuel Reynolds. 2014. *ISIS Governance in Syria*. Institute for the Study of War Middle East Security Report, no. 22 (July).

Carroll, Leah Anne. 2011. *Violent Democratization: Social Movements, Elites, and Politics in Colombia's Rural War Zones, 1984–2008*. Notre Dame, IN: University of Notre Dame Press.

Castro Caycedo, Germán. 1996. *En secreto*. Bogotá: Planeta.

Cederman, Lars-Erik, Kristian Skrede Gleditsch, and Halvard Buhaug. 2013. *Inequality, Grievances, and Civil War*. New York: Cambridge University Press.

Cederman, Lars-Erik, Kristian Skrede Gleditsch, and Simon Hug. 2013. "Elections and Ethnic Civil War." *Comparative Political Studies* 46 (3): 387–417.

Cepeda Castro, Iván. 2006. "Genocidio político: El caso de la Unión Patriótica en Colombia." *Revista Cejil* 1 (2): 101–12.

Cepeda Castro, Iván, and Claudia Girón Ortiz. 2005. "La segregación de las víctimas de la violencia política." In *Entre el perdón y el paredón: Preguntas y dilemas de la justicia transicional*, edited by Angelika Rettberg, 259–82. Bogotá: Universidad de los Andes.

Chacón, Mario. 2013. "In the Line of Fire: Political Violence and Decentralization in Colombia." SSRN Working Paper. http://dx.doi.org/10.2139/ssrn.2386667.

Chernick, Marc W. 1988. "Negotiated Settlement to Armed Conflict: Lessons from the Colombian Peace Process." *Journal of Inter-American Studies and World Affairs* 30 (4): 53–88.

———. 1999. "Negotiating Peace amid Multiple Forms of Violence." In *Comparative Peace Processes in Latin America*, edited by Cynthia J. Arnson, 159–95. Stanford, CA: Stanford University Press.

CIA. 1967. "Foreign and Domestic Influences on the Colombian Communist Party, 1957—August." US Central Intelligence Agency. Case number EO-1999-00625 (March 1).

Clavijo Ardila, Adolfo. 1996. "Estudio sociopolítico sobre Urabá." Report prepared for the Colombian army. From personal file.

Collier, Paul. 2009. *Wars, Guns, and Votes: Democracy in Dangerous Places*. New York: Random House.

Comisión Interamericana de Derechos Humanos. 1997. "Informe No. 5/97." Caso sobre admisibilidad. Organización de los Estados Americanos.

Comisión Intercongregacional de Justicia y Paz, Instituto Latinoamericano de Servicios Legales Alternativos, and Instituto Interamericano de Derechos Humanos. 1992. "El desplazamiento interno en Colombia." Memorias, Seminario-Foro Nacional "El desplazamiento interno en Colombia." Bogotá.

Comisión Nacional de Reparación y Reconciliación (Colombia), Grupo de Memoria Histórica. 2013. *¡Basta ya! Colombia: Memorias de guerra y dignidad*. Bogotá: Centro Nacional de Memoria Histórica.

Crisp, Jeff. 2000. "Who Has Counted the Refugees? UNHCR and the Politics of Numbers." In *Humanitarian Action: Social Science Connections*, edited by Stephen C. Lubkemann, Larry Minear, and Thomas G. Weiss, 33–62. Occasional Papers 37. Brown University, Thomas J. Watson Jr. Institute for International Studies.

Cubides, Fernando. 2001. "From Private to Public Violence: The Paramilitaries." In *Violence in Colombia, 1990–2000: Waging War and Negotiating Peace*, edited by Charles Bergquist, Ricardo Peñaranda, and Gonzalo Sánchez, 127–50. Wilmington, DE: Scholarly Resources.

Cusano, Chris. 2001. "Displaced Karens: Like Water on the Khu Leaf." In *Caught between Borders: Response Strategies of the Internally Displaced*, edited by Marc Vincent and Birgitte Refslund Sørensen, 138–71. London: Pluto Press.

Daly, Sarah Zukerman. 2016. *Organized Violence after Civil War: The Geography of Recruitment in Latin America*. New York: Cambridge University Press.

Darby, John P. 1990. "Intimidation and Intersection in a Small Belfast Community: The Water and the Fish." In *Political Violence: Ireland in Comparative Perspective*, edited by John P. Darby, Nicholas Dodge, and A. C. Hepburn, 83–102. Ottawa: University of Ottawa Press.

Darden, Keith A. Forthcoming. *Resisting Occupation: Mass Schooling and the Creation of Durable National Loyalties.* New York: Cambridge University Press.

Davenport, Christian, Will H. Moore, and Steven C. Poe. 2003. "Sometimes You Just Have to Leave: Domestic Threats and Refugee Movements, 1964–1989." *International Interactions* 29 (1): 27–55.

Deng, Francis. 1994. "Internally Displaced Persons: Report of the Representative of the Secretary-General. Addendum: Profiles in Displacement: Colombia." *Refugee Survey Quarterly* 14 (1).

Departamento Administrativo Nacional de Estadística (DANE). 2010a. "Indicadores demográficos y tablas abreviadas de mortalidad nacionales y departamentales 1985–2005." March. Bogotá. https://www.dane.gov.co/files/investigaciones/poblacion/. . ./8Tablasvida1985_2020.pdf, last checked June 18, 2010.

———. 2010b. "Series de población 1985–2020." March. Bogotá. https://www.dane.gov.co/files/investigaciones/poblacion/. . ./5Mortalidad85_05.pdf.

Douglas, Farah. 1999. "Massacres Imperil U.S. Aid to Colombia; Paramilitary Groups Linked to Army." *Washington Post*, January 31, A01.

Downes, Alexander B. 2007. "Draining the Sea by Filling the Graves: Investigating the Effectiveness of Indiscriminate Violence as a Counterinsurgency Strategy." *Civil Wars* 9 (4): 420–44.

———. 2008. *Targeting Civilians in War.* Ithaca, NY: Cornell University Press.

Dube, Oeindrila, and Suresh Naidu. 2015. "Bases, Bullets and Ballots: The Effect of US Military Aid on Political Conflict in Colombia." *Journal of Politics* 77 (1): 249–67.

Dudley, Steven S. 1997. "US Interests in Colombia." *Progressive* 61 (2): 26.

———. 2002. "Bad Timing for U.S. Bid to Extradite Warlord: Decision Could Prolong Colombia's Civil War." *Houston Chronicle*, October 2.

———. 2006. *Walking Ghosts: Murder and Guerrilla Politics in Colombia.* New York: Routledge.

Duncan, Gustavo. 2006. *Los señores de la guerra: De paramilitares, mafiosos y autodefensas en Colombia.* Bogotá: Planeta.

Eaton, Kent. 2006. "The Downside of Decentralization: Armed Clientelism in Colombia." *Security Studies* 15 (4): 533–62.

Echandía, Camilo. 2006. *Dos decadas del conflict interno en Colombia: 1986–2006.* Bogotá: Universidad de Externado.

Edwards, Scott. 2007. "A Composite Theory and Practical Model of Forced Displacement." PhD diss., University of Illinois at Urbana-Champaign.

El Espectador. 2015. "El rompecabezas del despojo." May 17.

———. 2009. "Castaño y Chiquita Brands." *El Espectador*, September 20. http://www.elespectador.com/impreso/articuloimpreso162489-castano-y-chiquita-brands.

El Tiempo. 1991. "A partir de hoy, no más intendencias ni comisarías." October 5. http://www.eltiempo.com/archivo/documento/MAM-166769.

———. 2000. "Paras quemaron cien casas en Ituango." September 9. http://www.eltiempo.com/archivo/documento/MAM-1271443.

———. 2013. "Condena a César Pérez por masacre de Segovia tardó 25 años." May 15. http://www.eltiempo.com/justicia/condenan-a-cesar-perez-por-masacre-de-segovia_12801023–4.

Esguerra, Adriana. 2009. *La paz frustrada en tierra firme: La historia de la Unión Patriótica en el Tolima.* Bogotá: Corporación Reiniciar.

Evans, Martin. 2007. "'The Suffering Is Too Great': Urban Internally Displaced Persons in the Casamance Conflict, Senegal." *Journal of Refugee Studies* 20 (1): 60–85.

Fajardo Landaeta, Jaime. 2009. "Por la paz de Colombia el EPL dispuso sus armas a discreción de la Constituyente." In *Biblioteca de paz, 1990–1994*, edited by Alvaro Villaraga Sarmiento. Vol. 3. Bogotá: Fundacion Cultura Democratica.

FARC-EP. 1997. "Pleno Ampliado Noviembre de 1997." http://www.farc-ep.co/pleno/pleno-ampliado-noviembre-de-1997.html.

Fariss, Christopher J., Fridolin J. Linder, Zachary M. Jones, Charles D. Crabtree, Megan A. Biek, Ana-Sophia M. Ross, Taranamol Kaur, and Michael Tsai. 2015. "Human Rights Texts: Converting Human Rights Primary Source Documents into Data." *PLOS ONE* 10 (9). http://humanrightstexts.org/.

Fattal, Alex. 2014. "Guerrilla Marketing: Information War and the Demobilization of FARC Rebels." PhD diss., Harvard University.

Fearon, James D., and David D. Laitin. 1996. "Explaining Interethnic Cooperation." *American Political Science Review* 90 (4): 715–35.

Fellman, Michael. 1989. *Inside War: The Guerrilla Conflict in Missouri during the Civil War.* New York: Oxford University Press.

Ferro Medina, Juan Guillermo, and Graciela Uribe Ramón. 2002. *El orden de la guerra, las FARC-EP: Entre la organización y la política.* Bogotá: Centro editorial Javeriano, CEJA.

Fjelde, Hanne, and Lisa Hultman. 2014. "Weakening the Enemy: A Disaggregated Study of Violence against Civilians in Africa." *Journal of Conflict Resolution* 58 (7): 1230–57.

Flores, Thomas Edward. 2014. "Vertical Inequality, Land Reform, and Insurgency in Colombia." *Peace Economics, Peace Science and Public Policy* 20 (1): 5–31.

Flores, Thomas Edward, and Irfan Nooruddin. 2012. "The Effect of Elections on Post-conflict Peace and Reconstruction." *Journal of Politics* 74 (2): 558–70.

Galula, David. 1963. *Pacification in Algeria, 1956–1958.* Santa Monica, CA: Rand Corp.

Gettleman, Jeffrey. 2008. "Rebels Kill Nearly 200 in Congo, UN Says." *New York Times*, December 30. www.nytimes.com/2008/12/30/world/africa/30uganda.html.

Gilhodés, Pierre. 2007. "El ejército colombiano analiza la violencia." In *Pasado y presente de la violencia en Colombia*, edited by Gonzalo Sánchez and Ricardo Peñaranda, 3rd ed., 297–320. Medellín: La Carreta Editores.

Gill, Stephen. 2016. "21 Colombia Soldiers Convicted of Executing Civilians in Iconic 'False Positives' Case." *Colombia Reports*, November 18. http://colombiareports.com/21-soldiers-convicted-executing-civilians-iconic-false-positives-case/.

Giraldo, Fernando. 2001. *Democracia y discurso político en la Unión Patriótica.* Bogotá: Centro Editorial Javeriano (CEJA).

Goodwin, Jeffrey, and Theda Skocpol. 1989. "Explaining Revolutions in the Contemporary Third World." *Politics and Society* 17:489–509.

Gottwald, Martin. 2003. "Protecting Colombian Refugees in the Andean Region: The Fight against Invisibility." New Issues in Refugee Research Working Paper Series, no. 81.

Gould, Roger V. 1991. "Multiple Networks and Mobilization in the Paris Commune, 1871." *American Sociological Review* 56 (6): 716–29.

———. 1995. *Insurgent Identities: Class, Community, and Protest in Paris from 1848 to the Commune.* Chicago: University of Chicago Press.

Granovetter, Mark. 1978. "Threshold Models of Collective Behavior." *American Journal of Sociology* 83 (6): 1420–43.

Greenhill, Kelly. 2010. *Weapons of Mass Migration: Forced Displacement, Coercion, and Foreign Policy.* Ithaca, NY: Cornell University Press.

Gutiérrez Sanín, Francisco. 2003. "Heating Up and Cooling Down: Armed Agencies, Civilians, and the Oligopoly of Violence in the Colombian War." Paper presented at the workshop on Obstacles to Robust Negotiated Settlements, hosted by the Santa Fe Institute and Universidad Javeriana, Bogotá.

———. 2004. "Criminal Rebels? A Discussion of Civil War and Criminality from the Colombian Experience." *Politics & Society* 32 (2): 257–85.

Gutiérrez Sanín, Francisco, Tatiana Acevedo, and Juan Manuel Viatela. 2007. "Violent Liberalism? State, Conflict, and Political Regime in Colombia, 1930–2006." Crisis States Programme Working Papers Series, no. 19 (November).

Gutiérrez Sanín, Francisco, and Elisabeth J. Wood. 2014. "Ideology in Civil War: Instrumental Adoption and Beyond." *Journal of Peace Research* 51 (2): 213–26. doi:10.1177/0022343313514073.

———. 2017. "What Should We Mean by 'Pattern of Political Violence'? Repertoire, Targeting, Frequency, and Technique." *Perspectives on Politics* 15 (1): 20–41.

Guzmán Campos, Germán, Orlando Fals Borda, and Eduardo Umaña Luna. 1962. *La violencia en Colombia: Estudio de un proceso social.* Vol. 2. Bogotá: Universidad Nacional.

Harff, Barbara. 2003. "No Lessons Learned from the Holocaust? Assessing Risks of Genocide and Political Mass Murder since 1955." *American Political Science Review* 97 (1): 57–73.

Heilbrunn, Otto. 1962. *Partisan Warfare.* London: George Allen & Unwin.

Helguera, J. León. 1961. "The Changing Role of the Military in Colombia." *Journal of Inter-American Studies* 3 (3): 351–58.

Henderson, James D. 1985. *When Colombia Bled: A History of La Violencia in Tolima.* Tuscaloosa: University of Alabama Press.

Hirschman, Albert O. (1970) 1980. *Exit, Voice, and Loyalty.* Cambridge: Cambridge University Press.

Hobsbawm, Eric J. 1963a. "The Revolutionary Situation in Colombia." *World Today* 19 (6): 248–58.

———. 1963b. "The Anatomy of Violence." *New Society* 28 (April): 16–18.

———. 1996. *The Age of Extremes: A History of the World, 1914–1991.* New York: Vintage Books.

Human Rights Watch. 1998. "War without Quarter." *Human Rights Watch Reports.* http://www.hrw.org/legacy/reports98/colombia/.

———. 2003. "Stolen Children: Abduction and Recruitment in Northern Uganda." *Human Rights Watch Reports* 15 (7). http://www.hrw.org/reports/2003/uganda0303/.

Hyde, Susan D., and Nikolay Marinov. 2012. "Which Elections Can Be Lost?" *Political Analysis* 20 (2): 191–210.

Ibáñez, Ana María. 2008. *El desplazamiento forzoso en Colombia: Un camino sin retorno a la pobreza.* Bogotá: Universidad de los Andes.

Ibáñez, Ana María, and Andrea Velásquez. 2006. "El proceso de identificación de víctimas de los conflictos civiles: Una evaluación para la población desplazada en Colombia." Documento CEDE. https://economia.uniandes.edu.co/components/com_booklibrary/ebooks/d2006-36.pdf.

IDMC. 2006. *Nepal: IDP Return Still a Trickle Despite Ceasefire.* Internal Displacement Monitoring Centre Report, October 16. http://www.refworld.org/docid/4550556f4.html.

———. 2008. *Challenges of Forced Displacement within Iraq: A Profile of the Internal Displacement Situation.* Internal Displacement Monitoring Centre Report, December 29. http://www.internal-displacement.org/middle-east-and-north-africa/iraq/2008/challenges-of-forced-displacement-within-iraq.

———. 2009. *Need for Continued Improvement in Response to Protracted Displacement.* Internal Displacement Monitoring Centre Report, October 26. http://www.refworld.org/docid/4ae574852.html.

———. 2010. "Internal Displacement: Global Overview of Trends and Developments in 2009—Yemen." Internal Displacement Monitoring Centre, May 17. http://www.refworld.org/docid/4bf252700.html.

———. 2011. "Syria: Displacement Continues as Anti-Government Protests Grow." Internal Displacement Monitoring Centre, July 15. http://www.refworld.org/docid/4e3944ce2.html.

———. 2012a. "People Internally Displaced by Conflict and Violence—Côte d'Ivoire." Internal Displacement Monitoring Centre Global Overview 2011, April 19. http://www.refworld.org/docid/4f97fb6328.html.

———. 2012b. "People Internally Displaced by Conflict and Violence—Nigeria." Internal Displacement Monitoring Centre Global Overview 2011, April 19. http://www.refworld.org/docid/4f97fb582b.html.

———. 2013. "People Internally Displaced by Conflict and Violence—Occupied Palestinian Territory." Internal Displacement Monitoring Centre Global Overview 2012, April 29. http://www.refworld.org/docid/517fb05918.html.

———. 2014a. "Global Overview 2014: People Internally Displaced by Conflict and Violence—Thailand." Internal Displacement Monitoring Centre Global Overview 2014, May 14. http://www.refworld.org/docid/5374746a3b2.html.

———. 2014b. "People Internally Displaced by Conflict and Violence—Thailand." Internal Displacement Monitoring Centre Global Overview 2014, May 14. http://www.refworld.org/docid/5374746a3b2.html.

International Crisis Group. 2006. *The Next Iraqi War? Sectarianism and Civil Conflict.* International Crisis Group Middle East / North Africa Report No. 52 (February 27).

https://www.crisisgroup.org/middle-east-north-africa/gulf-and-arabian-peninsula/iraq/next-iraqi-war-sectarianism-and-civil-conflict.

Isacson, Adam, and Abbey Steele. 2001. *"Steel Magnolias": Adjusting to Reality in Putumayo.* Center for International Policy Conference Report, December 14. http://www.ciponline.org/research/entry/steel-magnolias-reality-in-putumayo.

Jaramillo, Daniel García-Peña. 2005. "La relación del estado colombiano con el fenómeno paramilitar: Por el esclarecimiento histórico." *Análisis Político,* no. 53: 58–76.

Jennings, E., A. Birkenes, J. H. Eschenbacher, M. Foaleng, and K. Khalil. 2008. *Internal Displacement: Global Overview of Trends and Developments in 2007.* Internal Displacement Monitoring Centre. April. http://www.internal-displacement.org/publications/2008/internal-displacement-global-overview-of-trends-and-developments-in-2007.

Jentzsch, Corinna, Stathis N. Kalyvas, and Livia I. Schubiger. 2015. "Militias in Civil Wars." *Journal of Conflict Resolution* 59 (5): 755–69.

Kalyvas, Stathis N. 1999. "Wanton and Senseless? The Logic of Massacres in Algeria." *Rationality and Society* 11 (3): 243–85.

———. 2003. "The Ontology of 'Political Violence': Action and Identity in Civil Wars." *Perspectives on Politics* 1:475–94.

———. 2005. "Warfare in Civil Wars." In *Rethinking the Nature of War,* edited by Isabelle Duyvesteyn and Jan Ångström, 88–108. Abingdon, UK: Frank Cass.

———. 2006. *The Logic of Violence in Civil War.* New York: Cambridge University Press.

———. 2008. "Ethnic Defection in Civil War." *Comparative Political Studies* 41 (8): 1043–68.

Kalyvas, Stathis N., and Laia Balcells. 2010. "International System and Technologies of Rebellion: How the Cold War Shaped Internal Conflict." *American Political Science Review* 104 (3): 415–29.

Kalyvas, Stathis N., and Matthew Adam Kocher. 2007. "Ethnic Cleavages and Irregular War: Iraq and Vietnam." *Politics and Society* 35 (2): 183–223.

Kaplan, Oliver. 2013. "Protecting Civilians in Civil War: The Institution of the ATCC in Colombia." *Journal of Peace Research* 50 (3): 351–67.

Karl, Robert A. 2011. "The Fearful Night Continues: Displacement and Citizenship in Late Violencia Colombia." Paper presented at the University of Chicago Latin American History Workshop. November 17.

———. 2017. *Forgotten Peace: Reform, Violence, and the Making of Contemporary Colombia.* Berkeley: University of California Press.

Keefer, Philip. 2010. "Database of Political Institutions: Changes and Variable Definitions." Development Research Group, World Bank.

Keegan, John. 1994. *A History of Warfare.* New York: Vintage Books.

King, Gary, Michael Tomz, and Jason Wittenberg. 2000. "Making the Most of Statistical Analyses: Improving Interpretation and Presentation." *American Journal of Political Science* 44 (2): 347–61.

Kocher, Matthew Adam. 2002. "The Decline of PKK and the Viability of a One-State Solution in Turkey." *International Journal on Multicultural Societies* 4:1–20.

———. 2004. "Human Ecology and Civil Wars." PhD diss., University of Chicago.

Korn, David A. 2001. *Exodus within Borders: An Introduction to the Crisis of Internal Displacement*. Washington, DC: Brookings Institution Press.

Kunz, Egon F. 1973. "The Refugee in Flight: Kinetic Models and Forms of Displacement." *International Migration Review* 7 (2): 125–46.

Kuran, Timur. 1991. "The East European Revolution of 1989: Is It Surprising That We Were Surprised?" *American Economic Review* 81 (2): 121–25.

LeGrand, Catherine. 1984. "Labour Acquisition and Social Conflict on the Colombian Frontier." *Journal of Latin American Studies* 16:27–49.

———. 1992. "Agrarian Antecedents of the Violence." In *Violence in Colombia: The Contemporary Crisis in Historical Perspective*, edited by Charles Bergquist, Ricardo Peñaranda, and Gonzalo Sánchez, 31–50. Wilmington, DE: Scholarly Resources.

———. 2003. "The Colombian Crisis in Historical Perspective." *Canadian Journal of Latin American and Caribbean Studies* 28 (55–56): 165–209.

Lichbach, Mark I. 1994. "What Makes Rational Peasants Revolutionary? Dilemma, Paradox, and Irony in Peasant Collective Action." *World Politics* 46 (3): 383–418.

Lipset, Seymour M., and Stein Rokkan. 1967. "Cleavage Structures, Party Systems, and Voter Alignments: An Introduction." In *Party Systems and Voter Alignments: Cross-National Perspectives*. Toronto: Free Press.

Lischer, Sarah Kenyon. 2005. *Dangerous Sanctuaries: Refugee Camps, Civil War, and the Dilemmas of Humanitarian Aid*. Ithaca, NY: Cornell University Press.

———. 2008. "Security and Displacement in Iraq: Responding to the Forced Migration Crisis." *International Security* 33 (2): 95–119.

Llorente, María Victoria. 2005. "Demilitarization in Times of War? Police Reform in Colombia." In *Public Security and Police Reform in the Americas*, edited by John Baily and Lucia Dammert, 180–212. Pittsburgh: University of Pittsburgh Press.

Lomo, Zachary, and Lucy Hovil. 2004. "Behind the Violence: The War in Northern Uganda." Institute for Security Studies Monographs, no. 99. Sabinet Online.

López Hernández, Claudia. 2005. "Del control territorial a la Acción Política." *Revista Arcanos* 11:39–47. http://www.verdadabierta.com/documentos/politica-ilegal/el-estado-y-los-paras/708-del-control-territorial-a-la-accion-politica-arcanos-11-arco-iris.

———. 2010. "La refundación de la patria: De la teoría a la evidencia." In *Y refundaron la patria: De cómo mafiosos y políticos reconfiguraron el estado colombiano*, edited by Claudia López Hernández, 29–78. Bogotá: Debate.

Lubkemann, Stephen C. 2005. "Migratory Coping in Wartime Mozambique: An Anthropology of Violence and Displacement in 'Fragmented Wars.'" *Journal of Peace Research* 42 (4): 493–512.

———. 2008. *Culture in Chaos: An Anthropology of the Social Condition in War*. Chicago: University of Chicago Press.

Lupu, Noam, and Susan Stokes. 2010. "Democracy, Interrupted: Regime Change and Partisanship in Twentieth-Century Argentina." *Electoral Studies* 29 (1): 91–104.

Lyall, Jason. 2009. "Does Indiscriminate Violence Incite Insurgent Attacks? Evidence from Chechnya." *Journal of Conflict Resolution* 53 (3): 331–62.

Machiavelli, Niccolò. (1532) 1910. *The Prince*. Edited by S. T. More, M. Luther, and W. Roper. New York: P. F. Collier & Son.

Mampilly, Zachariah Cherian. 2011. *Rebel Rulers: Insurgent Governance and Civilian Life during War*. Ithaca, NY: Cornell University Press.

Mann, Michael. 2005. *The Dark Side of Democracy: Explaining Ethnic Cleansing*. Cambridge: Cambridge University Press.

Margesson, Rhoda, Andorra Bruno, and Jeremy M. Sharp. 2009. *Iraqi Refugees and Internally Displaced Persons: A Deepening Humanitarian Crisis?* Congressional Research Service Report for Congress. Order Code RL33936 (February). Washington, DC. http://fpc.state.gov/documents/organization/82978.pdf.

Marks, Tom. 2003. "Colombian Army Counterinsurgency." *Crime, Law and Social Change* 40 (1): 77–105.

Martínez, Ariel Fernando Ávila. 2010. "Injerencia política de los grupos armados ilegales." In *Y refundaron la patria: De cómo mafiosos y políticos reconfiguraron el estado colombiano*, edited by Claudia López Hernández, 79–214. Bogotá: Debate.

Marulanda, Elsy. 1991. *Colonización y conflicto: Las lecciones del Sumapaz*. Bogotá: Universidad Nacional de Colombia—IEPRI.

Mason, T. David, and Dale A. Krane. 1989. "The Political Economy of Death Squads: Toward a Theory of the Impact of State-Sanctioned Terror." *International Studies Quarterly* 33 (2): 175–98.

Masullo, Juan. 2015. *The Power of Staying Put: Nonviolent Resistance against Armed Groups in Colombia*. Washington, DC: International Center on Nonviolent Conflict Monograph Series. https://www.nonviolent-conflict.org/wp-content/uploads/2016/01/The-Power-of-Staying-Put.pdf.

———. 2017. "The Evolution of Noncooperation in Civil War." PhD diss., European University Institute.

McDermott, Jeremy. 2014. "The Bacrim and Their Position in Colombia's Underworld." Insight Crime: Investigation and Analysis of Organized Crime, May 2. http://www.insightcrime.org/investigations/bacrim-and-their-position-in-colombia-underworld.

Medina Gallego, Carlos, and Mireya Téllez Ardila. 1994. *La violencia parainstitucional, paramilitar y parapolicial en Colombia*. Bogotá: Rodríguez Quito Editores.

Melander, Erik, and Magnus Oberg. 2007. "The Threat of Violence and Forced Migration: Geographical Scope Trumps Intensity of Fighting." *Civil Wars* 9 (2): 156–73.

Metelits, Claire. 2009. *Inside Insurgency: Violence, Civilians, and Revolutionary Group Behavior*. New York: NYU Press.

Molano, Alfredo. 1987. *Selva adentro: Una historia oral de la colonización del Guaviare*. Bogotá: Ancora.

———. 1992. "Violence and Land Colonization." In *Violence in Colombia: The Contemporary Crisis in Historical Perspective*, edited by Charles Bergquist, Ricardo Peñaranda, and Gonzalo Sánchez, 195–216. Wilmington, DE: Scholarly Resources.

———. 1994. *Trochas y fusiles*. Bogotá: Instituto de Estudios Políticos y Relaciones Internacionales.

Molina, Mauricio Aranguren. 2001. *Mi confesión: Carlos Castaño revela sus secretos*. Bogotá: La Oveja Negra.

Monroy Giraldo, Juan Carlos. 2009. "Fiscalía investigará denuncias de alias Zamir." *El Colombiano*, July 19. http://www.elcolombiano.com/historico/fiscalia_investigara_denuncias_de_alias_zamir-DIEC_52023.

Moore, Will H., and Stepen M. Shellman. 2004. "Fear of Persecution: Forced Migration, 1952–1995." *Journal of Conflict Resolution* 48 (5): 723–45.

National Security Archives. 2011. "The Chiquita Papers." April 7. http://nsarchive.gwu.edu/NSAEBB/NSAEBB340/.

Nossiter, Adam. 2013. "In Nigeria, 'Killing People without Asking Who They Are.'" *New York Times*, June 6. http://www.nytimes.com/2013/06/06/world/africa/nigerian-refugees-accuse-army-of-excess-force.html?hp\&_r=0.

Ocampo, Gloria Isabel. 2003. "Urbanización por invasión: Conflicto urbano, clientelismo y resistencia en Córdoba." *Revista Colombiana de Antropología* 39.

Oppenheim, Ben, Abbey Steele, Juan F. Vargas, and Michael Weintraub. 2015. "True Believers, Deserters, and Traitors: Who Leave Insurgent Groups and Why." *Journal of Conflict Resolution* 59 (5): 794–823.

Oquist, Paul H. 1978. *Violencia, conflicto y política en Colombia*. Bogotá: Instituto de Estudios Colombianos.

Ortiz Sarmiento, Carlos Miguel. 1985. *Estado y subversión en Colombia: La violencia en el Quindío, años 50*. Vol. 4. Serie Historia Contemporánea, Universidad de los Andes.

——. 2007. *Urabá: Pulsiones de vida y desafíos de muerte*. Medellín: La Carreta Editores.

Paine, Thomas. (1776) 1998. *Rights of Man, Common Sense, and Other Political Writings*. New York: Oxford University Press.

Parsons, James J. 1967. *Antioquia's Corridor to the Sea: An Historical Geography of the Settlement of Urabá*. Berkeley: University of California Press.

——. 1968. *Antioqueño Colonization in Western Colombia*. Berkeley: University of California Press.

Pastoral Social. 2001a. *Desplazamiento forzado en Antioquia: Magdalena Medio. 2.* Bogotá: Conferencia Episcopal de Colombia.

——. 2001b. *Desplazamiento forzado en Antioquia: Urabá. 9.* Bogotá: Conferencia Episcopal de Colombia.

Pécaut, Daniel. 1989. *Crónica de dos décadas de política colombiana 1968–1988*. Bogotá: Siglo Veintiuno.

——. 1992. "Guerillas and Violence." In *Violence in Colombia: The Contemporary Crisis in Historical Perspective*, edited by Charles Bergquist, Gonzalo Sánchez, and Ricardo Peñaranda, 217–40. Wilmington, DE: Scholarly Resources.

Peñaranda, Ricardo. 2007. "La guerra en el papel: Balance de la producción sobre la violencia durante los años noventa." In *Pasado y presente de la violencia en Colombia*, edited by Gonzalo Sánchez and Ricardo Peñaranda, 3rd ed., 33–46. Medellín: La Carreta Editores.

Pérez Murcia, Luis Eduardo. 2001. "Una mirada empírica a los determinantes del desplazamiento forzado en Colombia." *Cuadernos de Economía* 20 (35): 205–43.

Petersen, Roger Dale. 2002. *Understanding Ethnic Violence: Fear, Hatred, and Resentment in Twentieth-Century Eastern Europe*. New York: Cambridge University Press.

Petersen, William. 1958. "A General Typology of Migration." *American Sociological Review* 23 (3): 256–66.

Pizarro Leongómez, Eduardo. 1992. "Revolutionary Guerrilla Groups in Colombia." In *Violence in Colombia: The Contemporary Crisis in Historical Perspective*, edited by Charles Bergquist, Ricardo Peñaranda, and Gonzalo Sánchez, 169–94. Wilmington, DE: Scholarly Resources.

———. (1986) 2007. "La insurgencia armada: Raíces y perspectivas." In *Pasado y presente de la violencia en Colombia*, edited by Gonzalo Sánchez and Ricardo Peñaranda, 3rd ed., 321–38. Bogotá: La Carreta Editores.

Price, Megan, and Anita Gohdes. 2014. "Searching for Trends: Analyzing Patterns in Conflict Violence Data." Political Violence at a Glance. April 2. https://political violenceataglance.org/2014/04/02/searching-for-trends-analyzing-patterns-in-conflict-violence-data/.

Przeworski, Adam. 1991. *Democracy and the Market: Political and Economic Reforms in Eastern Europe and Latin America*. Cambridge: Cambridge University Press.

Ramírez Tobón, William. 2001. "Colonización armada, poder local y territorialización privada." *Journal of Iberian and Latin American Studies* 7 (2): 63–81.

Reiniciar. 2006. *Historia de un genocidio: El exterminio de la Unión Patriótica en Urabá y el plan retorno*. Bogotá: Corporación Reiniciar.

———. 2009. *Relatos de mujeres: De viva voz, memorias del genocidio de la Unión Patriótica*. Bogotá: Corporación Reiniciar.

Restrepo, Luís Alberto. 1992. "The Crisis of the Current Political Regime and Its Possible Outcomes." In *Violence in Colombia: The Contemporary Crisis in Historical Perspective*, edited by Charles Bergquist, Ricardo Peñaranda, and Gonzalo Sánchez, 273–92. Wilmington, DE: Scholarly Resources.

Reyes Posada, Alejandro. 1994. "Territorios de la violencia en Colombia." In *Territorios, regiones y sociedades*, edited by Renán Silva. Cali: Universidad del Valle.

———. (1991) 2007. "Paramilitares en Colombia: Contexto, aliados, y consecuencias." In *Pasado y presente de la violencia en Colombia*, edited by Gonzalo Sánchez and Ricardo Peñaranda, 3rd ed., 353–61. Bogotá: La Carreta Editores.

———. 2009. *Guerreros y campesinos: El despojo de la tierra en Colombia*. Bogotá: Grupo Editorial Norma.

Reyes Posada, Alejandro, and Hernán Correa. 1992. *Pacificar la paz: Lo que no se ha negociado en los acuerdos de paz*. Bogotá: Universidad Nacional de Colombia—IEPRI, CINEP, Comisión Andina de Juristas y Centro de Cooperación al Indígena.

Rich, Paul B., and Richard Stubbs. 1997. "Introduction: The Counter-Insurgent State." In *The Counter-Insurgent State: Guerrilla Warfare and State Building in the Twentieth Century*, edited by Paul B. Rich and Richard Stubbs, 1–25. New York: St. Martin's.

Robinson, James A. 2013. "Colombia: Another 100 Years of Solitude." *Current History* 112 (751): 43–48.

Rodríguez-Franco, Diana. 2016. "Internal Wars, Taxation, and State Building." *American Sociological Review* 81 (1): 190–213.

Roldán, Mary. 2002. *Blood and Fire: La Violencia in Antioquia, Colombia, 1946–1953*. Durham, NC: Duke University Press.

Romero, Mauricio. 2000. "Political Identities and Armed Conflict in Colombia: The Case of the Department of Córdoba." *Beyond Law* 7 (21): 81–101.

———. 2003. *Paramilitares y autodefensas 1982–2003*. Bogotá: IEPRI-Editorial Planeta.

——, ed. 2007. *Parapolítica: La ruta de la expansión paramilitar y los acuerdos políticos*. Corporación Nuevo Arco Iris. Bogotá: Intermedio Editores.

Ron, James. 2003. *Frontiers and Ghettos: State Violence in Serbia and Israel*. Berkeley: University of California Press.

Ronderos, María Teresa. 2014. *Guerras recicladas: Una historia periodística del paramilitarismo en Colombia*. Bogotá: Aguilar.

Salehyan, Idean, and Kristian Skrede Gleditsch. 2006. "Refugees and the Spread of Civil War." *International Organization* 60 (2): 335–66.

Sánchez, Fabio, and Mario Chacón. 2005. "Conflict, State and Decentralisation: From Social Progress to an Armed Dispute for Local Control, 1974–2002." Crisis States Research Centre Working Paper. Crisis States Research Centre, London School of Economics; Political Science.

Sánchez, Fabio, and María del Mar Palau. 2006. "Conflict, Decentralisation and Local Governance in Colombia, 1974–2004." Documento CEDE. Universidad de los Andes.

Sánchez, Gonzalo. 1992. "The Violence: An Interpretive Synthesis." In *Violence in Colombia: The Contemporary Crisis in Historical Perspective*, edited by Charles Bergquist, Ricardo Peñaranda, and Gonzalo Sánchez, 75–124. Wilmington, DE: Scholarly Resources.

——. 2001. "Introduction: Problems of Violence, Prospects for Peace." In *Violence in Colombia, 1990–2000: Waging War and Negotiating Peace*, edited by Charles Bergquist, Ricardo Peñaranda, and Gonzalo Sánchez. Wilmington, DE: Scholarly Resources.

Sánchez, Gonzalo, and Donny Meertens. 1983. *Bandoleros, gamonales y campesinos: El caso de la violencia en Colombia*. Bogotá: El Ancora.

Schemo, Diana Jean. 1998. "A Coca-Trade Jungle Town Trapped by Colombia's Strife." *New York Times*, October 11, 3.

Schoultz, Lars. 1972. "Urbanization and Changing Voting Patterns: Colombia, 1946–1970." *Political Science Quarterly* 87 (1): 22–45.

Schubiger, Livia I. 2015. "One for All? State Violence and Insurgent Cohesion." Paper presented at the Kobe University Satsuki Political Science Meeting, May 14.

Scott, James C. 1998. *Seeing Like a State: How Certain Schemes to Improve the Human Condition Have Failed*. New Haven, CT: Yale University Press.

——. 2009. *The Art of Not Being Governed: An Anarchist History of Upland Southeast Asia*. New Haven, CT: Yale University Press.

Secretariat, AI International. 2008. "Leave Us in Peace: Targeting Civilians in Colombia's Internal Armed Conflict." Amnesty International. https://www.amnesty.org/en/documents/AMR23/023/2008/en/.

Semana. 1988. "Misterio antropológico." June 13. http://www.semana.com/nacion/articulo/misterio-antropologico/10329-3.

——. 1989. "El 'dossier' paramilitar." June 12. http://www.semana.com/especiales/articulo/el-dossier-paramilitar/11674-3.

——. 1998. "La tierra del olvido." July 13. http://www.semana.com/nacion/articulo/la-tierra-del-olvido/26655-3.

——. 2008. "El 'Negro Vladimir' reconocerá el asesinato de 14 miembros de la UP." September 8. http://www.semana.com/on-line/articulo/el-negro-vladimir-reconocera-asesinato-14-miembros-up/95145-3.

Sepp, Kalev I. 1992. "Resettlement, Regroupment, Reconcentration: Deliberate Government-Directed Population Relocation in Support of Counter-Insurgency Operations." Master's thesis, US Army Command, General Staff College.

Seybolt, Taylor B., Jay D. Aronson, and Baruch Fischhoff, eds. 2013. *Counting Civilian Casualties: An Introduction to Recording and Estimating Nonmilitary Deaths in Conflict*. Oxford: Oxford University Press.

Shugart, Matthew Soberg. 1992. "Guerrillas and Elections: An Institutionalist Perspective on the Costs of Conflict and Competition." *International Studies Quarterly* 36 (2): 121–51.

Skarbek, David. 2014. *The Social Order of the Underworld: How Prison Gangs Govern the American Penal System*. Oxford: Oxford University Press.

Snyder, Jack L. 2000. *From Voting to Violence: Democratization and Nationalist Conflict*. New York: Norton.

Staniland, Paul. 2014. *Networks of Rebellion: Explaining Insurgent Cohesion and Collapse*. Ithaca, New York: Cornell University Press.

———. 2015. "Armed Groups and Militarized Elections." *International Studies Quarterly* 59 (4): 694–705. doi:10.1111/isqu.12195.

Steele, Abbey. 2009. "Seeking Safety: Avoiding Displacement and Choosing Destinations in Civil Wars." *Journal of Peace Research* 46 (3): 419–29.

———. 2011. "Electing Displacement: Political Cleansing in Apartadó, Colombia. *Journal of Conflict Resolution* 55 (3): 423–45.

———. 2017. "IDP Resettlement and Collective Violence during Civil Wars: Evidence from Colombia." Unpublished paper. University of Amsterdam.

Steele, Abbey, and Livia I. Schubiger. 2015. "Democracy and Civil War: The Case of Colombia." Paper presented at the Universidad del Rosario, December 9.

Steiner, Claudia. 2000. *Imaginación y poder: El encuentro del interior con la costa en Urabá, 1900–1960*. Medellín: Editorial Universidad de Antioquia.

Stepputat, Finn. 1999a. "Dead Horses?" *Journal of Refugee Studies* 12 (4): 416–19.

———. 1999b. "Politics of Displacement in Guatemala." *Journal of Historical Sociology* 12 (1): 54–80.

Straus, Scott. 2001. "Contested Meanings and Conflicting Imperatives: A Conceptual Analysis of Genocide." *Journal of Genocide Research* 3 (3): 349–75.

———. 2006. *The Order of Genocide: Race, Power, and War in Rwanda*. Ithaca, NY: Cornell University Press.

Stubbs, Richard. 2004. *Hearts and Minds in Guerrilla Warfare: The Malayan Emergency, 1948–1960*. New York: Marshall Cavendish Academic.

Suárez, Andrés Fernando. 2007. *Identidades políticas y exterminio recíproco: Masacres y guerra en Urabá 1991–2001*. Medellín: La Carreta Editores.

Sweig, Julia. 2002. "What Kind of War for Colombia?" *Foreign Affairs* 81 (5): 122–41.

Tajima, Yuhki. 2014. *The Institutional Origins of Communal Violence: Indonesia's Transition from Authoritarian Rule*. Cambridge: Cambridge University Press.

Tate, Winifred. 2001. "Paramilitaries in Colombia." *Brown Journal of World Affairs* 8 (1): 163–76.

Taussig, Michael T. 2005. *Law in a Lawless Land: Diary of a "Limpieza" in Colombia*. Chicago: University of Chicago Press.

Tilly, Charles. 1992. *Coercion, Capital, and European States: AD 990–1992.* New York: Wiley-Blackwell.

Tilly, Charles, and Sidney Tarrow. 2007. *Contentious Politics.* Oxford: Oxford University Press.

Tolnay, Stewart E., and E. M. Beck. 1992. "Racial Violence and Black Migration in the American South, 1910 to 1930." *American Sociological Review* 57 (1): 103–16.

Trinquier, Roger. 1964. *Modern Warfare: A French View of Counterinsurgency.* London: Pall Mall.

UNHCR. 2000. "'Return Is Struggle, Not Resignation': Lessons from the Repatriation of Guatemalan Refugees from Mexico." http://www.refworld.org/docid/4ff585ad2.html.

———. 2001. "The Repatriation Predicament of Burmese Refugees in Thailand: A Preliminary Analysis." http://www.refworld.org/docid/4ff5661a2.html.

———. 2003. "Protecting Colombian Refugees in the Andean Region: The Fight against Invisibility." http://www.refworld.org/docid/4ff3f1372.html.

———. 2006. "UNHCR Position on the International Protection Needs of Asylum-Seekers from Sri Lanka." http://www.refworld.org/docid/459a1fcb2.html.

———. 2010. "Definitions and Obligations." http://www.unhcr.org.au/basicdef.shtml.

———. 2012. "State of the World's Refugees: In Search of Solidarity." http://www.unhcr.org/4fc5ceca9.html.

———. 2015. "World at War: UNHCR Global Trends Forced Displacement 2014." http://unhcr.org/556725e69.html.

Valentino, Benjamin. 2004. *Final Solutions: Mass Killing and Genocide in the 20th Century.* Ithaca, NY: Cornell University Press.

Vargas, Gonzalo. 2009. "Armed Conflict, Crime and Social Protest in South Bolívar, Colombia (1996–2004)." Crisis States Programme Working Papers Series, no. 65.

Varshney, Ashutosh. 2003. *Ethnic Conflict and Civic Life: Hindus and Muslims in India.* New Haven, CT: Yale University Press.

Velásquez, Carlos Alfonso. 1996. Informe. May 31. http://nsarchive.gwu.edu/NSAEBB/NSAEBB327/informe_sobre_carrera_militar_general_rito_alejo_del_rio.pdf.

VerdadAbierta.com. 2009. "El dinero del banano sirvió para financiar la guerra." *Verdad Abierta,* February 16. http://www.verdadabierta.com/victimas-seccion/asesinatos-colectivos/859-ni-las-balas-acabaron-con-sintrainagro.

———. 2010. "Raúl Jazbún habla de los 'paras' y los negocios del banano y la palma." *Verdad Abierta,* June 3. http://www.verdadabierta.com/negocios-ilegales/otros-negocios-criminales/2492-los-paras-y-los-negocios-del-banano-y-la-palma.

———. 2014. "Los políticos capturados del Urabá antioqueño." *Verdad Abierta,* August 28. http://www.verdadabierta.com/politica-ilegal/parapoliticos/5423-el-aleman-y-su-proyecto-politico-en-uraba.

Villarraga Sarmiento, Alvaro. 1996. "Pluralización política y oposición." In *La oposición política en Colombia,* 47–72. Bogotá: Fescol IEPRI—Universidad Nacional de Colombia.

Vincent, Marc. 2001. "Introduction and Background." In *Caught between Borders: Response Strategies of the Internally Displaced,* edited by Marc Vincent and Birgitte Refslund Sørensen, 1–12. London: Pluto.

Weidmann, Nils B., and Idean Salehyan. 2013. "Violence and Ethnic Segregation: A Computational Model Applied to Baghdad." *International Studies Quarterly* 57 (1): 52–64.

Wilkinson, Steven. 2006. *Votes and Violence: Electoral Competition and Ethnic Riots in India*. Cambridge: Cambridge University Press.

Wood, Elisabeth Jean. 2003. *Insurgent Collective Action and Civil War in El Salvador*. New York: Cambridge University Press.

——. 2006. "Variation in Sexual Violence during War." *Politics and Society* 34 (3): 307–42.

——. 2010. "Sexual Violence during War: Variation and Accountability." In *Collective Crimes and International Criminal Justice: An Interdisciplinary Approach*, edited by Alette Smeulers and Elies Van Sliedregt, 295–322. Antwerp: Intersentia.

Zhukov, Yuri M. 2014. "Population Resettlement in War: Theory and Evidence from Soviet Archives." *Journal of Conflict Resolution* 59 (7): 1155–85.

INDEX

CPSIA information can be obtained
at www.ICGtesting.com
Printed in the USA
LVHW021634210920
666684LV00002B/24/J